What Makes Ryan Tick?

A Family's Triumph over Tourette Syndrome and Attention Deficit Hyperactivity Disorder

by

Susan Hughes

Foreword by James McCracken, M.D.

©1996

What Makes Ryan Tick?

by *Susan Hughes*

Published by **Hope Press** P.O.Box 188
Duarte, CA 91009-0188 U.S.A.

Other books by Hope Press:
Tourette Syndrome and Human Behavior
by *David E. Comings, M.D.*
Search for the Tourette Syndrome and Human Behavior Genes
by *David E. Comings, M.D.*
**The Gene Bomb Does Higher Education and Advanced Technology Accelerate the
Selection of Genes for Learning Disorders, ADHD, Addictive and Disruptive Behavior?**
by *David E. Comings, M.D.*
Teaching the Tiger
by *Marilyn P. Dornbush, Ph.D* and *Sheryl K. Pruitt, M.Ed.*
RYAN A Mother's Story of Her Hyperactive/Tourette Syndrome Child
by *Susan Hughes*

(to order these and others see back leaf form)

Copyright © 1996 by Susan Hughes
Printed in the United States of America

Library of Congress Cataloging-in-Publication Data

Hughes, Susan, 1949-
What makes Ryan tick? : a family's triumph over Tourette syndrome and attention
deficit hyperactivity disorder / by Susan Hughes :
Foreword by James McCracken.
p. cm.
ISBN 1-878267-35-3
1. Hughes, Ryan James. 1979- --Health.   2. Tourette syndrome in adolescence
-- Patients--United States--Biography. 3. Attention-deficit disorder in adolescence
-- Patients--United States--Biography.   I. Title
RJ496.T68H844 1996
362.1'9683--dc20
[B]   96-17637
                                                                          CIP

Table of Contents

Dedicated to:

My mother

whose help supported us, whose love sustained us,

and whose faith in Ryan and me never failed.

Foreword

Tourette syndrome is at its core a family disorder. In spite of greater awareness of its manifestations, and moving first-person accounts of individual acceptance, triumph, and restored identity, the impact of a child with Tourette on parents and family is largely absent from our literature on the condition. This book, written with remarkable honesty by the mother of a child with Tourette, captures the experience of a mother and her family's struggle with the disorder. There are many pearls to be discovered here for parents, patients, and professionals alike. Above all, it is a testimony to the dedication of a mother to her son, and should offer hope to all of those who have wrestled with the many manifestations of the disorder, and have discovered it to be the tenacious opponent that it is.

In many ways Ryan's story embodies the extraordinary range of problems that Tourette can contain, and the varying reactions that these lead to in parents and family members. Perplexing tics, extreme activity, labile moods, low frustration, and the frequent associated features of fears, compulsions, inattention, explosive behavior, discouragement and depression, alienation, and even hopelessness can represent a disorder as severe as any neuropsychiatric illness. For families, the boundaries between Tourette and other behaviors are often blurry. Faced with public and professional misunderstandings of Tourette in individuals, parents, like Ryan's are frequently confused, humiliated, discouraged, and, in this account, eventually hopeful. Though each parent also differs in their response to the presence of such a disorder, Susan Hughes' analogy of the family reaction to their son's problems as equivalent to grieving is well taken. Fortunately, one message from this book is the importance of perserverance, and how a

1

mother's efforts impacted on various school, mental health, and other professionals along the way. Ultimately, greater knowledge feeds back to the individual in the form of more appropriate care, greater support, and improved outcomes.

For professionals, Ryan's story should serve to remind us of our need for humility, the toll that Tourette's can exact from families, and the importance of support. Powerful treatments do exist, but failures are common. For every individual and family, the impact of the disorder is unique, and must be carefully appreciated. Treatments provided in the absence of a strong partnership existing between parents and practitioners are likely to fall short. This book also reminds us of the common experience of many parents of feeling blamed for the frustrating problems of their children, generally springing from the frustration of the clinician. Ryan's mother teaches us that knowledge is empowering, and hope in the face of adversity follows closely thereafter.

Though not a scientific history, the book serves to chronicle the significant progress that has been made in the understanding and treatment of this disorder. Not long ago, appreciation of the range of TS and related problems was limited. For the medical professional, the focus of treatment was often restricted to the suppression of tics, with little appreciation of the larger impact of the disorder on behavior and adaptation. Today, the unfortunate frequency with which disorders such as ADHD and obsessive compulsive disorder co-occur is well known, but knowledge as to the successful management of these problems in persons with TS is accumulating rapidly, and new treatments continue to be proposed.

James McCracken, M.D.
Director, Child Psychiatry
Neuropsychiatric Institute,
UCLA

Chapter 1

Introduction

*"Life consists not simply in what heredity
and environment do to us but in what we
make out of what they do to us."*[1]
Harry Emerson Fosdick

The majority of children with Tourette syndrome (TS) go undiagnosed. Their symptoms are mild and do not interfere with their daily lives. Others have mild to moderate motor and vocal tics that can easily be controlled with medication.

This book is about a "different" type of Tourette syndrome—perhaps the severest form. A significant group of children with TS have what is known as "associated behavioral problems." Some of these behaviors occur with such frequency that many now accept them to be "associated disorders." Some in the Tourette syndrome community refer to this form of TS as TS+.

Most people know very little about Tourette syndrome. Ask the "average" person on the street about TS and he or she may respond vaguely about some weird disease that makes people twitch, jerk, shout obscenities and do bizarre things.

Tourette syndrome is not a rare disease; instead it's a very common neurobiological disorder that affects as many as three to five percent of the population. TS normally appears during childhood, usually before the age of twenty-one. Contrary to popular belief, most children or adults with TS do not shout obscenities or shake uncontrollably. In a child with TS+ there are less known, yet more common, characteristics involved in the disorder. These characteristics many times have a much more profound impact on children with TS and their families than the much-publicized tics. Although

3

the presence of motor and vocal tics are necessary for the diagnosis of TS, these may be mild for some children and secondary to other more disturbing problems involving the child's behavior. Many children with TS are hyperactive and have significant behavior and discipline problems. Attention Deficit Disorder (with or without Hyperactivity) is present in up to fifty percent of children diagnosed with Tourette syndrome. Many others may display symptoms of Obsessive Compulsive Disorder (OCD). They may feel as if they have to touch something a certain number of times or "even" things up. An increasing amount of research data now suggests that OCD may even be an alternative expression of TS in some people, especially females.

Dyslexia, learning disabilities, problems with math and handwriting and other associated school problems are also common, even though school children with TS have the same IQ range as the public at large.

This story is about our sixteen-year-old son Ryan and his struggle to cope with Tourette syndrome and its associated disorders. Ryan has certainly had his share of vocal and motor tics. They have included shrieking, spitting, screaming, coprolalia, stuttering, rapping, eye blinking, shoulder shrugging, foot dragging, toe tapping, sock pulling, and excessive touching. He's also had finger rubbing, headbanging, obnoxious kissing, clothes adjusting, shirt pulling, mouth wiping, hair swiping, copropraxia, and a variety of other insensible and purposeless movements and noises. As difficult as these have been for Ryan to experience and for our family to endure, motor and vocal tics have been the easiest part in dealing with Tourette syndrome.

The most difficult aspects of TS for Ryan and our family have been problems with hyperactivity, attention, impulsivity, explosive rage attacks and aggression. Second to those difficulties have been obsessions, compulsions, fears, and phobias. We have also suffered with other problems that some (but not all) children with TS experience. These have included sleep problems, mood swings, depression, inappropriate sexual behaviors, self-injurious behaviors and even suicidal thoughts and verbalizations.

Researchers are still involved in much debate over the frequency and even the true relationship between TS and these other "associated disorders." Since the time Ryan was diagnosed in 1988, knowledge regarding TS has been rapidly unfolding—but not quickly enough for those of us still living in the trenches.

I often wish doctors and researchers would leave the comfort of their laboratories and offices to spend time at a local TSA support group meeting. I believe they would gain more knowledge from listening to parents and hearing the family histories than they would learn from drawing another tube of blood, ordering another EEG or completing another questionnaire.

As a former Tourette Syndrome Association (TSA) support group leader, I heard the same refrain repeatedly from frustrated parents: "Tics aren't the problem. We can live with the tics. It's the ADHD, OCD and all the other behavioral stuff that causes all our trouble."

When I was growing up in the fifties and sixties, I never saw kids at school with disabilities. If children were physically handicapped, they were generally "put away" some place with "their own kind." I never saw kids with schizophrenia, autism, or Down's syndrome. They too were "put" into institutions or state mental hospitals. Children with severe behavior problems were likewise absent from my classes. None of us ever knew for sure, but there were whispers about "reform" schools and the awful kids who were sent there. Thanks to federal and state laws, children with physical and neurological challenges are no longer "sent away" to be with "their own kind." Despite the monumental changes, there is still much to be done.

Children with behavioral problems, such as those associated with Tourette syndrome, are often misunderstood. They are labeled by some psychiatrists, psychologists and educators as "bad" kids, when in fact they are "sick" kids who can often be successfully treated.

Getting that treatment for their child can be a nightmare for even the most dedicated parents. They are often accused of being the "cause" of their child's neurological problem. Professionals sometimes fail to acknowledge that there are children with neurological challenges that make it impossible for parents to manage—no matter how stable, loving and caring they may be. If parents appear very involved, they are considered "too controlling." If they seek to set firm limits or try to make their child be more responsible, they are accused of not giving the child "enough" attention.

Many times parents are "victims" of the various systems they turn to for help. They either make too much money or not enough to qualify for special programs. Their child is either "not far enough behind" or "too delayed" for various educational options. Their child either has "no label," the "wrong" label, or "too many labels." Parents are accused of being "dysfunctional" because they are unable to cope, when it is the frustration of dealing with the child and the "systems" that make them dysfunctional.

Getting help for Ryan was not always easy. Jim and I have had to push the boundaries many times to get appropriate services for him and for our family. It was always our desire and our belief that Ryan should be at home with his family, and be educated in our local schools.

I have struggled with how honest I should be in writing this continuation of Ryan's story—perhaps not so much honest as revealing. Many of the behaviors that parents of children with Tourette syndrome deal with are humiliating and shocking to most people. Some of us confide our problems reluctantly to various professionals, but seldom to friends or relatives, who see only a glimpse of what our lives are really like. Many of us are still living "in the closet," so to speak.

By sharing our brutally honest and sometimes shocking story, I hope to leave you with a broader knowledge of this complex and frustrating disorder, and a greater compassion for children with TS and their families.

I have written this book with Ryan's permission and his blessing. I must warn you that the language is not pretty. Tourette syndrome is not a pretty disorder.

Other than Dr. David Comings and Dr. James McCracken, I have chosen to conceal the names of all professional people such as doctors, psychologists, social workers and teachers, and also school districts, insurance companies and hospitals.

Ryan's story is about a teenager who has suffered the most ravage cruelties of Tourette syndrome, yet continues to defy the odds with brave determination. It is also a story about our family—a family that was forced to challenge doctors, hospitals, insurance companies, teachers, principals, school districts, bus drivers, police officers, residential treatment centers, neighbors, churches, relatives, and even each other, to make a place for Ryan.

It is a story of my struggle with the anger and hurt of having TS in the family. It is a story of frustration and fears, of lost hopes and dreams. It is a story of how one family, propelled by injustices and ignorance, was challenged to reach deep for raw courage and strength they never knew they had. It is a story of determination, setbacks, victories, and renewed faith.

Most of all, it is a story about love—a family's love for a good kid named Ryan who has overcome a bad case of Tourette syndrome.

Chapter 2

No Rotten Apple

*"Big sisters are the crab grass
in the lawn of life."*[1]
Charles Schultz

Let me introduce you to Ryan. To put it simply, he is a great kid. Ryan is the picture of health and has an impish charm that can melt the heart of any unsuspecting adult. He is strong and athletic, with Paul Newman-blue eyes and skin that stays tan all year.

Ryan is a typical teen. Just like many other adolescents his age, he is facing the challenge of crossing from boyhood to manhood. He struggles daily to understand his changing body and his world. He finds it confusing why, all of a sudden, taking a bath and smelling good is not such a bad idea after all—at least on some days.

Ryan is bright, inquisitive, very articulate and has a great sense of humor. He loves school and is working at or above grade level in every subject but math. He is fanatically honest, is proud of it and would never compromise his hard-earned reputation for honesty just to escape a punishment or reprimand.

He can locate a blank tape and set the VCR to record a program faster than his dad can open the drawer to look for the instruction book. He has mastered every Nintendo game he owns and can sit quietly for hours working on a new project that captures his attention. He is a whiz at puzzles and can put together a difficult model car in a just a matter of hours.

He is a very talented artist and creates beautiful lifelike sketches of tigers and lions with precision and great attention to detail. Ryan is also an apprentice of illusion. He has mastered dozens of magic tricks, becoming a proficient sleight-of-hand artist. He taught himself how to juggle in just one day and has learned to play many chords on the electric guitar.

He loves music, especially loud music. His personal library includes an odd assortment of Jerry Lee Lewis, the Beach Boys, Jon Bon Jovi, Alan Jackson, Guardian, and Weird Al Yankovic. Although curious about the hard rock and heavy metal sounds, he has been content to pursue Christian metal groups that offer wholesome lyrics mixed with screaming guitars. These seem to satisfy his teenage desire for electronic chaos.

Ryan's taste in movies is somewhat schizophrenic, with Disney's *Homeward Bound* and *Lion King*, Jean Claude Van Damme's *Lionheart* and *Tombstone* all attracting his equal loyalty.

He is an animal lover. He is an animal rights "activist" at heart and is quite vocal about anyone who would hurt or kill an animal. He finds hunters repulsive. He has been known to approach women at the shopping mall, suspiciously demanding to know if their handbags were "real" or "fake."

He is a consummate salesman who is always working an angle; he's usually quite successful. He can charm his way into and out of just about anything. He is a master at getting his grandmother to part with a twenty dollar bill to indulge his latest whim.

Ryan seems to have the luck of the Irish. He can take a single quarter into a video arcade and play for an hour. He is always finding money on the floors of stores, public phones or in parking lots. He can leave home with twenty-four bars of candy to sell and return in ten minutes with twenty-four dollars crumpled in his back pocket and some extra bars left.

His room decor is typical "boy." Stuffed tigers share a dresser top with a thin layer of dust. Large tiger prints line the walls along with a huge poster of his mentor, Dennis the Menace. An electric guitar sits on a stand next to a half-made bed and Energizer batteries dot the floor. Nine gleaming trophies representing nine years of Little League occupy the shelf, along with the game ball he captured after striking out twenty-one batters.

Baseball is only one of the many sports that Ryan enjoys. He is an avid swimmer and loves to water ski. He also loves basketball, tennis, Ping-Pong, roller hockey and the Los Angeles Kings. He hates football, soccer, waiting for dinner, waiting for holidays, or waiting in line for anything.

Some of his favorite things are: getting presents, spending money, playing with his remote control car, and wasting quarters in toy vending machines. Also high on Ryan's list of pleasures is dressing up for Halloween, going to Disneyland, ordering the number two "meal deal" at McDonald's, and provoking his older sister Julie. His favorite clothes are T-shirts with pictures of tigers or sharks, a Kings hat and any pair of athletic shoes that cost more than we can afford.

Ryan is very sensitive to spiritual things, demonstrating a sincere love for God and an unselfish willingness to help others less fortunate than himself. He enjoys going to youth group at church and he is quick to remind me to just "pray about it" when something goes wrong.

He also has a deep love for his family. Before she died last year, Ryan patiently took time to talk on the phone with his eighty-five-year-old great-grandmother and gladly tagged along when I visited her at the nursing home. He adores his older cousin Dorian, his best friend Joe, and his Grandma Polly. He is very affectionate and loving. He kisses me goodnight every night and reminds his dad and me at least several times a day that he loves us. He often hugs me spontaneously, with no strings attached.

Ryan is all the things I have described, but there is more. It is the "more" that is the most painful for me to share. Through his mother's eyes you have met Ryan and learned much about his life, yet there is much more to know.

After reading my introduction, it might be surprising to learn that for five years Ryan attended a special school for children with severe emotional or behavioral disorders. He was severely hyperactive and impulsive, extremely oppositional, defiant, had a very short fuse and was prone to having explosive rage attacks both at school and at home. He was loud and demanding. He never stopped talking, had irrational fears, wide mood swings, and was obsessive and compulsive.

Ryan also displayed mild vocal and motor tics such as wiping his mouth, adjusting his pants, rubbing his fingers together, tapping his foot, and tossing his head. Many of these tics one may not have particularly noticed—unless he got the urge to shriek. He usually had to do that one at least two, or three times before he felt completely satisfied.

He has also had much difficulty displaying appropriate social skills. He has had few friends his age because his behavior was annoying and at times unbearable. He pestered his dog, hit his mother, father, and teachers, spit in our faces, and called us horrible, unspeakable names. He was rude to people on the phone and in public. He verbally lashed out at strangers and flashed the finger sign to other parents, peers, neighbors, teachers and even police officers. Ryan had a "hair trigger" temper. He put holes in practically every room in our home and at school. During fits of rage, he often threw large pieces of furniture. Nothing we did made any difference in preventing the rages. For a while, he even had a "fascination" with knives and would threaten to kill us whenever something would set him off.

Despite being very bright, Ryan struggled at school due to problems with attention and hyperactivity. He felt convinced he was dumb and stupid. He displayed very poor self-control and had an even poorer self-image.

He felt he was a "freak" of sorts and suffered with the aftermath that remained as a result of his erratic and sometimes uncontrollable behavior. He would often exhibit tremendous remorse after unpredictable "episodes." During those times, however, he seemed totally unconnected to anyone else around. His eyes were vacant and we couldn't seem to reach him.

We were accused of "letting" him behave inappropriately. We were told that he misbehaved because he ate too much sugar and ingested too many food additives, that his behavior was surely the cause of his environment, allergies, lead poisoning, and lack of proper vitamins. It was suggested that he was demon-possessed and that we needed to have the "devil" cast out. Everybody, it seemed had a theory. What could have gone wrong? Was it something we did to cause Ryan to have so many difficulties? We searched for answers.

We had been married five years when he was born. His dad was a teacher and I stayed at home, happily caring for our two little babies, making homemade jelly and happy memories.

He was only seven weeks old when the pastor at our church held him up before the congregation to be dedicated to the Lord. We promised God that very day to follow the Bible's admonition to "raise him up in the way he should go" and we meant it.

Ryan never had any trouble bonding as an infant. He never knew a day without hugs and kisses. He was never molested or abused. He had all that we could physically, emotionally and spiritually offer, but somehow it was not enough.

His dad and I never experienced drugs. We did not smoke or use alcohol. We were mature, well-educated, and determined to be good parents. Our other child was perfectly normal. Julie and Ryan both lived with us in the same home—a home filled with love, where swear words and physical abuse were unknown.

Yet by the age of three he was severely hyperactive. He received medications and psychotherapy. By the age of seven, he was violent, oppositional, and defiant. He hit, kicked, threw objects, screamed, used profanity, and exploded with rage attacks. He was phobic and obsessive-compulsive. He was only ten years old when he expressed a desire to die because living was, as he put it, "just too hard."

We sought the best care available. Sometimes the "best" was awful. We attended dozens of parenting classes. We joined support groups. We spent years with psychologists, neurologists, and psychiatrists. The insurance company spent hundreds of thousands of dollars for hospitalizations. He exhausted all school options. When he was thirteen years old I quit my job, because the school officials thought that sending him home every day was better than keeping him at school. The day he went to live at a residential treatment center I felt as if someone ripped my heart from my chest with no anesthesia.

I cried a river of tears.

Today, Ryan is sixteen years old and doing extremely well. He is still handsome, bright, charming, and loving. He is a high school sophomore, attends school on a regular campus and gets good grades. What is more important, he expresses his feelings appropriately, controls his anger, and (this is a big one) takes responsibility for his actions.

It's been a long, hard, sometimes unbearable journey. A healthy spurt of maturity combined with multiple medications have helped to make a difference. Skillful doctors, devoted teachers, caring mental health professionals, and the prayers and unceasing love from his family have all contributed to helping Ryan become the extraordinary young man he is today—the very same boy who was trapped for many years in the complex and mysterious jungle of Tourette syndrome.

Chapter 3

No Stone Unturned

*"Determine that the thing can and shall be done,
and then we shall find the way."*[1]
Abraham Lincoln

It was five years ago that I published my first story about Ryan. We had been through many ordeals before Ryan received a diagnosis of Tourette syndrome at the age of nine.

Ryan was our second child. His sister Julie was born two and a half years earlier. We were a happy young family, full of hopes and ambitions. We certainly were unprepared for the turbulent years that lay ahead.

By the time Ryan was three years old, Jim and I knew we could no longer dismiss his exceptionally high activity level with the excuse that he was just "all boy." He set off the fire alarm at church, broke mirrors and windows, and caused his sister a trip to the emergency room. His hyperactive antics were driving us crazy. We struggled to find something that worked. Nothing Jim and I tried, however, seemed to curb Ryan's frantic, impulsive behavior.

In 1982 at the age of three and a half, a pediatrician diagnosed Ryan with Minimal Brain Dysfunction, now more appropriately called Attention Deficit Hyperactivity Disorder. He began a treatment program that included counseling and the controversial stimulant medication, Ritalin.

We labored with feelings of helplessness, guilt and despair, especially when criticized by outsiders who hinted they would never "let" a child of theirs behave so horribly. It was even worse when other people criticized us for giving "unnecessary" medication to such a young child.

Dramatic and positive results from Ritalin gave us a few hours of normalcy throughout each day; counseling, however, was not as success-ful. Ryan was all over the psychologist's office. He jumped up on her desk, the filing cabinet, opened all the drawers and knocked the plants off the tables.

The beginning of kindergarten opened up a new world for us. We learned about diagnostic testing, dyslexia, learning disabilities, and Indi-vidualized Education Programs (IEPs). Frequent meetings with the teacher, principal, and school psychologist became the norm.

By the end of kindergarten it was obvious Ryan was not ready for the challenges of first grade. We collaborated with the school staff and created an individualized program that allowed him to attend a kindergarten class in the morning and a regular first grade class in the afternoon. We called this the transition year and it was highly successful. The following year, Ryan completed a full year of first grade with no major problems.

His success in school was due, in large part, to an increase in medica-tion. From an original five milligrams of Ritalin per day, the dosage had climbed to forty-five milligrams, a larger-than-normal amount for his small size of forty pounds. The doctor cautioned us his very slow growth could be a result of using the stimulant medication. Unfortunately, Ryan's in-creasingly violent behavior required its continued use.

Using Ritalin scared us. We pressed the doctor for more information. Other hyperactive children we had seen never seemed quite as severe as Ryan. Even with a structured behavioral program and the medication, Ryan was still unable to behave like a normal child.

Because our health insurance program was an HMO (health mainte-nance organization), any referral to an "outside" specialist needed to be authorized by the pediatrician. Ryan's doctor, however, refused to make a referral to a specialist outside the HMO group, despite our repeated con-cerns.

By the age of seven, Ryan had become increasingly violent. He was having "babbling spells" and was wetting his pants numerous times a day. Eventually, the pediatrician agreed to authorize a referral for Ryan to see a neurologist. We were disappointed when the brusque and insensitive spe-cialist spent less than five minutes with Ryan. He admonished us to be grateful that he had not been born before there were medications to help hyperactive kids.

We plodded on, doing our best to deal with Ryan's behavior. The Ritalin dosage crept up to sixty milligrams per day, despite suppressed growth and body weight that still hovered around forty pounds.

Shortly before second grade, we moved to a new home in a nearby community. Although Ryan had received special education services since kindergarten, the staff at the new school determined Ryan did not qualify for services. We were shocked when the new school staff wanted to exclude Ryan from the special education program. We knew his limitations and were certain he needed the benefit of being in a resource room for tutoring.

We scrambled to learn about special education laws. We studied Public Law 94-142 and decided to pursue Ryan's legal rights to a free and appropriate education. Eventually, the school district's special education director agreed to conduct a full-scale evaluation and scheduled Ryan for diagnostic testing.

The results of their study confirmed what we had known all along. Ryan did indeed have learning disabilities and would qualify under our state's guidelines to receive special education services. We provided the staff with information about problems common in children with attention deficit disorder, such as low frustration, intolerance to discipline, volatile temper, low stress threshold, and tendencies for depression. We offered suggestions for intervention therapies and those were incorporated into Ryan's new IEP.

When Ryan had started on Ritalin six years earlier, I questioned the pediatrician about a disturbing article I saw in a woman's magazine. The article cited a possible correlation between Ritalin and the onset of a tic disorder known as Tourette syndrome. The pediatrician dismissed my concerns and admonished me that *Better Homes and Gardens Magazine* had never been an authority on pediatric neurology. He also cautioned that I not be so quick to believe everything I read. I obediently took the doctor's advice and forgot the subject until several years later, when Ryan's behavioral difficulties became even more severe.

At a teaching conference in Los Angeles, Jim heard a geneticist speak about Tourette syndrome. The doctor described some of the symptoms of TS such as spitting and compulsive swearing, both behaviors Ryan had been displaying for many months. Many of the doctor's descriptions fit Ryan exactly, so we questioned Ryan's psychologist about TS at our next visit. He doubted the possibility of Tourette syndrome, but suggested we have Ryan evaluated by a child psychiatrist. He felt Ryan's problems had become too complex for him.

Shortly after starting with the new psychiatrist, Ryan's symptoms began to worsen, despite a change in medication. By this time Jim and I had reached the edge of burnout in trying to handle Ryan's difficult behavior. When I learned about a research study for eight-year-old boys with ADHD, I called the number immediately.

We were disappointed again when the research doctor rejected Ryan for the program. According to him, Ryan most likely had Tourette syndrome. The doctor encouraged us to demand a new referral from our HMO doctor for a complete neurological evaluation. He suggested we go to a facility familiar in treating Tourette syndrome, such as the City of Hope National Medical Center.

We were eager to call Ryan's pediatrician with the news regarding TS. Although he readily agreed that Tourette syndrome was a distinct possibility, he again refused to authorize an outside referral. He insisted the local "group-approved" doctor could make the diagnosis. Jim and I were discouraged but agreed to see the doctor again.

When the psychiatrist vehemently denied the evidence of Tourette syndrome in Ryan, we were dismayed and confused. He acknowledged his opinion was in conflict with the "big city doctor" but maintained Ryan was suffering only from ADHD. He suggested adding another medication, Stelazine, to the daily doses of Ritalin. He sent us home, more exasperated than ever, to deal with a child whose behavior was becoming increasingly worse as each month passed.

Ryan continued to have severe difficulties both at home and school. His behavior was regressing and he acted more like a three-year-old than a nine-year- old. He was wetting his pants daily, crying incessantly, hanging on to me, and afraid to be in a room alone.

He was unable to sit still, was hostile to everyone, and was violent toward his dad and me. Along with hitting, biting, kicking, throwing, spitting, and cursing, on several occasions Ryan threatened us by waving a kitchen knife.

Desperate, I called the psychiatrist again, pleading for his help. He advised me to get some Benadryl, an over the counter allergy medicine that had a side effect of drowsiness. He suggested that Benadryl, combined with Stelazine and Ritalin, might make Ryan more manageable.

Instead, I picked up the phone and dialed the Tourette syndrome clinic at the City of Hope National Medical Center. I spoke with Dr. David Comings, the Director of Medical Genetics, who specializes in treating patients with Tourette syndrome. Dr. Comings seemed to perceive my despair. Despite the normal wait of three months, he offered to work us in for an appointment within the next two weeks.

When we arrived at the hospital, a nurse took seven vials of blood from Jim, Ryan and me. We later learned the samples were for a large, ongoing research project.

After examining Ryan and reviewing a detailed history of our family, Dr. Comings made the easy and obvious diagnosis. Nine-year-old Ryan was suffering from a full-blown, classic case of Tourette syndrome.

We felt enormous relief as we drove away from the hospital that day. After years of suffering guilt from being unable able to control Ryan's behavior, we finally had an answer. What is more important, we finally felt there was hope—hope that with the proper help, Ryan would be able to lead a normal life.

My first story ended with Ryan newly diagnosed with Tourette syndrome. He was taking medication and had started third grade in a regular classroom with minimal special education services. It also ended with me naively believing (hoping) that our problems were over because he had a diagnosis of TS.

Little did I know that our troubles in raising a child with a severe case of Tourette syndrome and ADHD had just begun. Our battles with school and medical professionals were really a "honeymoon" compared to what was yet to come.

Getting the diagnosis of Tourette syndrome was a welcome relief; however, it was not a magic wand we could wave over each new crisis. Each new year has brought a new set of challenges, heartaches, disasters, and small victories.

Parenting a normal adolescent is no easy job. Throw in Tourette syndrome with a hefty dose of ADHD, a pinch of obsessive compulsive symptoms, then mix them up with a generous helping of medication side effects, and you have created instant parental insanity.

Chapter 4

Coming to Grips

"Twas but my tongue,
'twas not my soul that swore."[1]
Euripides

When Ryan entered third grade in the fall of 1988, his behavior was under fairly good control. This was due to the success of a behavioral modification plan we were using at home and the medications Stelazine and Ritalin.

"Fairly good" meant he was manageable some, but not all of the time. We were spending a good bit of effort using various behavior management techniques we had learned through the years. There were still many times of the day, however, when Ryan's behavior challenged our capabilities and pushed our patience to the limit.

These difficult times usually occurred thirty to forty minutes before his next scheduled dose of Ritalin. Just like "Old Faithful" at Yellowstone Park, Ryan would "go off" with alarming predictability. We never had to rely on our watches to know when the next dose was due. Ryan's entire appearance and demeanor would change dramatically. He became loud and his speech was more rapid and intense. He became irritable and demanding, restless and agitated.

Within fifteen to twenty minutes after taking Ritalin, Ryan transformed again into a pleasant, calm, but energetic, young boy. It was like riding an elevator that kept going up and down but never stopped.

As always, tics were mild. To the casual observer they went mostly unnoticed, except for the spitting. Coprolalia, the repetition of foul words, seemed to come and go. This was most noticeable in the early morning before medications and at bedtime.

Much to his dad's and my dismay, our precocious, hyperactive nine-year old often let loose with horrible words. Other times he would chant the words repeatedly. We would often find pieces of paper in his room with three or four "choice" words (usually misspelled) written repeatedly. Sometimes he directed the words at his father or me. We tried everything imaginable to stop him from saying the bad words. Another TS mother suggested that putting a drop of Tabasco sauce on Ryan's tongue would stop the swear words. The first time I used Tabasco sauce he screamed and called me a "mother-fucking bitch." When I tried to get close enough to put another drop on his tongue, he kicked and bit me.

I tried the Tabasco approach for several weeks but it did not work. I usually ended up getting it in *my* eyes instead of his mouth. As with other acts of misbehavior, nothing we could say or do, nothing we could take away, and no amount of time-outs seemed to diminish the undesirable conduct. Even so, we considered things to be going "fairly well."

Although we previously had trouble with our local school district in obtaining special education services for Ryan, extending those services to third grade did not prove to be a problem. The IEP team consisted of the school psychologist, principal, teacher, resource specialist, and Jim and me. All of us agreed it was best for Ryan to remain in a regular education classroom. In addition, we all agreed he could benefit with extra help from the resource specialist in math and handwriting. We scheduled the tutoring for thirty minutes a day.

When Ryan entered third grade, he had the labels of ADHD, Tourette syndrome and learning handicapped. For some parents, labels attached to their child are a big concern. For me, these labels seemed to provide a shield between behavior that was expected from him—a child who appeared normal—and whatever might go wrong. Of course, no one who spent more than a few hours with Ryan could escape without knowing something was wrong.

His teacher, Mrs. Terry, seemed pleasant. She was small in stature and very soft-spoken. I wondered silently how she and Ryan would get along. I learned from another parent that Mrs. Terry had previously taught at a high school and I marveled that she could make such a drastic transition to teaching elementary students. I was optimistic she would prove to be a strong disciplinarian and provide a structured classroom that would be suitable for Ryan.

Shortly after school started in early September, I started to receive phone calls and notes from the teacher. Over the next few weeks I learned Ryan was having difficulty sitting still, paying attention, writing his assignments, and playing cooperatively with the other children. Mrs. Terry informed me he was impulsive and constantly acting out, calling other students' names, spitting on the floor, and throwing pencils. Practically every day we communicated either by note, phone or in person.

I don't remember exactly when I first learned that Mrs. Terry was sending Ryan out of class to work in the teacher's copy room. Mrs. Terry had mentioned she had sent him to the office a few times to finish his work, but I did not realize until later the extent of his trips to the office. I was just grateful he was able to stay in school for a full day without being suspended or sent home. Despite our valiant attempts to maintain control, Ryan was having increased difficulty at home. I didn't know what I would do if he couldn't stay at school.

At the time I was working full time as a real estate agent and relocation manager. My work, plus Ryan's special demands and the needs of a husband and teenage daughter, were certainly a challenge, even for a self-professed Super Mom.

To build my client base, I often walked through the neighborhood passing out flyers and promotional items. I usually "farmed" on Saturday mornings when most people were outside washing their cars or working in the yard. It was a good opportunity for me to meet the neighbors and determine if they were considering a future move. I was able to generate many promising leads that way.

What I did not expect was having potential clients call me about Ryan. Neighbors soon made the association between my name and picture on the promotional flyers and the little boy who was riding his bike through their yards and throwing clods of dirt at their front doors.

I started to feel self-conscious when I made my rounds, feeling as if there were a sign around my neck saying, "Lousy mother-Lousy agent." I soon discovered I was doing more on my walks to educate people about Tourette syndrome than about real estate. Fortunately, most people were understanding.

As fall approached, Ryan became excited about Halloween. His class was planning a party and the whole school was having a costume parade.

He spent weeks working on his cowboy costume, practicing how to tie the neck scarf and making fake bullets for his holster.

The days preceding Halloween were particularly difficult for Ryan. His tics had become more frequent. Episodes of pencil throwing and copropraxia (giving the "finger sign") were irritating the teacher. His repeated offenses resulted in his spending many days confined in the school office. Not sure what to do with her resident "prisoner," the principal set up a desk for Ryan in the teacher's copy room where he could do his assignments without bothering anyone.

When Halloween finally arrived, Ryan's hyperactivity escalated. He had a hard time containing his exuberance and excitement about the class party. He also found it impossible to stay in his seat or concentrate on work.

On the short walk to the resource room that morning, Ryan impulsively knocked on another teacher's door. When she opened it, Ryan darted inside the room, gave her class the finger sign, and quickly ran back outside. The teacher (who did not know Ryan) was aghast. She became livid when he continued to run, despite her urgent demands to stop.

Again, Ryan landed in Principal Hunt's office. She scurried him off to the teacher's copy room where he spent the rest of the school day, including lunch. There was no Halloween party for Ryan that day. Mrs. Terry did not permit him to participate in or even watch the costume parade.

When I arrived to pick him up from school that afternoon Ryan walked to the car slowly, his head hanging. He was clutching the rumpled brown bag that held his unworn cowboy costume. As he dropped into the seat beside me I could tell something was terribly wrong. His eyes were red and tears began rolling down his pale cheeks.

"I can't take this anymore, Mommy. Why me, why me?" he cried. "Why do I have to have this stupid Tourette stuff?" When we got home I got a washcloth and sponged his face. It was hours before he was able to settle down and stop the bouts of sobbing.

Ryan's behavior was certainly inappropriate and he deserved consequences. A more experienced and sensitive teacher, however, may have handled the situation differently. If I had not been so new to the world of Tourette syndrome, maybe I could have provided more information to the teacher and principal about the hallmarks of the disorder. Perhaps I could have suggested other interventions or consequences that would have been more appropriate and less devastating for Ryan.

Holidays have always been very difficult for Ryan, as they are for many children with ADHD and Tourette syndrome. He seems to completely lose what little patience he has and finds it impossible to wait for the big day to arrive. Birthdays and Christmas are usually the worst because they involve the magic word—presents! For Ryan, life can be no better than when he is sitting in front of an unwrapped gift.

Unfortunately, part of Ryan's learning disorder involves a memory disability. Although he could remember and recite the names of all the Teenage Mutant Ninja Turtles (and their enemy counterparts), he often could not remember how much two times two was.

As Christmas day drew near, Ryan's problems with distractibility and hyperactivity increased, much the same as they did with Halloween. He was especially excited about a class party the teacher was planning. As I tucked him into bed the night before the big party he nonchalantly asked, "Did you get the cookies for the party yet, Mom?"

"What cookies, Ryan?" I asked, holding back an urge to scream.

"I told the teacher you would make all the cookies for the party tomorrow, Mommy," he beamed proudly.

"Why didn't you tell me, Ryan?" I yelled loudly. "How on earth can I bake cookies at this hour?"

He looked up at me sadly. I knew why he hadn't told me about the cookies—he has ADHD. He simply forgot. I knew I was wrong to yell at him, but it was so frustrating! He was always forgetting and losing everything. It was driving me crazy.

Fortunately, the local market still had an assortment of decorated cookies. Before going to bed that night, I arranged the cookies on a beautiful Christmas plate, wrapped it in plastic and topped it off with a big red bow.

I had no trouble waking Ryan up for school the next morning. He bounced out of bed, raring to go. He was jubilant as he walked into school, proudly carrying his festive plate of cookies and small Christmas gifts for his teacher, tutor and the health aide who administered his medications.

When I arrived at school to get him that afternoon, I expected him to be extra "hyper" after such an exciting day. I was shocked when I saw him running toward the car in tears.

"Everybody got a present but me, Mommy!" he cried, tears streaming down his face. He was distraught, his body heaving as he stuttered, trying hard to force out the words.

"What do you mean, Ryan? What happened?" I asked in disbelief. "What present are you talking about?"

Through the stuttering and tears Ryan explained there had been a gift exchange. Mrs. Terry had sent the students home with a notice about the gift exchange the week before. Evidently, on the day Mrs. Terry sent the notes home, Ryan had left school early for a doctor's appointment and did not get his notice. The teacher had forgotten to give him his note the following day.

As he burst forth with more details it became apparent that the gift exchange was the major activity of the afternoon. Passing out the gifts was a game, with each child taking a turn selecting a gift, then choosing to keep or trade it with another child. Ryan, who had an immature passion for presents, sat in the corner alone and watched in agony as the other students enjoyed an afternoon of fun and games.

I had heard enough. My protective motherly instincts were in high gear as I made my way to the classroom to see Mrs. Terry. I needed to ask her what really happened. Things could not possibly have happened the way he described. He must have left something out of the story. I was eager to hear the teacher assure me none of the things Ryan described had happened—that he was just overreacting to an imagined injustice.

Unbelievably, Mrs. Terry's explanation matched Ryan's exactly. When I asked why she had not given Ryan a note about the gift exchange, Mrs. Terry explained that she had simply forgotten. She assured me she had *verbally* reminded the class to bring in their gifts. Then, she turned to Ryan and said, "Maybe this will teach you to pay more attention in class next time."

I was appalled by the teacher's lack of empathy. She was well aware Ryan had Attention Deficit Disorder, a learning disability in processing information, and poor memory retention. When I tried to explain how much being excluded from the gift exchange had hurt Ryan, she responded defensively.

"Oh, come on now, he's playing on you," she scolded. "I don't think it's right you are spoiling my vacation over this. I even spent my own money buying candy for the kids. Besides, I already go above and beyond for Ryan the way it is. I can't believe you are making such a big thing out of a lousy three dollar gift. After all, he did get to have cookies and punch."

Mrs. Terry's remarks and her lack of sensitivity stunned and angered me. I could imagine how hurt Ryan must have felt as he sat watching the other children unwrap their gifts.

I left her room, walked quickly to the main office, and asked to speak with the principal, Mrs. Hunt. I struggled to remain calm and composed as

I related the incident to her. I was extremely upset and she knew it.

Mrs. Hunt was apologetic and assured me she would resolve the situation with Mrs. Terry when school resumed after the winter break. I liked Mrs. Hunt and felt assured she would do as she promised.

I hoped the spirit of the holidays and the passing of time would ease my feelings of betrayal and anger. As Ryan and I left the principal's office and walked toward the car, my eyes were stinging with tears. I felt sad that the teacher had excluded my child and I was angry at her for being so insensitive.

"Why can't people just understand?" I thought to myself.

I was glad it was time for Christmas vacation and that Ryan would not have to go back to school for two weeks. I was glad he did not have to go back to face the unforgiving teacher and back to long days and lunch times spent isolated in the teacher's copy room.

I knew for Ryan's sake I would need to put my feelings of anger aside and find a way to make things better for him and Mrs. Terry. Somehow I needed to conjure up fresh optimism and make sure that Ryan could finish third grade without any further damage to his self-esteem—at least not at the hand of his teacher. I determined to make sure that nothing like the Halloween and gift exchange fiascoes would ever happen again.

Chapter 5

Sink or Swim

*"Love demands that I learn to focus my attention
on the needs of those I love."*[1]
John Powell

Despite the incident with Mrs. Terry, Christmas of 1988 held special excitement for us. I was fortunate to earn a commission that was totally unexpected and I decided to do something extra special for our family. I investigated vacation possibilities and finally settled on a family cruise.

Premier's "Big Red Boat," as they called it, seemed perfect for a once-in-a-lifetime family vacation. The offer included a three-day cruise to the Bahamas plus four days at Disney World and Epcot Center in Florida. The price included airfare from Los Angeles and first class accommodations near all the major attractions.

Although it would exhaust every penny of my unexpected windfall, this vacation seemed like a dream come true. The promise of supervised programs for the kids sold me. I envisioned Jim and myself cruising to Nassau, basking in the warm sun and enjoying some well-deserved quiet time, while Ryan was being entertained and contained.

Our flight left at 11:00 P.M. on Christmas Eve. I planned it that way, thinking Ryan would sleep from Los Angeles to Orlando. Assuming Ryan would sleep was my first mistake—I had forgotten to factor his anxiety and obsessions into the travel itinerary.

When we got to the airport he began to worry about how Santa would find him all the way in Florida. He worried about the plane. Would we crash? When could he eat? How long would it take to get there? How would he be able to go to the bathroom? Would he be able to buy a water bottle at Disney Wor—he didn't just worry about these things a little bit. He worried about them repeatedly and always out loud.

I should have begged the pilot to turn around over Arizona. Ryan was on my lap, then he was off my lap. He was up and then he was down again. He was hungry and thirsty. He was hot, then he was cold. He was bored and antsy. He was everything but sleepy.

Flying east we lost three hours with the time change. By the time I staggered off the plane that morning I felt terrible. I have never had a hangover but I am sure I was feeling something close to it. To make matters worse, Julie had started to sniffle and wheeze.

"My throat hurts, Mom," she said with a weak and scratchy voice. "I don't feel very good."

The bus ride to the rental car lot seemed to take forever. By the time we rented the car and found our way to the hotel, we were ready to collapse. Well, at least three of us were ready to collapse. Ryan was raring to go. It did not matter that he hadn't slept for the last three thousand miles. He was ready to see Mickey Mouse and buy a water bottle.

We had not been in Florida twenty-four hours when I found myself chasing Ryan around the dark, dreary emergency room at the hospital in Kissimee, Florida. Julie's sniffles and scratchy throat had turned into an ear infection and asthmatic bronchitis. Several hours later, armed with antibiotics, antihistamines and a cortisone inhaler, we ate dinner with the Colonel at a Kentucky Fried Chicken restaurant and made plans for the next day at Epcot Center.

I felt excited about taking the kids to Epcot Center. There was so much to see, so much to learn. It would be a wonderful educational opportunity and I couldn't wait for them to absorb every enlightening attraction. Unfortunately, there were thousands of other mothers there with the same idea! When I made plans for our wonderful Christmas vacation I hadn't considered crowds. There were so many people at Epcot that day that you couldn't see over the heads in front of you. A few million people were not about to stop Ryan, though. The money he had gotten for Christmas was burning a hole in his pocket and he was eager to hit the souvenir shops.

What we didn't know was that shopping was the *only* thing on Ryan's mind that day. None of the attractions, none of the exhibits, none of the rides or entertainment or even the restaurants could capture his attention. He was "stuck" on shopping and he seemed driven to dash from one shop to another. Every time we stopped to see an exhibit, Ryan loudly voiced his disapproval. He was perseverating on shopping and the obsession didn't stop, even after he had spent all his money.

The next two days at Disney World were about the same. Then, to make matters worse, he found a twenty dollar bill on the ground and the shopping obsession started again. Energized by finding the twenty dollars, Ryan decided he needed a plastic sword from the pirate shop. The three of us tried to explain that the swords were not very sturdy and looked as if they would break easily. No amount of reasoning could change Ryan's mind. He had to have a sword. We decided to use the sword as leverage. We set some limits for his behavior that would allow him to get the sword later in the day, but only if he earned it.

When he finally had the prized sword in hand, we walked out of the shop believing that our nightmare with his shopping obsessions was over. We had barely gone a few steps from the door of the shop when Ryan made a swift sweeping motion in the air with his sword.

"Ryan, you need to keep the sword inside the case while you are around all these people," I began.

Before I could say any more, Ryan made another quick swiping motion and slammed the sword into the ground. It immediately snapped in half. He began crying and demanded that we go back inside and buy him another sword. We tried again to explain that the swords were made out of cheap plastic and that another sword would break just as easily as the first one.

He only became angrier and sobbed even louder. He screamed and cried, stomped his feet and ran around in circles. People were staring, dozens of people. Jim picked Ryan up, still kicking and screaming, and hauled him off to the nearest restroom until he was able to calm down. We knew from experience that any inappropriate reaction to his outburst could "fuel the flame" and make the situation even worse. Spanking would have escalated the tantrum. We were firm advocates of spanking when Ryan was younger. We learned, however, that it never worked and that it made him even angrier and more aggressive. Spanking worked on Julie but never for Ryan.

When we finally left the Magic Kingdom and headed back to the hotel, I was still crazy enough to be optimistic that the upcoming three-day cruise would be better. Julie, full of antibiotics, was feeling great and even Ryan seemed excited about our new adventure.

"The Oceanic" was sitting in port when we arrived and it looked huge. The large red boat seemed majestic and inviting. Visions of Kathie Lee Gifford floating around the deck singing "If They Could See Me Now" invaded my thoughts as we slowly climbed the long gangplank on our way to temporary paradise.

We hurriedly checked out our small cabin and figured out how to work the strange-looking toilet. We also settled a big fight between Julie and Ryan over who was going to get the top bunk. Ryan won, only because he was smaller, weighed less and wasn't prone to sleepwalking like Julie.

The kids approved of the ship right away. There was nonstop food available like hamburgers, pizza, ice cream, and all the sodas you could waste. Ryan was a little worried at first and started obsessing about the swimming pools because they were all empty. We assured him they would be filled with water when we were out at sea, but he worried nonetheless. He worried again when we had to don life preservers for a routine emergency drill. He was certain we were going to drown, just because we tried on the life jackets. I spent the first few hours trying to calm him down and shut him up.

We had signed up for the early dinner schedule. I was relieved when we arrived in the huge dining room to see that our dinner companions were another couple with kids. They looked friendly but I secretly worried about what Ryan might do or say. I wondered if I should say something about him having TS. I decided to give him the benefit of the doubt and act as if nothing were wrong. After all, there was a chance, however small, that he would behave well and no one would suspect that he was hyperactive or had Tourette syndrome.

Our dinner companions were a cordial couple from Canada with two young daughters, nine and six years old. Both girls were attractive and extremely well-mannered. They placed their napkins on their laps and quietly sat through dinner acting prim and proper.

Ryan behaved well, too, but he was like an octopus reaching for everything. He spilled his chocolate milk about two minutes after we started eating. Other than that, there were no major events. He talked a lot but was very appropriate and, thankfully, did not speak too loudly. As we were leaving the table, the girls' mother commented on how "active" Ryan was. If she only knew.

The next day at sea was wonderful, at least for a while. We swam, sunned, played bingo, watched movies, and ate (a lot). The kids' counselors had a special program planned for the evening—a picnic dinner and a scavenger hunt. We had informed the counselors that Ryan had ADHD and made sure they could give him his medications at the appropriate time. They assured us they had experience in taking care of kids and that there would be no problem. I felt good that Julie would be close by, even though

Ryan would be in a group of younger kids.

Jim and I were looking forward to a quiet, peaceful dinner away from our two little blessings for a couple of hours. We enjoyed every quiet moment, especially the stroll around the deck in the moonlight. Even so, we couldn't keep from wondering out loud about Ryan and how he was doing. It's a good thing we didn't know what was happening three decks above.

According to Julie, big sister and eager news reporter, the evening was a total disaster. Ryan didn't eat dinner and wouldn't (couldn't?) settle down. He would not listen to the counselors and engaged in many inappropriate behaviors. During the scavenger hunt, the counselors put Julie in charge of a group and then assigned Ryan to her group. As the kids made their way down the various decks, in search of items for the scavenger hunt, Ryan ran wildly, yelling and screaming. As Julie told it, passengers were opening their cabin doors to see what was going on and becoming quite upset. I did not have any problem getting the picture.

The more Julie tried to calm Ryan the wilder he got. When they finally returned to the counselors, he grabbed a can of Coke and threw it at Julie, soaking her clothes with sticky soda. Jim and I, three levels below, were oblivious to what was happening. No one attempted to contact or page us and Ryan remained out of control until we arrived at the appointed time. Of course, that was the end of the "supervised" kids' activities for Ryan. After what happened, we were afraid to let him out of our sight. So much for the wonderful family cruise we had imagined after reading the slick brochures.

New Year's Eve was our final night at sea. After a long day of shopping in Nassau, we were looking forward to a formal dinner with the captain and a New Year's Eve Party to welcome in 1989. When we arrived back on board the ship, all four of us hurried to our cabin to get ready for the big night. Jim was the last to shower. By the time he finished, the kids and I were ready to go.

Jim called out from the bathroom and asked me to bring his suit from the closet. When I opened the closet door my heart sank. There was no suit. My mind began spinning. Where was Jim's suit? Did we leave it at the hotel in Florida?

"Jim," I shouted, "your suit is not here! Where is it?" I was afraid to hear the answer.

With more than a hint of annoyance Jim responded, "I don't know. You're the one who packed it."

"I didn't pack it!" I snapped. "You were responsible for packing your clothes. I packed for the kids and me. The last time I saw your suit, it was hanging behind the bedroom door at home."

The realization hit us both like a rock between the eyes. Jim's suit was at home in California. The kids and I were ready for dinner with the captain and Jim's suit was four thousand miles away.

Ryan started yelling. "Come on. Let's go. I'm hungry!"

Julie was saying, "It's okay, Daddy, just wear something else."

I don't remember exactly what I said but I am sure it didn't come close to terms of endearment.

Jim didn't even have a decent pair of trousers with him. His wardrobe for the trip consisted of shorts and T-shirts, a pair of gray cotton Dockers, a long-sleeved gray striped shirt, a casual belt and no tie.

There were close to 1800 passengers on board the Oceanic that New Year's Eve. My husband was the only man on board who showed up for dinner with the captain with no suit or tie. To make matters worse, we had to stand in a long line to shake hands with the captain before entering the dining room. As luck would have it, a photographer was there to capture the occasion. At the time, I found not even a shred of humor in the situation. I was still steaming because Jim blamed me for not remembering to bring his suit.

Our Canadian dinner partners were gracious. By this time, they knew all about Ryan having ADHD and Tourette syndrome. The girls had told them about the scavenger hunt disaster. There had also been some other table antics and tics that we needed to explain. Generally though, the eight of us had enjoyed a pleasant time together.

The girls were especially lovely that night. Each was wearing a fancy, very expensive-looking dress with full petticoats and matching bows in their hair. Their mom looked beautiful too—and their dad was wearing a suit. They all looked stunning.

We made it through dinner with no catastrophes. Afterwards, we moved to the lounge area where a magician was performing tricks and illusions for the kids. The room was crowded but we managed to find the kids a table up close. As usual, waiters were milling around and passing out soft drinks. The kids each ordered a Coke and placed their drinks on the small round table in front of them.

I remember the scene unfolding as if in slow motion. I was frozen, powerless to stop what was happening. Ryan jumped up from his seat, stretching to see the magician's trick a little closer. As he leaned forward, his leg bumped the table, causing it to tip. Julie and each of the two girls in their beautiful fancy dresses were instantly soaked with Coca Cola.

"It was an accident, Mommy, it was an accident!" Ryan yelled.

Everyone was staring. The girls jumped up and the Coke ran down their legs and onto their fancy ruffled socks. They quickly began wiping the sticky soda off their taffeta skirts. I was mortified.

Ryan apologized, I apologized, Jim apologized, and Julie apologized. We all felt terrible. We offered to have the dresses dry-cleaned, but the Canadians were merciful. They tried to put us at ease and politely refused our offer to have the dresses cleaned.

We went back to our room for Julie to change clothes and to take some time for us all to recoup before the New Year's Eve party began. Jim and I were hoping Ryan would fall asleep and we could forget the party. He didn't and we couldn't.

As we joined the other passengers later that evening, we danced and sang. We wore funny-looking hats, blew horns, drank a ginger ale toast and ushered in the New Year floating on a big red boat somewhere off the coast in the Bahamas.

We were a family—through thick and thin, asthmatic bronchitis, obsessive spending sprees, hyperactive outbursts, spilled soda, and forgotten suits. Somehow, I felt at peace. I was thankful for our many blessings and hopeful that 1989 would bring a year of peace and happiness for our family—and a miracle cure for Ryan.

Chapter 6

Laying Down the Law

"God grant me the serenity to accept the things
I cannot change, the courage to change
the things I can, and the wisdom to know the difference."[1]
Reinhold Neibuhr

The end of the cruise also signaled the end of 1988. As we boarded the plane and headed home to California, I felt totally exhausted from the trip and emotionally drained. Yet, the beginning of 1989 offered me hope that Ryan would settle down and be better in the new year. Little did I know the roller coaster we were riding had only reached a small, temporary peak on its journey. Unfortunately, we were in for a long downhill ride.

After the Christmas gift exchange incident, my relationship with the third grade teacher, Mrs. Terry, improved dramatically. I was sure the principal's involvement contributed to the improvement and I felt satisfied things were moving in the right direction. Ryan's behavior, though, continued to deteriorate, not only at school, but at home.

We decided to consult another doctor after a disappointing experience with the psychiatrist that originally failed to diagnose TS in Ryan. We hoped the new psychiatrist would have a broader knowledge of ADHD and Tourette syndrome.

We were still seeing Dr. Comings at the City of Hope Medical Center for medication monitoring and were grateful for his continuing concern and generous availability to help, even after normal office hours. His clinic, however, was sixty-five miles from home, making it difficult to go frequently.

Until this time, Ryan's medication regime was fairly simple, consisting of Ritalin and Stelazine.

By spring there had been a rapid flurry of medication changes that included trials of Haldol (halperidol), Tofranil (imiprimine), Elavil (amitriptyline), and Catapres (clonidine). Dr. Comings prescribed the medications in a variety of combinations that most often included Ritalin.

The hyperactivity was indomitable and seemed to be the antecedent for verbal and eventually physical aggression. Ryan was often unreasonable and oppositional. Coprolalia, which we tried so hard to extinguish with Tabasco sauce, was becoming a bigger challenge. He was also flashing the "finger sign" impulsively and frequently.

During this time Ryan seemed to have additional problems. He was obsessed about some things and compulsive about others. Along with the erratic and horrible behavior, he would constantly kiss me, saying he felt as if he "had" to do it. He would say "I love you" repeatedly. He became fearful of bugs, to the point of having what I would describe as "panic attacks" at the sight of even a small fly.

Most concerning of all was the self-abusive behavior that had started for the first time. Ryan would often try to hurt himself when frustrated or angry. It began with hitting himself in the head with his closed fist and then progressed to hitting himself in the face, sometimes until his nose would bleed. Other times he would purposely do dangerous things like throwing himself off high places or riding his bike into the street in front of oncoming cars. During these episodes, he had no sense of danger.

Jim and I searched for solutions throughout this difficult time. We attended parenting classes and workshops on learning disabilities. We joined Ch.A.D.D., a support group for parents of children with ADHD. I read every book I could find that mentioned anything about raising a difficult child and I talked with anyone who would listen. We tried new behavioral modification programs. We used check marks, happy faces, stars, stickers, and poker chips. We tried to ignore the negative behaviors and reward the positive; sometimes we had to search hard for those.

Ryan ripped the point sheets off the wall and threw them in our faces. A "feelings" chart depicting various emotions was the focus of many discussions in our vain attempts to take his "emotional temperature" at different times. He quickly became bored with the feelings chart.

We had learned from experience that spanking did not work with Ryan—it only fueled the fire. We'd tried spanking when he was younger, but it didn't work. It seemed that he never reacted to pain in a normal way. It scared us when we discovered our spankings never provoked tears or a change in Ryan's behavior.

We initiated "time-outs" that were sometimes successful, but many times he would trash the time-out area, kicking the chairs and putting marks or holes in the walls. Then we designated the bathroom as the time-out room, believing that he could do less damage there—it wasn't necessarily so.

The psychiatrist offered little in the way of direction or advice. A problem with both psychiatrists we had seen was conflicting advice. No matter what we did, it was never the "right" thing.

If we were low-key and tried not to overreact to Ryan's misbehavior, the psychiatrists told us to be more assertive. If we were assertive, the doctors said we were being too confrontational. If we responded to Ryan's outbursts, we were "reinforcing" the negative behavior. They told us to ignore him. If we tried to ignore the behavior, they told us we should be more nurturing—after all, he probably wasn't getting enough attention.

We were damned if we did and damned if we didn't. I found myself trying to analyze my every response to Ryan's actions and I was driving myself crazy in the process. Did I do the right thing? Did I do the wrong thing? All I knew for sure was that I was doing the best I could, and so was Jim.

We continued to burn up the phone lines to Dr. Comings—adding, increasing or deleting medications, and hoping to find a perfect balance that would spell relief. By April of 1989 Ryan's behavior was so out of control we felt compelled to try something different.

We consulted a new therapist, a psychologist who treated children and adults with Tourette syndrome. Although distance was an obstacle, especially for any type of long-term therapy, we decided to give the therapist a try. We were desperate for help.

The doctor was warm and friendly, and she asked that we call her Liz. I had prepared well for the visit, writing down Ryan's medication schedule and a long list of the problematic behaviors. At the time of our visit Ryan was taking Haldol, Tofranil and Ritalin.

The behaviors I had documented were (in no particular order):

1. Cursing
2. Name-calling
3. Defiance
4. Banging his head on the wall
5. Hitting himself in the head and face (really hard)

6. Threatening to kill himself
7. Threatening to kill us
8. Saying he wants to die—to just get it over with
9. Constantly kissing us and saying "I love you"
10. Extreme and unreasonable fear of bugs
11. Afraid to be out of the room and away from us (this was new)
12. Going crazy every time the phone rings
13. Jerking the steering wheel while we're driving
14. Hitting and punching us and Julie
15. Fixated on trying to kick us between the legs
16. Giving us and everyone else the "finger" sign
17. Having a seemingly "I don't care" attitude
18. Showing remorse but usually much later after episodes
19. Going berserk in a store when he can't get what he wants
20. Unacceptable social behavior
21. Throwing furniture

Liz was extremely valuable in helping us sort out which behaviors were TS-related, and which of Ryan's behaviors were attention-seeking and manipulative. She is a proponent of cognitive behavioral therapy and expressed her belief that children with TS respond best to that type of therapeutic intervention.

Liz suggested a "tough love" type of approach to get a handle on a situation that had spiraled dangerously out of control. Although I was confident in her knowledge, some of the suggestions seemed unconventional and extremely harsh. Jim and I listened intently and, despite some hesitation, we finally agreed to follow through with her recommendations.

When Ryan became aggressive and combative, Liz suggested we remove all toys and other goodies from his room until he could earn them back. If he continued to be noncompliant and abusive, she suggested that we remove everything from his room, even the furniture, leaving only his mattress and bedding on the floor. As a final consequence she proposed that we remove the pillows and bedding, leaving only a bare mattress on the floor of a totally bare room.

She asked what Ryan might do in response to such actions and we both answered at the same time, "He'll jump out the window!" Because Ryan's room was on the second floor, Liz suggested we put bars on his window to prevent him from jumping out and hurting himself.

I also complained that Ryan threw fits at the dinner table about the food. He was always complaining that he didn't like what I served (even if he really did). Then he would cry for a snack later in the evening because he was hungry. Liz suggested that we give Ryan the opportunity to eat dinner with the family first, but if he was inappropriate and disruptive, we should take him to his room. If he later complained of being hungry, she recommended we offer him some slices of bread with water, but nothing else.

Jim and I drove home with a sense of hope and confusion. We felt confused because some of the suggestions seemed so drastic, almost inhumane and certainly not nurturing. Interspersed with feelings of hope was a sense of dread. I had read about "Tough Love" meetings for parents of delinquent teenagers. I had also heard stories of parents who had changed the locks on their doors and not allowed their abusive or drug-addicted teens to return.

I tried to reason it out and convince myself that Liz was right. Perhaps a little "tough love" now at the age of nine would prevent more extreme measures when Ryan became older. I accepted trying the drastic consequences she suggested, but I still did not feel good about it. At the time I was sure of only one thing—something had to change. If it took serving my son bread and water instead of cookies and milk, then I would make myself do it. I was determined to help Ryan, even if the process was painful for all of us.

Jim and I stopped at the hardware store on the way home. We could not bring ourselves to buy bars, but we did buy a metal screen that would cover the entire bedroom window. When we got home and realized all the furniture we would have to move, we decided instead to use our extra bedroom for Ryan's new room.

Jim spray painted the metal screen a matching cream color and bolted it securely to the wall above and below the window. We removed everything from the room except a twin mattress with a pillow and blanket.

Later that day we informed Ryan about the new "quiet room" and took him upstairs for a look. While he surveyed the room, we laid down the ground rules and were very clear about our expectations for his behavior.

We informed Ryan about the consequences for disrupting dinner, refusing food, or knocking over his plate. He seemed unfazed when we told him about the prospects of eating only bread and water.

We explained that the "quiet room" was a place for him to go where he could be alone and regain his self-control. We told Ryan if he went to the quiet room and stayed inside for the required number of minutes, we would allow the door to remain open. He would be free to come out when the timer sounded.

We also told him we would have to close the door if he refused to stay inside. We warned him that if he persisted in trying to come out of the room, we would need to lock the door during the time-out period. Except for a slight curiosity about the metal screen on the window, Ryan appeared bored with the whole presentation. The fireworks began the next night.

Chapter 7

Blood, Sweat and Tears

"There are times when parenthood seems nothing more than feeding the mouth that bites you."[1]
Peter DeVries

It started out as a typical day with Ryan. He began the morning with cursing and verbal threats. He refused to get up and became physically abusive when I tried to assist. He settled down a short time after taking his pills and seemed under control and in good spirits when I dropped him off at school.

Nothing remarkable happened during class that day. He was on the "chip" system and Mrs. Terry's note home reflected he had earned most of his chips.

When Ryan came home from school he was irritable, edgy, and restless. He complained of being bored and flitted from one activity to another. Playing Nintendo, which used to be a calming activity for Ryan, now seemed to set him off, especially if he could not achieve the level he wanted. He followed me from room to room, whining, complaining, and throwing himself around on the floor. An offer to ride bikes together was rejected, as were my suggestions for a number of other activities.

Over the past few weeks, dinner time had been the most trying and difficult time with Ryan. Although we reminded him about the ground rules we had set the night before, he continued to monopolize the dinner conversation. He complained about the "sucky" food I had fixed, demanded that I fix something different and was generally loud and obnoxious.

We warned Ryan again, reminding him he would need to take five minutes "time-out" in the quiet room if he did not comply. His response was to escalate even further. Then he took the time-out, only to return again and engage our attention by outrageous behavior.

We told Ryan that because of his unacceptable behavior he would have to sit away from us, over at the kitchen bar area. He then began cursing, threatening us, and shaking the table, causing the drinks to spill. When Jim and I attempted to physically remove him, he jumped on top of the table, knocking over bowls of food, and escaped by running away before we could grab him.

When we tried to stop him in the hallway, he dodged us and ran out the front door. We soon realized the more we attempted to chase him, the farther he would run. We chose to wait inside. Ryan came back a few minutes later and started crying, saying he was sorry.

"I'm just a no-good, Mommy," he cried. "I don't know why I did that."

I was mad and so was Jim. Ryan knew it. When I brushed away his numerous attempts to hug me he didn't argue. We explained that he could not finish eating dinner with the family because of his inappropriate behavior. Instead, he would need to spend ten minutes alone in the "quiet room." I suggested he use the time to think of what he had done and of other behaviors that would have been more appropriate. He obediently followed me up the stairs to the sparse room and sat on the mattress in the middle of the floor.

"Don't shut the door, Mommy," he said. "You aren't going to shut the door, are you?" I assured Ryan the door could remain open as long as he stayed inside and remained quiet for the full ten minutes. He nodded that he understood. I left him sitting quietly on the mattress and returned downstairs to see what was left of dinner.

I had barely sat down when I heard him sneaking down the steps. As I jumped up to investigate, I saw him run down the hall and dart back inside the room. When I entered the bedroom he was jumping up and down on the mattress and giggling. I asked if he remembered what would happen if he chose not to stay inside the room. He just kept jumping up and down, repeating "fart, fart, fart" between giggles. I sternly reminded him that if he came outside the room again it would be necessary for me to shut the door. Before I even reached the bottom, Ryan was standing at the top of the stairs, swinging his feet through the spaces in the banister.

"I'm sorry, Ryan," I said, climbing back up the stairway. "Because you have decided to disobey and continue to come out, I will have to shut the door."

"No, Mom, no," he cried. "Please don't shut the door! Please don't shut the door. I'll stay this time," he promised. "Just don't shut the door."

I explained it was not *my* decision to shut the door, that I would have preferred it to remain open. "*You* made the decision to have the door closed, Ryan," I told him. "By deliberately disobeying, not once, but twice, you are the one who decided the door needs to be closed."

As I attempted to pull the door closed, he grabbed the handle from inside and pulled hard. It quickly became a tug of war. I wedged my foot against the doorjamb and I pulled the handle again as hard as I could. I tried my best to pull the door closed. Ryan, however, was on the inside doing the same, and unfortunately, doing a much better job.

I refused to go along with the game. I informed Ryan I would have to lock the door if he did not leave it closed. He went ballistic, calling me a "mother-fucking shit ass."

I tried warning Ryan that we would increase his time in the quiet room if he continued, but he zoned out at that point. I knew I could not reach him. He had "the look" in his eyes—the look I had seen many times before. He was physically in the room but appeared totally unaware of what was happening. He continued to curse and spit. As I attempted to shut the door one more time, he spit in my face and then released the handle.

I quickly took advantage of his releasing the handle and closed the door, quickly turning the lock. I listened but didn't hear anything for a few seconds. I called through the door to tell Ryan I would be back when he had completed his ten minutes of quiet time. He responded by shouting, "Fuck you, bitch."

I paused outside the door briefly, listening for his reaction. After hearing nothing, I started away from the door when I suddenly heard something hit the wall. As I walked back toward the room I realized he was banging his head into the wall! Ryan hit his head against the wall harder and harder and began to make crying noises. I wasn't sure what to do. I knew if I opened the door I would be "giving in," yet my motherly instincts were compelling me to stop the loud jolts that were ripping at my heart with each loud thud. I gave in quickly and opened the door. Ryan was standing nearby, his face bright red and puffy with a dark streak across his forehead.

He grabbed me around the waist and said, "I just want to die, Mom. Just let me die and get it over with!"

I returned his hug briefly and then moved him away. I began to lecture him sternly. "Ryan, I know what you are doing. I understand you feel upset, but hurting yourself will not solve the problem. I am going to close this door and lock it until you are able to stay away from the door, remain quiet and stop banging your head."

"If you choose to bang your head on the wall," I warned him, "that's your decision. I will not allow you to manipulate me by threatening to hurt yourself. If you choose to continue this way, I will increase your time in the quiet room to twenty minutes instead of ten." With that, I walked out the door, closing and locking it behind me.

I felt sick to my stomach. I was petrified he would start banging his head again. I kept thinking about the visit with Liz, and the words "tough love" kept running through my mind.

The banging started up again, accompanied by a plaintive "ow" with each of the next few blows. Then it stopped. I listened closely, straining to hear what was happening in the room. Apart from soft whimpering, all was calm. I waited a few seconds longer and then set the timer on my watch for ten minutes.

I felt emotionally drained and my eyes were blurred with tears. Had I done the right thing? Could I go through an episode like this again? I wasn't sure. I really wasn't sure about anything at that point, except that I loved Ryan and he needed my help. He needed everyone's help.

Maybe Liz was right. Making him take responsibility for his behavior made sense, yet, he was my *baby*. In those long ten minutes I silently grieved for the normal little boy I had envisioned during my pregnancy. What had happened? What went wrong? The shrill beeping of the timer jolted me back from my mental haze.

When I unlocked the door to the quiet room Ryan looked sullen. He was lying very still on top of the mattress.

"Good job, Ryan," I said. "Your time is up."

Ryan slowly got up and hugged me, repeating again that he was sorry and that he was just a "no-good."

I assured him the episode was in the past and that he was starting over with a clean slate. He seemed satisfied with my assurances and went to his room to play Nintendo. All was well until a short time later when he came downstairs to announce he was going to have some cereal. I felt my stomach tighten as I realized what was about to happen.

"I'm sorry, Ryan," I said. "You won't be able to have cereal tonight." I asked if he remembered the rules we had discussed the night before about mealtimes. He didn't answer. I reminded him of the rule that he would give up his right to eat dinner and the right to have a snack later on if he did not eat what I served.

"But I'm starving," he bellowed. "You can't make me starve or I'll die!"

Little voices were going off in my head saying, "What's the big deal, give the kid some cereal." Then another voice responded, "Tough love, bread and water, tough love, bread and water."

"You know, Ryan," I began. "I have no intentions of making you starve. You are welcome to have some slices of bread and butter—as many as you like to fill you up."

"I'm not eating that crap," he persisted. "I'm going to get me some cereal."

"You are not allowed to have cereal tonight, Ryan," I continued. "You can have a big bowl for breakfast, but if you are hungry tonight, you will have to settle for bread and butter."

He started to whine, complaining that I was a horrible mother—that no decent mother would do that to her kid. I held firm and reminded him that if he continued to rant he would need to take another brief time-out in the quiet room until he could regain control and act appropriately.

"Well, make me the stupid bread then," he snapped, "and get me some milk."

"I will be glad to help you make the bread and butter, Ryan, if you ask me in a polite way. But you'll have to settle for water tonight instead of milk."

"Pleeeeeeze get me the bread and butter, big Mama," he said, "but I don't want any stupid water."

He ate one slice of bread with butter and a few bites of another. I sat with him as he ate and he chatted as if nothing had ever happened.

We went through the usual ups and downs the rest of the evening. When he was finally in bed and sound asleep I tiptoed in, kissed his head as I have done every night since his birth, and whispered, "I love you, Ryan."

Chapter 8

No Laughing Matter

*"Hope is the feeling you have that
the feeling you have isn't permanent."*[1]
Jean Kerr

The "quiet room" proved to be anything but quiet. The following six days offered more of the same difficult behaviors and challenges to our authority. The aggression worsened, followed by bouts of self-recrimination that resulted in self-abusive behaviors.

The self-injurious behavior had started several months earlier with Ryan biting his arm until it bled, hitting himself in the head with his fist, and banging his fist into the wall. It then progressed to hitting himself in the face with both fists, butting his head into the wall and running head first and full force into the wall. When he was outdoors, he would often lay down and bang his head onto the concrete. Although you could plainly see he was feeling the pain, it was almost as if he obtained relief by being in pain. It was frightening.

Ryan's self-injurious behavior also escalated into life-threatening situations. He would often become angry at himself or someone else while we were driving, impulsively grabbing the steering wheel and jerking it while the car was moving. Other times he would open the car door while the car was moving, even if we were on the freeway. We learned to drive in the slow lane, have someone in the back seat and avoided taking him alone whenever possible.

Putting Ryan into the "quiet room" proved to be too much for me. With his behavior deteriorating rapidly, the necessity of putting him in "the room" became more frequent. Instead of complying or adjusting, he resisted even more. Instead of just banging his head on the wall, he slammed

47

his head into the wall and huge purple "goose eggs" would appear.

He hit the doorjamb with his fist so hard that his hand would swell and turn various shades of red and purple. He refused the bread and water on the nights he lost his dinner privileges and became nauseated after taking his medications on an empty stomach.

Crying and whining were constant.

"I'm just a no-good. I can't learn. I'm not worth anything. I'm stupid and dumb. I'm going to go to hell." Ryan repeated these words over and over.

When he wasn't crying or throwing a tantrum, his general hyperactivity caused major problems. If he wasn't spilling a drink on purpose, Ryan's inability to sit still usually resulted in an "accident" of one sort or another. He then would become angry at himself and the self-denigration would start all over again.

He would become angry and hit me, his dad or Julie, and then become remorseful and depressed. Sometimes he would become angry at an inanimate object and vent his anger by hitting or throwing something at the person closest to him. Sometimes he would scream at us for looking at him the "wrong way."

After a week of trying the "tough love" approach, I couldn't stand it any more. Ryan had an appointment scheduled with Dr. Comings for Wednesday of that week. The sixty-five mile trip to the medical center was horrible and this day I had no one to ride along in case I needed help.

Ryan began pulling my hair on the freeway when I said something he didn't like. He tried to jerk the steering wheel but I was able to pull off to the side and "talk him down."

When we finally arrived at the hospital we found the large waiting room crowded with people. There were at least eight or ten other young boys with Tourette syndrome in the waiting area and they were all ahead of us on the schedule. I settled down on one of the few empty chairs and prepared for a long and miserable wait.

Ryan behaved well, considering the stimulation in the waiting room. He seemed content to watch the other boys and they entertained him with their activities. At one point, he leaned close and whispered, "Look at that stupid kid over there, Mom. I think he has Tourette's."

Once we made it into the small examining room Ryan was all over the place. He wheeled around on the doctor's stool, wadded up the paper on the exam table, and opened every cabinet door that didn't have a lock. He was like an octopus while I was trying to contain him. I eventually got him to sit on my lap until the doctor came into the room.

Dr. Comings entered cheerfully and said, "Hi, Ryan! How are you doing?"

"Fine," Ryan said, still sitting on my lap.

"How's it going at school?" the doctor inquired.

"Fine," Ryan replied.

"How about at home—is that going fine, too?" asked Dr. Comings as he sorted through the file.

"Yep," said Ryan convincingly. "Everything's fine."

The doctor could tell by the contortions of my face that everything was not fine. What was so confusing was that Ryan was not a child who lied. His replies to the doctor's questions were genuine. On the surface he seemed oblivious to all that was happening. Yet I knew deep inside he was accumulating emotional scars—wounds that would surface during bouts of self-abusive behavior and depression about his failures.

Dr. Comings suggested we begin Ryan on an anti-seizure medication called Tegretol. Although previous EEG's (electroencephalographs) had shown no abnormal seizure activity, the doctor explained that rage attacks and aggression are similar to seizure activity. The type of seizure or misfiring occurs too deep in the brain to be detected by conventional testing. He assured me that medications such as Tegretol often have a positive effect in treating severe aggression in children with Tourette syndrome and ADHD. He recommended Ryan also continue with Haldol, Ritalin and Tofranil.

Although at the time I was desperate to try anything, I was nervous about adding a fourth medication. Dr. Comings tried to allay my fears by explaining that fighting a severe case of Tourette syndrome was like fighting a war. He explained our country must depend on not just the Army when fighting a war—it also uses the Navy, Marines and Air Force to effectively fight the battle.

In fighting TS and its associated behaviors, he explained, we need medications that will address each of the different areas involved, such as tics, hyperactivity, depression, obsessions, and aggression. It was a simple analogy that satisfied my overwhelmed brain. I left the doctor's office clutching a tiny piece of paper that would order the pharmacist to send out the fourth battalion.

Our ride home was uneventful—which in itself was an event. Dr. Comings had cautioned that the 100 mg. tablets of Tegretol he prescribed might be hard to find, so I decided to let my fingers do the walking. I made calls to half a dozen local pharmacies and found that a nearby Thrifty Drug Store had the pills in stock.

It was around four o'clock in the afternoon when Ryan, Julie and I left to get the prescription. Ryan was hyper on the way, but not abusive—at least not physically. The three of us went inside and my heart sank when I saw the crowd of people lingering at the pharmacy counter. The pharmacist saw me walk up and immediately reached out to take the prescription I was holding. As I extended the paper across the counter, he snapped, "If you're going to wait for this, it will be an hour wait, maybe longer."

What on earth am I going to do with Ryan for an hour?, I worried to myself. Out of earshot from Ryan, who was busy investigating a nearby display of toys, I took a chance and approached the pharmacist again.

"Is there any possibility it may be ready sooner?" I asked in a pleading tone.

"Look, lady," he snapped. "I've got twenty of these ahead of you. You have to wait your turn like everybody else."

I walked away, embarrassed that I had asked and annoyed that he was so rude. I needed those pills, though, and knew there were no other pharmacies close by that had them in stock. I gathered up Julie and Ryan and decided we would go to the library. It wasn't far away and Ryan loved to get books. I thought it might be a good way to spend the hour.

Ryan was agreeable about going to the library and the three of us headed for the door. On the way out, a toy vending machine caught his eye and he stopped, hastily pulling all the change out of his pocket. The machine held a variety of small plastic toys, encased in plastic bubbles. The toy ring piqued Ryan's interest.

Before I knew it, he dropped a quarter in the machine. When the plastic bubble dropped, he anxiously ripped it open to see his prize. He didn't get the ring, but instead he got a small piece of paper with a cartoon on it. He sorted through his change for another quarter but had only nickels and pennies left.

"Come on, Ryan," I coaxed. "Let's go to the library."

"I want a ring!" he shouted while shaking the machine. "It shows you get a ring. Gimme a quarter!" he demanded.

I took his hand and urged him to come with me. I tried to explain about the vending machines—how you usually don't get what you expect.

Ryan would have no part of it.

As the automatic doors of the store opened to let us out, he hurled the remaining coins he was holding in his hand. He threw them full-force into the crowded parking lot and began shouting obscenities at the top of his lungs.

As usual, people were staring. I strengthened my grip on his hand and sped up the pace toward our Suburban, parked a considerable distance away. Ryan continued to shout, and his face was full of rage. He went from calm to ballistic in a matter of seconds.

Once inside the truck he continued the tirade. Julie tried to comfort him but he lashed out at her and called her names. I began to slowly back out of the parking space, hoping that a change in scenery would distract him and stop the obsessing about the ring.

Just as I pulled the truck out of the parking lot and onto the street, Ryan lunged at me. He physically attacked me, hitting me in the head and shoulders with his fist. I stopped abruptly, just short of a busy intersection. I tried to block his attack by holding my arm up in front of my face. When that failed, I started hitting back at him, desperately trying anything to get him to stop. He grabbed my hair and jerked my head back. Then, before I could realize what was happening, he threw open the door of the Suburban, put his foot on top of the open window and vaulted to the top of the large truck.

I was stunned. I looked around at the traffic moving all around us and realized Ryan was really on top of the truck. I shifted into park, shut off the motor and motioned for the cars behind us to go around, but no one moved.

When I got out of the truck Ryan continued his verbal attack. I climbed on the running board and reached my hand toward him. He kicked at me, still screaming about the toy ring. It must have only lasted a couple of minutes but it seemed like an eternity. I shouted for Julie to run back to the drug store to call the police. I didn't know what else to do. When Julie started across the street, Ryan leaped from the top of the truck, ran across the street and into the parking lot. I yelled for Julie to keep her eye on him until I could move the truck out of traffic. When the light changed, I made a U-turn in the intersection and pulled the truck back into the store's parking lot. I pulled into the nearest parking space and jumped out of the truck. When I started toward Ryan he began to dart between the cars. I knew that chasing him would only prolong the agony.

I broke down and started to cry. Julie offered to call Grandma to come and help us. "No honey," I cried. "Call Aunt Sally." She lives closer and can get here faster." Julie ran inside the store; in just a few minutes she returned and announced that my sister was on her way. I plopped back down inside the truck, shaking uncontrollably and crying while I watched Ryan through the tears.

Just a few minutes later he walked toward the truck and said, "I'm sorry, Mommy. Can we go to the library now?" I couldn't believe it. For him it was no big thing. He didn't seem to realize the magnitude of what he had done. To Ryan, it was as if nothing had even happened.

My hair was a tangled mess from being pulled, my dress was torn at the neck, and I had red marks on my arms and face. Mascara was dripping down my cheeks from crying and he wondered if we could go to the library!

As hard as this was to believe, it was certainly not the first time Ryan switched moods so quickly. Many times after a tantrum or rage he would suddenly change his whole demeanor. He would transform before our eyes into a calm, controlled child with little realization of the previous episode.

By the time Aunt Sally arrived, Ryan was perfectly calm. I asked if she would take him to her home for the evening and she said she would. I explained to Ryan that I just didn't feel like being with him for a while and that he would have to stay with Aunt Sally until I was feeling better. As they pulled out of the parking lot, I broke down and cried again.

Poor Julie. I felt so sorry for her. She hugged me and assured me everything was going to be all right. For a moment, she was the mother and I was the child. Finally, I pulled myself together and we walked hand in hand back into the drug store. The prescription was ready, but I don't remember seeing the pharmacist or even paying for it. I was emotionally numb. I felt like the walking dead.

After getting the Tegretol, Julie and I drove home. We found Jim home from work and waiting for dinner.

"What have you guys been up to all day?" he asked innocently. "Where's Ryan?"

Chapter 9

On Pins and Needles

*"Man sees your actions,
but God sees your motives."[1]*
Thomas á Kempis

The results of using Tegretol seemed apparent within the first week. Although there were no dramatic personality changes, the frequency of aggressive episodes seemed to lessen. Also, the length of time he was out of control seemed much shorter.

Despite all the horrible acting out and embarrassing behaviors, I was determined to not hide Ryan away or shut him out from normal life experiences. When Little League began that spring, we registered him with a youth baseball team in a nearby city.

Ryan loved playing baseball practically more than anything. He had played on a Little League team since the age of four and had developed quite a strong arm. Early during practice sessions, before the regular season began, Ryan made his mark as a promising pitcher. The coach bragged on several occasions about his star "lefty." He was sure Ryan would psyche out the other players because he looked so small but had such a powerful throw.

Ryan behaved fairly well and kept himself under control during most of the practices. We would always time his Ritalin to get the best advantage. Most of the time it seemed to work. Unfortunately, delaying Ritalin until time for practice meant that Ryan did not have the benefit of the medication for an hour or two *before* practice.

Many times we suffered a major episode at home and then gave him

Ritalin as he went out the door. Then, over the next two hours of baseball practice, he would act as calm and normal as the other boys. There were times, though, during the practices that we were really "sweating bullets." We never knew when he would explode with an expletive or annoy or provoke the other players.

Jim and I had been doing our homework about Tourette syndrome. We started attending support group meetings at the City of Hope and we read everything we could find. We decided it would be best to inform the coach and other parents about Ryan having TS and ADHD. We have always felt that honesty is the best policy and that having a neurological condition is nothing to be ashamed about.

When we told the coach, he seemed appreciative, understanding, and very supportive. We encouraged him to treat Ryan exactly the same as the other boys—no special favors.

Everything seemed to go well for the first few games. Ryan got to pitch and did remarkably well. He always did well when he was on the field, but the bench was a different story. If Ryan wasn't playing, he wasn't interested. He couldn't sit still and refused to watch his teammates up at bat. His mind was constantly spinning and his body was constantly moving. When the coach ordered him to sit still, he couldn't. He would talk to the other players, flip their hats off, pull their shirt-tails out, and kick dirt on their shoes.

When the coach asked the other kids to "knock it off," they did, but Ryan couldn't. When he failed to comply with the demands to stop whatever annoying thing he was doing, the coach got angry—rather quickly too. The coach's appreciation for knowing about the disorder, and the understanding and support he had previously pledged, soon gave way to furious irritation. He still used Ryan to pitch occasionally but had little use for him otherwise. He ignored him whenever possible.

We were glad Ryan even got to play at all. We were happy he was getting a chance to learn the meaning of sportsmanship. He made some progress at establishing peer relationships, even though it was rocky at times.

By the end of April, Ryan seemed to have taken one step forward and two steps back. He was having less frequent episodes of aggression and the head banging and wall hitting had decreased. The tics, however, had gotten worse. He had started a new tic of rubbing his fingers together. This may not have seemed like much of a problem on the surface, but it was seriously interfering with his ability to do things. Even playing Nintendo, Ryan would have to stop frequently to rub his fingers together, causing him to misfire or have a delayed response.

It was extremely irritating when he had to stop his activities to tic. Ryan's frustration about constantly rubbing his fingers together usually reached a point of annoyance that quickly escalated into anger. Angry episodes would often escalate to aggression and then to full-blown rage attacks that could last anywhere from a minute to ten or fifteen minutes.

Another problem that had become more disturbing was the escalation of self-reproach and what seemed, at least to me, to be serious depression. He began to talk more and more about wanting to die. One day after a fit of rage he screamed, "I want to kill myself. Kill me, Mommy, kill me. I'm going to hell anyway. Just kill me."

I held him close for a long time and did my best to assure him everything was going to be okay. When it was over, Ryan seemed fine. He was back to being happy-go-lucky, acting as if nothing had happened.

Mrs. Hunt, the school principal, was becoming better acquainted with Ryan during this time. Although he was in special education and had a resource teacher for tutoring, Mrs. Hunt arranged for the SST (student study team) to assess Ryan. The purpose of the assessment was to evaluate his learning and behavioral problems at school. The SST determined that Ryan was definitely an "at risk" student and recommended him for a ten-week group counseling program at school.

The purpose of the sessions was to help the children explore their feelings, practice communication skills, work on building self-esteem and to learn decision-making skills and more appropriate behavior.

I readily gave permission for Ryan's participation. I requested the counselor notify me when sessions would begin, how long each would last, and the frequency of the meetings. I also wanted to know if Ryan would have any individual goals. I asked if I could receive feedback throughout the sessions that I could share with Ryan's psychiatrist, and if I could receive a written report at the conclusion of sessions.

Apart from any feedback I could elicit from Mrs. Terry, I heard nothing about the sessions. At the end of the ten-week period, I received a photocopied form letter from the counselor. It said the sessions had come to a close and that she had enjoyed having the children in her group. At the bottom of the form letter she had written, "Ryan needs to work on taking responsibility for his actions."

That was it. After ten weeks, all the counselor offered was that Ryan needed to take responsibility for his actions. I got the impression the counseling sessions were more of a learning exercise for the counselor than a benefit for the students.

Ryan also experienced his first suspension from school that spring. Mrs. Hunt was aware of Ryan's increasing difficulties and was extremely sympathetic. She became very involved in trying to help him and initiated several calls to Dr. Comings on behalf of Ryan. She too seemed confused about how to handle a child who could swing from being charming and delightful to hyper, aggressive and, at times, totally irreverent and disrespectful. Dr. Comings advised Mrs. Hunt to treat Ryan as a normal child at school—to isolate him for swearing, but to give him the same consequences as the other children for other infractions.

One day the principal called to say she was suspending Ryan for trying to "choke" another child. I left work immediately to meet with Mrs. Hunt to discuss the incident and the suspension.

Mrs. Hunt appeared uncomfortable when she opened the door to her office. "I'm sorry Mrs. Hughes," she began, "but I will have to suspend Ryan from school for one day for choking another child." She handed me a copy of the school district's suspension form with the box checked next to "physical injury to another student."

When I entered the office I saw Ryan sitting quietly at a big round table, his head bent and his eyes focused on the floor.

"Hi, honey," I said. "What happened?"

"I didn't choke her, Mom," Ryan said calmly. "We were just playing ball and I was trying to get the ball away from her. Mrs. Hunt says I choked her but I didn't. I didn't choke anybody."

Confused, I looked at Mrs. Hunt and waited for an explanation.

"I believe Ryan is telling us the truth," she began. "I think he just was caught up in trying to get the ball back and got a little too rough. I don't think he intentionally meant to hurt the other student. But he was also rude to the student's mother and she was not pleased with Ryan's attitude."

I glanced at the official-looking suspension form. It was a multicolored quadruplicate document and the formality of the form struck me as to the seriousness of documenting incidents correctly. I told Mrs. Hunt I was uneasy because the form did not seem to accurately depict what happened. It was my concern, I explained, that someone unfamiliar with the incident could read the report and infer that Ryan had purposefully and deliberately caused an injury to another student. It appeared to me that was not the case at all.

Mrs. Hunt agreed to clarify the incident on the report. She wrote a better explanation on the form:

> Ryan jumped on a female student's back while playing ball. She was hurt, had a red mark on her neck and was upset by momentary loss of breath. In the classroom after the incident, the student's mother asked him why he had done it. Ryan responded with an obscenity. Ryan later apologized to the student. He maintained that he did not intend to hurt her.

I felt comfortable that the form more closely reflected what happened. It was certainly very different from the previous implication that Ryan had purposefully "choked" another student.

I took Ryan home and tried to impress upon him the seriousness about what had happened—that he had hurt another student and was suspended from school. He seemed contrite and remorseful about being suspended but couldn't seem to get over Mrs. Hunt thinking he had choked someone.

Along with problem solving about the incident, I informed Ryan he could not play outside the rest of the afternoon or the next day. He didn't like it, but at least he didn't blow up at me. I felt I was making some progress in teaching him to take responsibility for his actions.

His behavior continued to be up and down. At home we were walking on eggs, doing our best to head off any potential "episodes" and trying to keep one step ahead of the next "rage attack." Some days were better than others, but Jim and I were aware that none of our days with Ryan were normal.

We were grateful for the occasional good times we had. We just kept clinging to the hope that something (a new medication) or someone (a new teacher) would make a difference. The good times kept us going and kept us from giving up hope.

One morning while going through his backpack for school I found this note he had written the day before:

Dear Mom I had a good day
at school I did lot g of
thangs today and I didint
have to writ standerds
and didit get my name on her
list. and had a good day
I still have a reses to go,
love Ryan

(Dear Mom, I had a good day at school. I did lots of things today and I didn't have to write standards and didn't get my name on her list and had a good day. I still have a recess to go. Love, Ryan)

Love, Ryan. Yes, Ryan did love us. He told us so every day, even though he didn't (couldn't) show us. It was Ryan's love that made it possible for me to get up each morning and face again the uncertainty of his unpredictable behavior.

Chapter 10

Heaven Help Us

"There is nothing the body suffers
that the soul may not profit by."[1]
George Meredith

Ryan's behavior continued to be erratic and unpredictable that spring. My notes, though sporadic, reflected a two-week period that showed days of good behavior interspersed with days of outrageous misconduct.

Wednesday, April 26

Had a good morning. Flipped off several people at school. Was a little "edgy" after school but calmed down quickly. Went to Little League game and did very well. Best day we have had in a long time.

Thursday, April 27

Woke up cursing and angry. Came out of school cursing and giving people the finger. Called another student's mother a "shit ass." Went to Little League game and did well. Had a good evening.

Friday, April 28

Had difficulty waking. Some cursing but calmed down after taking his pills. Came out of school kicking and cursing. I took him to the park and he played well for an hour. Then started cursing and threw a Coke can at me. Extremely hyper at dinner—talkative, demanding, threatening, weepy, remorseful. Was provoking most of evening. We went out for pizza and he became angry and pushed, shoved and hit us. Cried all the way home saying, "I'm stupid and dumb. I can't learn. I'm no good. I'm going to die and go to hell, etc."

Saturday, April 29

Woke up cursing—had a "wild" look in his eyes. Laughing and goofy. He was defiant all morning. Would not stay in his room. We had to hold him down to keep him from hurting himself or us. A horrible day. Very violent and abusive. Hurt his hand hitting the door. Cried a lot. Vacillated from being demanding and violent to weepy and clinging. Dr. Comings recommended putting him back on the clonidine patch. He fell asleep on the couch after we put the patch on.

Sunday, April 30

Good behavior. Slept all the way to Knott's Berry Farm. A little cursing during noon hour. Tried pulling dad's hair on the way home but quit. Good behavior the rest of the evening. Overall good day.

Tuesday, May 2

Cursing when he first got up. Okay by the time he left for school. Principal called at 11:30 saying he was "out of control." I brought him home for lunch and he settled down—was active but not wild. I returned him to school and learned there had been a bomb threat at school that morning. Ryan and the other students had been outside on the playground for two hours and he got really "wound up." The teacher reported there was much cursing and that he was making "strange" sounds. At home he did fairly well. He was rubbing his fingers together a lot.

Wednesday, May 3

Hard to get up but his behavior was good. Very talkative but able to settle down after school. When Dad came home, Ryan demanded to play basketball. When his dad could not take him right that minute, Ryan started badgering, cursing, yelling, hitting, and kicking. There was a lot of spitting in our faces and he began to yell, "I'm going to kill, I'm going to kill." He would settle down for a few seconds and then shout "fuck" repeatedly. He seemed to be coming "in and out" of reality. Toward the end of the episode he started crying and begged, "Kill me, Mommy, kill me." The whole episode lasted about fifteen minutes. He finally accepted a five minute time-out. When that was over he was fine again, acting as if nothing had happened.

Thursday, May 4

Very hard to get up. Much cursing. Had a great day at school. At baseball practice he started trying to hit kids between the legs and was cursing. When his dad went over to intervene he started hitting and spitting at him. He took a time-out, took his Ritalin and continued practice with no problems. He lost control again later that evening. He started hitting, cursing and yelling "kill me, kill me" while I was attempting to hold him down. The episode lasted about ten minutes. After it was over, he settled down. He went to bed and I held him close, prayed with him and assured him he would do better the next day. I encouraged him to work on controlling his anger.

Monday, May 8

He was good in the morning. At school he deliberately kicked the soccer ball over the fence. He had trouble calming down. He bothered other students and was unable to focus on his work. He acted up a little at ball practice. There was some name calling and cursing. He was very "antsy."

Tuesday, May 9

Had a good morning. Some trouble focusing on his work at school and bothered the other students. He threw a ruler across the room. His behavior was good all evening. We went shopping and he was excellent.

Wednesday, May 10

Had a good morning. Bad day at school. He could not settle down and was sent to the office in the morning. Took him to the dentist in the afternoon and he was very hyper, never stopped talking. He crawled around on the floor of dentist's office, then kicked my eyeglasses under the dentist's sofa (on purpose). He was irritable and argumentative. He went to bed kicking, cursing and spitting.

Saturday, May 13

He woke up loud and very hyper. Could not calm down. He was this way all day long. He talked constantly, even to strangers at the store. He was good at ball game in the afternoon and had good behavior in the evening. He seemed much more calm.

Monday, May 15

Good behavior at school. In the evening we went to the store to buy a music tape. When the store did not have the tape he wanted in stock, he started screaming, cursing and hitting us. He could not accept that he wasn't able to get the tape and blamed it on us. It was nearly forty minutes before he regained total control.

Tuesday, May 16

It was a good morning. He was good on the field trip at school. He was also good after school. He went for a blood test and did well. We ate dinner out and Ryan did very well. Only a few minor outbursts of cursing in the evening.

Thursday, May 18

Had an okay morning. Bad behavior at school. Hitting, kicking, cursing and throwing. Hit another student during recess. He was hyper at ball practice. There was a lot of cursing and hitting at home during the evening.

Friday, May 19

Good morning and good at school. Good behavior the rest of the day and evening. Great day.

Tuesday, May 23

Good behavior at school in morning. Had a ninety minute recess at school and became hyper. Was sent to the office and stayed there the rest of the afternoon. Was hyper, defiant, hitting, etc. at home. Evening was okay.

Wednesday, May 24

Difficulty in getting dressed in morning. At school he threw crayons at the other students. He was isolated but continued to throw objects. He was sent home from school at 12:30. Behavior at home was good in the afternoon. Good behavior the rest of the day.

Throughout this time Ryan was taking four medications: Haldol, Ritalin, Tegretol and half of a clonidine patch. When a severe skin reaction occurred with the patch, we substituted oral clonidine.

What was so remarkable was the erratic pattern of his behavior. Although the medications did not change, Ryan's behavior was good some mornings and horrible on others. Some evenings were wonderful but other evenings were unbearable. There were no unusual circumstances at home and nothing we could pinpoint on the bad days to explain the extreme behavioral differences. He was clearly Dr. Jekyll and Mr. Hyde, and we never knew which one would wake up in his bed each morning.

The aggressive behavior was terrible to handle. It was the depression and self-abusive behaviors, however, that tore at my heart more. Ryan was ten years old and still wetting his pants daily.

He was extremely impulsive because of the ADHD and was unpredictable in nearly every situation. He would lash out at us and then feel horrible about what had happened. When his talk of wanting to die became more frequent, I knew we needed more help than the doctors could offer.

Chapter 11

Church Chat

*"I thank God for my handicaps, for,
through them, I have found myself,
my work, and my God."*[1]
Helen Keller

I admit I did not give Liz's recommendations a fair chance to work. To me, putting Ryan in the "quiet room" seemed to do much more harm than good. Instead of quieting down, he became self-injurious. He would bang his hand, head and face into the wall, often causing bruising, swelling and bleeding.

I also could not, in good conscience, give him only bread and water to eat, even if he had been a horrible brat at dinner. I struggled with my feelings and emotions. I knew I needed to be strong and consistent, yet I was sure there must be a better way.

I knew Ryan needed to accept responsibility for his conduct; however, I knew there were many times he truly could not help the outrageous behavior. I just did not feel harsh responses were appropriate for Ryan, especially given his tendency for hurting himself and his ongoing self-recrimination and depression.

Some could argue, I suppose, that I failed by not following through—that Ryan "won the battle" so to speak. Right or wrong, Jim and I made the decision to surrender this one particular battle and concentrate instead on winning the war. In doing so we knew we would need a new battle plan.

Our new plan of attack focused on the real enemy, Tourette syndrome, and not just the individual behaviors. We kept in close contact with Dr. Comings, adjusting the medication doses up or down as side effects occurred or new symptoms developed. We implemented a revised behavior modification plan at home using "poker chips" as a reward for appropriate behavior and brief time-outs for acting out behaviors.

We continued to consult the pediatric psychiatrist for support during the difficult times. Jim and I attended support groups for Tourette families at the City of Hope Medical Center, driving sixty-five miles each way without a thought given to the distance. We were hungry for any information we could get. We read everything we could get our hands on about parenting techniques.

We also prayed. Although there were times we were unable to attend church due to Ryan's difficult behavior, we never surrendered our faith in God. We taught both of our children to pray at an early age, and to trust God in all situations.

Since Ryan was born we had a nightly bedtime ritual of tucking him into bed, talking about whatever was on his mind and then sharing a bedtime prayer. Many nights we talked about God and heaven and what you have to "do" to get there.

Sometimes we looked up Bible verses that talked about what happens when we die and what a wonderful place heaven will be for those who believe. Because my faith had always been a source of strength and comfort to me, I naturally assumed it would be the same for my children.

Julie was always interested in spiritual things. She loved Sunday school, enjoyed being involved in church activities, was a devout Bible reader and very outspoken about her beliefs.

Ryan, too, loved Sunday school, although he did not always socialize well with the other kids. He also embraced our Christian faith with little more than the usual questions children have when trying to comprehend the unknown. I often wondered exactly how much he really understood. I never realized that our teachings about God and heaven would someday compound his emotional difficulties.

It began with a boating trip we had taken a year earlier with some other family members. Ryan was eight years old and beginning to show the first signs of coprolalia. I wasn't there when it happened, but Ryan told me about the incident later that night during our bedtime chat.

Evidently, Ryan had been using inappropriate words in front of another family member and her daughter. The child's mother warned Ryan if he did not stop cursing he wouldn't go to heaven. Even Ryan could figure out what that meant—if you weren't going to heaven, that meant you were going to hell.

When he told me about the incident that night, Ryan asked me if it was true—that if you cussed you wouldn't go to heaven. I reassured him cussing would not keep him from going to heaven and that God understands we are not perfect as human beings. I told him we must try our best to avoid doing something we know is wrong, but when we make a mistake, we can ask God to forgive us and He will. Ryan seemed to understand and accept my explanation and soon fell asleep.

I could not sleep though. I was angry that someone in my family could be so ignorant about Tourette syndrome. I had tried to explain repeatedly about the inappropriate behaviors—the cursing, the impulsivity, etc. I thought I had gotten through to everyone but I obviously had not. I don't think the child's mother said it to be cruel; I only know the painful repercussions of her words.

Unfortunately, the seeds of doubt were planted. For months Ryan anguished over every episode of misbehavior, fearful that he was doomed to hell. Over and over he agonized: "I can't go to heaven because I say bad words. I'm just a no-good. God can't love somebody as bad as I am. I'm going to go to hell because I'm so bad." Many times Jim and I would have to hold and comfort him, reassuring him of God's love and forgiveness while encouraging him to work on changing the behaviors that he could. He was continually plagued with self-doubt.

By the spring of 1989 the self-recriminations escalated even further. During the bad episodes he would beg us to "kill him," to "just get it over with." There were times when he seemed obviously depressed, but other times, within the same day, he seemed jubilant and carefree. We could never predict which way the pendulum would swing. When he began talking incessantly about wanting to die, I felt as if I wanted to die too. Ryan was barely ten years old and he truly believed that dying was better than living. Few things can break a mother's heart more than hearing her child crying that he wants to die or begging for his parents to kill him.

It was during this time that I, too, had feelings of inadequacy in the face of God. I had raised my son in faith, dedicating him to the Lord as an infant. I trusted that God would honor that faith.

Once, after a particularly heart-wrenching episode, instead of praying, I challenged God. "How can you do this," I shouted in anger. "What could we have possibly done that was so wrong that we deserve to live like this? I can understand if you want to punish Jim or me for something, but why him? Why Ryan? He's just a little boy!"

I was standing in my bedroom screaming the words upward with tears pouring down my face, challenging God's wisdom and feeling desperately helpless and alone. I am ashamed to admit it was quite a long time before I apologized to God. Yet, I believe He understood my pain. There were many times after that episode I came close again to being angry with God. During some of my bleakest moments, when prayer should have been a refuge, I somehow found myself unable to pray.

Ryan never really used the word suicide—he just talked about wanting to die. "After all," he construed in his mind, "if heaven's such a wonderful place, I'll just go now." This kind of talk, combined with his desire to hurt himself, and his impulsive behaviors, such as riding his bike out in front of cars and jumping off high places, frightened me.

What if? I thought. What if he impulsively or accidentally kills himself?

The thoughts tormented my mind. My anger with God eventually, in time, turned into quiet resolve and acceptance. Despite how lonely and inadequate I felt, I was certain God had not forsaken me. Sometimes I dropped into bed at night, totally exhausted and feeling quite certain that I could not endure another day like the one I had just finished. Yet somehow, I awoke with renewed faith and just enough energy to make it through another day.

One of the pastors from our church attended a local baseball clinic where I took Ryan and he seemed to establish a good rapport with all the boys. When Ryan's talk of wanting to die became increasingly worrisome, I called the pastor, James Swanson, and set up an appointment for us to visit.

When we entered the office Ryan was immediately transfixed with the pastor's aquarium of fish. There was an assortment of brightly colored fresh water fish moving about the tank and a big ugly brown one hanging on the side.

"That's an algae-eater," explained the pastor. "He keeps things clean in there."

Ryan was mesmerized by the fish. Except for a few goldfish I had accidentally killed off over the years, our family had little experience with fish of any kind.

"Did you see the snake in there?" The pastor pointed to the corner of the tank.

Ryan leaned over for a closer look. "There's no snake in there," he said. "Snakes don't live in fish tanks."

"There he is, right there, peeking out from under the rock," the pastor said. He tapped on the glass tank. Sure enough, a long skinny snakelike thing darted out from under the colored rock.

"He is really a Kuli loach," the pastor explained.

The fish fascinated me too and I wondered if having a fish tank might be comforting for Ryan.

After exhausting all possible conversation about the fish, the pastor gently approached the subject that had brought us to his office—Ryan's desire to die and go to heaven.

Although the pastor had no personal knowledge about Tourette syndrome, he did a wonderful job counseling Ryan about his feelings about having TS. He talked about how hard things must be at times and Ryan nodded in silent agreement.

Ryan offered little unless prodded, but when it came to talk about heaven he had many questions. The pastor agreed with Ryan that yes, it's a wonderful, glorious place, but that heaven can wait. He explained that heaven is a place for us to look forward to when our lives are over, but that God does not want us to come until He is ready for us.

Ryan hung on every word. When Pastor Swanson finished and asked if he understood, Ryan nodded and said that he did.

I will be forever grateful for the pastor's wise counsel. Although we were to face many more difficult and extreme times ahead, Ryan never again obsessed over wanting to die.

Chapter 12

The Pain of a Broken Brain

"To every one of my oppressors
I am contemptible,
loathesome to my neighbors;
to my friends a thing of fear.
Those who see me in the street
hurry past me;
I am forgotten, as good as dead in their hearts,
something discarded."[1]

Psalm 31:11-12

Ryan left the church office in a good mood that lasted for several days. He had learned a valuable lesson about suicide, dying and heaven during his visit with the pastor. He also caught the fish bug.

Ryan's fascination with the pastor's aquarium quickly turned into an obsession. For the next few days he talked of nothing but fish. I remembered my thought that having an aquarium might be comforting for Ryan, so Jim and I decided we would give him the opportunity to earn one. We made the goal rather easy and we made it clear we would not give in to his constant obsessing over getting the fish.

Ryan had grandiose ideas about what kind of aquarium we should buy. After seeing the expensive models at the fish stores, we decided to go to Kmart and get a "starter" tank. It wasn't exactly what Ryan had in mind, but at least he didn't blow up over it.

We bought colored rocks for the bottom of the tank and ceramic statues for the fish to swim around. We also bought artificial plants, a fish net, a thermometer to make sure the temperature was just right, a filter pump, and some chemicals to remove chlorine from the water. Fifty dollars later we were ready to buy the fish.

I had no idea there were so many different kinds of fish. We settled on a few fluorescent tetras, a Kuli loach, and an algae-eater. The fish cost an additional $16.57.

I was sick at the thought of spending so much money on a tank of fish. I reasoned that watching the fish swimming around the aquarium might be calming for Ryan. He had been waking many times through the night with night terrors. He would usually wake up shouting and screaming for a few seconds and then go right back to sleep. I thought maybe the light from the aquarium would be a comfort during those times. Besides, getting the fish eased my feelings of guilt over not letting Ryan have the dog, cat, rabbit, guinea pig, and hamster he had been wanting.

The first night with the aquarium didn't go so well. The light bothered Ryan, the sound of the filter bothered Ryan and the thought of having the snake (Kuli loach) in the tank scared him.

I was mad. I know I should have been patient and understanding but I felt exhausted from having the whole day consumed with fish activities and fish talk. Why couldn't he have been afraid of the Kuli loach when we were at the store?

We talked, we prayed, we talked some more and finally, we decided to name the fish. For some reason, giving them names seemed to take the fear away and he was able to settle down and fall asleep. Bubbles, Fred, Spike, Sharkey Larkey, and Snakey officially became part of the family.

Jim and I regretted that Ryan had had such a bad experience with the baseball coach that spring. Little League had always been successful for him. He was good at baseball and it was the one area in which he could feel good about himself. When we saw a bulletin about a summer baseball camp at The Master's College in Newhall, I called for more information.

The baseball camp was for one week. The boys had an option of spending the night or attending camp daily. Along with a full day of baseball, there was swimming too. Because The Master's College is a Christian College, there were also devotional times scheduled. It sounded like a great program, with one-on-one instruction in the morning and baseball games in the afternoon.

There was just one problem—distance. Newhall was about forty-five miles from our house. We were positive we could not trust Ryan to stay overnight for the full week. Even though he was having some good days, his behavior was still erratic. We certainly could not risk having him stay in a dorm overnight with other boys.

Jim and I decided we should go ahead and give Ryan the experience of being at baseball camp with other kids—even though it would be a little uncomfortable for us. So we drove him forty-five miles to the college at eight o'clock every morning and dropped him off for camp.

Ryan thought we left to drive back home but we really didn't. Each day after dropping him off, Jim and I went out for breakfast and then parked in a hidden area close by the ballfield and watched him play ball. For some parents, hanging around a ballfield for five days would be awful, but for us it was great. Just seeing Ryan doing well, playing normally with other kids and not getting into trouble was worth every mile we drove and every hour we waited.

As long as he was playing ball and everything remained structured, he behaved superbly. The only time he had any difficulty was in the afternoon when everyone went to the pool. Practically every day, Ryan became over-excited and had to sit out on the side. He ran around the pool instead of walking. He jumped in the pool after the coach warned him not to. He had difficulty waiting in line for the slide and wanted to slide down backward instead forward. He splashed the other boys and squirted water in their faces.

Yet, when it came to baseball, he was right on target. The coaches told him to forget playing third base and to concentrate on pitching. From then on, that's all he wanted to do.

Jim and I were proud of Ryan and pleased he was able to participate in the camp. I almost wished it could have been longer so that he could have had more chances to socialize with other kids.

When we first bought our house we liked the family atmosphere of the neighborhood. We also liked having a community pool just a few doors away. Ryan did not have any friends in our neighborhood. His behavior always got in the way of friendships. Although he was friendly and outgoing, he usually got too rough and was too hyper for most kids to put up with for long.

One day that summer, after "earning" the privilege of going swimming, Julie, Ryan and I packed some drinks and headed down to the pool. As usual, there were many kids of all ages swimming and playing.

Both kids jumped in the water and I settled down on a lounge chair next to two other mothers I had met previously during my monthly real estate rounds.

We had only been at the pool about ten minutes when Ryan became "overexcited" and became very aggressive toward Julie. I cautioned him to settle down but he didn't and I reminded him he would need to take a time-out if he didn't stop. Instead of stopping, Ryan expanded his victim list to include several other children who were close by, splashing water in their faces and making inappropriate comments.

"Ryan," I began, "you need to come out of the pool and sit out a few minutes."

"Try to make me," he taunted loudly, as he swam farther away from the edge of the pool.

Embarrassed, I looked around and realized I had a full audience. All the kids were looking up at me and their moms were watching too.

"Ryan," I said sternly. "Get out of this pool immediately, and I *mean* it." I wasn't prepared for what happened next.

Instead of coming out of the pool, Ryan shouted, "Shut up, you fucking asshole!"

I wished at that moment the ground would have opened up and swallowed me. I just wanted to die. I felt humiliated and embarrassed. All the kids in the pool were giggling and looking at me to see what I was going to do next. The moms I had just been talking with were glaring at me in shocked disbelief.

No parenting class I had taken or child psychiatrist I consulted had prepared me for what to do in this situation. I knew at that moment that nothing I could do would be enough.

Each time I moved toward Ryan he swam away. I did not have on a swimsuit and even if I had jumped in, I knew I would not be able to physically drag him out of the pool. I repeated my demand for him to come out of the pool several more times, to no avail. Finally, Julie was able to swim nearby Ryan and persuaded him to get out of the water.

I began to gather our things while Ryan continued his tirade. I reached to grab his arm and he began kicking and pulling my hair. It seemed like an eternity until I heard the pool gate slamming shut behind me.

When we reached the house I went ballistic. I was crying and started to scream at Ryan. He swung at me and I raised my arm to block his punch. He hurt his hand on my arm and started cursing again. He grabbed my hair and I grabbed his hair, pulling it as hard as I could until he let go of mine.

"Don't you ever hit me again, you little brat!" I cried. "Don't you ever hit me again! I will not let you hit me anymore!" I screamed.

Ryan gave me the finger sign all the way up to his room. I was angry, hurt, and humiliated. Ryan had embarrassed me many times before. He was always doing things in public that made us the objects of humiliation. This time was different though. It was in front of our neighbors—people we had to see every day.

After he calmed down, Ryan apologized profusely.

"I am so sorry, Mommy," he pleaded. "I don't know why I did that. I love you, Mom. Please forgive me." Then he started to "obsess" on if I could ever forgive him and if he was going to go to hell for what he had done.

Ryan lost the privilege to swim for a month. I also grounded him from riding his bike and playing Nintendo, the two things he liked the most. He took the consequences well, although the outbursts continued. I never knew when he was going to freak out. Even when everything seemed to be going well, we were always waiting for the "other shoe to drop."

Several months after the pool incident, Ryan was riding his skateboard down the street. When he got near the pool, he walked up to the gate to see who was there. It was a hot day and there were many families with young kids at the pool.

As he approached the gate, Rita, one of the neighborhood moms, yelled, "Hey you, get away from here. You're sick in the brain and I don't want you around my children. Go away from here."

Ryan ran home in tears.

"Phillip's mom said I was sick in the brain," he cried. "It's not true, is it, Mom? Am I? Am I sick in the brain?"

He cried off and on the rest of the evening. I sat and held him for a long time, stroking his head, and trying my best to soothe the sting of Rita's cruel remarks.

I had my own feelings to deal with too. I almost hated Rita for hurting Ryan. Didn't she know how blessed she was to have two normal, healthy children? Why couldn't she show some compassion? Why couldn't everyone just have more compassion?

As difficult as it was for me to deal with the day-to-day challenges of Ryan's unpredictable behavior, the hardest thing was knowing I couldn't stop his pain. I tried to imagine the hurt in dealing with a body he could not always control—the pain of dealing with others who could not and would not try to understand, the pain of being a child accused of having a broken brain.

Chapter 13

Odd Man Out

"It isn't easy being green."[1]
Kermit the Frog

I was glad summer was over but I was also concerned about starting a new school year and having to "break in" a new teacher. To complicate matters, Ryan would also be attending a different school.

Fortunately, Mrs. Hunt, the principal from the old school collaborated with the new principal, Mrs. Berg. Together they identified a fourth grade teacher they thought would be good for Ryan. Mrs. Hunt also arranged for me to meet with Mrs. Berg before the start of school. I felt encouraged when she informed me that Ryan was getting a wonderful teacher, Mrs. Lewis. She cautioned, however, if Ryan became too disruptive, he would have to leave her class.

I liked Mrs. Lewis immediately. She was the kind of teacher every parent would pick if given the choice. Ryan liked her too. He was eager to start fourth grade and was motivated to do well.

I knew Mrs. Lewis had already learned quite a bit about Ryan from Mrs. Hunt so I decided to wait until after the first week before calling her. It was only four days after school began, however, when I received the first note home.

> Mrs. Hughes,
> I would like to set up a conference early in the week so Ryan will have every chance to begin his fourth grade year on a positive note.
> Mrs. Lewis

During our first conference I felt I was walking a very thin line with Mrs. Lewis. I did not want to scare her by exposing some of Ryan's past difficulties, yet I wanted to give her a clear picture so she could best help him.

The first meeting went well and I sensed Mrs. Lewis sincerely wanted to help Ryan succeed. His tutor, Mrs. Simms, was also very pleasant. She seemed to establish a good relationship with Ryan from the start.

Things went fairly well the first few weeks. It was a constant challenge, however, for the playground aides to keep Ryan from running on campus. Fortunately, though, nothing major happened.

Three weeks into the new school year Ryan had his first encounter with the principal, Mrs. Berg. The "Discipline Report" read as follows:

> Prone to mischief. Threw a rock and some sand at another boy. Ryan told another child to get off the rings on the playground. The boy did not want to and pushing began. Then Ryan threw a rock at his stomach. Later he picked up a handful of sand and threw it at Louis. Ryan understands that if this happens again, he will be suspended and will make up the day on a Saturday.

When I picked Ryan up from school he offered a different version than what Mrs. Berg had written on the report.

"It wasn't all my fault, Mom," Ryan began. "I wasn't the one who started it."

"If you didn't start the fight, then who did?" I asked suspiciously.

"Louis tried to take the rings away from me and Billy. Then he shoved me real hard."

I looked at him sternly. "Did you throw a rock at Louis' stomach, Ryan?"

"Yeah, 'cuz he shoved me first," Ryan said defensively.

"Did you explain to Mrs. Berg about Louis starting the fight?"

"No," Ryan said flatly, "cause she wouldn't believe me. I'm always getting in trouble with everyone. Everybody always thinks everything's my fault."

Jim and I were quite stern with Ryan that evening. We made it clear that throwing rocks was wrong, no matter what anyone else did to him. We talked about what happened and what would have been a more appropriate response to Louis instead of throwing a rock.

We also encouraged Ryan to tell the whole truth about what happened—

not to just sit by when others were not telling the whole story. Again Ryan said, "It wouldn't do any good, Mommy. Nobody's gonna believe me. I'm always the one getting into trouble."

When I went to bed that night, it troubled me that Ryan had not told his side of the story. It concerned me that Mrs. Berg did not have a clear picture about what really happened.

Remembering the "choking" incident back in third grade, I realized how incidents can become distorted when reduced to paper. I thought it was important to let Mrs. Berg know that Ryan felt reluctant to share his side of the story because of his assumption that no one would believe him.

I put my thoughts in a letter to Mrs. Berg, explaining the incident and asked that she include a copy of my letter in his file with the discipline report. Mrs. Berg called me soon after receiving my letter. After checking into the incident further, she discovered Louis had indeed started the altercation. Billy, Louis and the other boy had corroborated Ryan's story.

I was glad I took the time to write the letter to the principal. I could have let it go but I didn't. There were plenty of times Ryan did initiate problems, but this was not one of them. I didn't want him being blamed unjustly. More importantly, I did not want him to think the principal would not believe him.

Making friends did not come easily for Ryan. I understood why, but it was hard to watch him struggle to gain acceptance. There was a boy his age who lived only two doors away, but he ignored Ryan whenever possible.

"Why don't you go down to Jeff's house and ask if he can play today?" I asked. I hoped Ryan would be brave enough to make the first move.

"He can't," Ryan replied, dejectedly.

"How do you know that?" I asked. "You haven't even asked him yet."

"He already told me the other day, Mom. His Mom doesn't want him playing with me 'cause I say bad words."

It was true. Ryan had a problem with saying bad words. Although Jim and I did not tolerate the use of swear words in our home, Ryan continued to have outbursts of foul language.

"Fuck" was the most common and disturbing word for me. We tried everything imaginable to get him to stop (including the Tabasco sauce), but nothing worked. One day while cleaning, I noticed some blue ink markings on the mini-blinds. There, printed in his primitive scrawl, was the "f" word. If he wasn't saying them, he was writing the bad words, whenever and wherever he got the urge.

I had never met Jeff's mother but I couldn't really blame her for not wanting him to play with a boy who said bad words. I certainly didn't want Ryan to play with someone who said bad words either. I thought about talking with her, and explaining about Tourette syndrome. I was nervous, though, about how she would react.

How could I expect her to understand when I couldn't even understand myself? I decided it would be worth a try to talk with Jeff's mom—for Ryan's sake. That afternoon I slowly walked the short distance to their front door. Jeff was standing in the garage when I walked up the drive.

"Hi, Jeff, I'm Ryan's mom. Is your mother busy?" I asked, halfway hoping she would be.

Jeff opened the door and yelled, "Mom, Ryan's mother wants to talk to you." I felt a lump in my throat and my legs suddenly felt weak.

When she came to the door, I introduced myself and asked if I could have a few minutes to speak with her. She graciously invited me inside, asked me to call her Elise, and we sat down in the family room to talk.

I started out by saying I had heard that she did not want Jeff to play with Ryan because he said bad words. I assured her I completely understood her feelings but I wanted to explain why Ryan had difficulty with saying bad words.

For the next few minutes I explained about Tourette syndrome and shared with Elise some of the difficulties Ryan was experiencing. I had feared she would be cold and unsympathetic, but she was neither. Jeff's mother listened with compassion as I told her about Ryan's struggle with TS. She told me she had no idea that anything was wrong with Ryan because he looked normal.

We had a pleasant talk and I left Elise with a couple of brochures from the Tourette Syndrome Association. She promised me she would explain everything to Jeff, and I left feeling as if Ryan and I had each made a new friend. After my visit with Elise, Jeff and Ryan began to play together frequently and became fast friends.

Once Jeff started spending time with Ryan, a few of the other neighborhood boys began to accept him into their "inner" circle. Another change in medications (Prozac) seemed to improve Ryan's mood and I was starting to feel a little more comfortable about letting him play outdoors. I still made sure he stayed in front of the house, within view from our upstairs window.

One Saturday morning, Ryan got up early (as usual), and was eager to finish breakfast so he and Jeff could play. He wolfed down some cereal and raced across the neighbor's lawn to Jeff's house. Elise told him Jeff was down at Jarod's house, along with another boy, Gary.

Ryan quickly came home and asked permission to go to Jarod's house to see if the boys could come to our house to play. Because Ryan's behavior the past few days had been exemplary, Jim and I agreed he could walk one block to Jarod's house. He promised to come right back, even if the boys couldn't come back to play with him.

Just a few minutes later Ryan returned and quickly ran upstairs to his room.

"Did you find the boys?" I asked, as I pushed open the door to his room.

"I don't want to play with them," Ryan said, as he flipped on his Nintendo.

Knowing how much he had been looking forward to skateboarding with the boys, I knew something was wrong. I pressed Ryan for more information. The tears began.

"I can't play with them," Ryan sobbed. "Jarod's having a birthday party and they're going to Golf & Stuff and I can't go."

Realizing what had happened, I struggled to find words that would soothe the hurt he was feeling.

"Maybe Jarod's parents would only let him invite a couple of friends. It was probably just too much to invite all of his friends to Golf & Stuff," I reasoned.

Ryan began to cry harder and explained, "No, Mommy, it's because Jarod's mom doesn't like me. She told Jeff that I wasn't invited because I say bad words and she doesn't want me around Jarod."

I sat on the bed and tried to wipe his tears but he turned away.

"Why do they hate me, Mommy, why? I can't help saying the bad words. I can't help it, Mommy. How can I stop? How can I stop?"

We somehow made it through the rest of the day, but Ryan's words and the pain in his voice haunted me.

I decided I should talk with Jarod's parents too. Although we had never met, I picked up the phone one evening and called Jarod's house. His dad answered. I introduced myself as Ryan's mother and asked if I could come over to speak with him and his wife. The next thing I knew I was standing at their front door, my finger on the bell and a lump in my throat so big that I thought I was going to choke.

I felt as if I were walking into a lion's den. It took every bit of courage I could muster to walk into the home of strangers and bare my soul about Ryan's problems. I knew they had already prejudged my parenting abilities and had formed negative conclusions about Ryan and me. I did not know how they would receive my visit but I knew that I had to somehow try to make them understand about Tourette syndrome.

Jarod's parents listened intently as I explained about Ryan's difficulties with TS. They too were compassionate and seemed forgiving. Best of all, they were willing to give Jarod and Ryan the opportunity to play together.

Jarod and Gary skateboarded with Ryan a lot, although they sometimes lost patience with his immaturity and provoking behavior. It was Jeff, though, who stuck with Ryan. When Jeff got a hamster, Ryan wanted one too. They spent hours playing with their hamsters, making tunnels out of toilet paper rolls and building elaborate ladders for them to climb. Ryan and Jeff were inseparable or, as they liked to say, "We're best buds."

Having friends was a mixed blessing for Ryan. Most of the time he played well with the other boys, but there was usually one incident a day when his behavior would cause a problem. The other boys were more mature and responsible and had much more freedom than we were willing to give Ryan. Far too many times I had "trusted" him and been sorry later when one of the neighbors came to my door complaining.

Most of the time when Ryan was outdoors playing, Jim and I would take turns jumping in the car or on a bike to go and secretly check on him. We never knew when someone might say or do something that would set him off into a rage.

Things were just as unpredictable at school. Some days were very good, with Ryan working well and getting along with the other students. Other days he was unable to concentrate and became disruptive. In late November I received a note from Mrs. Lewis:

> Dear Mrs. Hughes,
>   I spoke to Ryan regarding his behavior. His interactions with other students have been in a negative manner. In math yesterday, he broke the teacher's pencil in half, tore up his paper and threw small scrap

balls at the students during the lesson. He was sent back to my class early.

As he went to get his medicine he grabbed his groin area in front of another student and laughed. The nurse spoke to him explaining that this was inappropriate.

During spelling yesterday he was off task. Mrs. Simms sat with him allowing Ryan to use the "word whiz." He put in dirty words so the spelling machine was taken away. I informed Ryan this morning that I expect appropriate behavior not only in my class but anywhere in the school. If he is not willing to work then I have told him he will work in a small setting with Mrs. Simms. Today Ryan made an effort and did his work. I will be talking with him daily.

Mrs. Lewis

Poor Mrs. Lewis. She still hoped that just talking to Ryan would persuade him to change his behavior. Jim and I knew all too well it was not as simple as that.

Chapter 14

Every Dog Has His Day

"Experience is the best teacher but the
tuition is very costly."[1]
Unknown

Despite problems at school and in the neighborhood, Ryan also had many positive things happen that year. His teacher, Mrs. Lewis, selected him to play the part of Mr. Sawyer in the school play, *Miracle on 34th Street*.

I wasn't sure what to think about him being selected for the part. I definitely wanted to encourage Ryan to be in the play but I was afraid he would be so nervous that he might start acting inappropriately.

Ryan was happy Mrs. Lewis chose him for the play. We helped him rehearse sporadically, whenever he felt like it. Although he could not remember any of his times tables in math, he had little difficulty remembering his lines for the play. On opening night, Jim, Julie and I sat with nervous anticipation waiting for "Mr. Sawyer" to make his debut.

It was over in a matter of minutes. Ryan marched on to the stage confidently. He recited his lines loudly and with great enthusiasm. He even did a pratfall and got a big round of applause and much laughter from the audience.

No family ever felt so proud! It was just a small part but it may as well have been the academy awards for us—especially after all we had been through. Ryan was also happy with his performance. He seemed to gain a little confidence in his abilities and a boost in his self-esteem.

In early January I succumbed to my better judgment and allowed discussion about getting a dog. We had tried having a dog a few years earlier and the result was disastrous.

We had only had Blacky a short time when we discovered the cocker spaniel was even more "hyper" than Ryan. He also barked a lot and caused general chaos in the house—something we did not need help with. We only kept Blacky a few weeks before finding him a new home. I thought at the time I would never consider getting another dog. Julie and Ryan, however, persuaded me to give it another try.

Jim wasn't crazy about the idea either, especially after Blacky. He reluctantly drove us to the animal shelter one Saturday afternoon just to "look."

There were one hundred forty dogs at the shelter that day. As we made our way up and down the rows of cages, Ryan would shout, "Let's get that one, Mommy."

Then Julie would see another and say, "Please, Mommy, let's get this one. He's sooo cute."

I saw practically all the dogs available that day and none of them swayed me with their sad pleas for our attention. Just as we were leaving, I spotted a small furry dog huddled at the end of a pen. It was shivering and looking up sadly out the corner of his eyes.

"Is that a cockapoo?" I asked the animal control officer.

"Yes, it is," she replied, "but I don't think he's available for adoption yet. I think we just got him in this week."

The officer left to check the records. Julie, Ryan and I tried to coach the shy dog to come toward us but he wouldn't budge. He was very dirty and just sat there shaking, looking quite pitiful and doing a good job of pulling my heartstrings. When the officer reported that the seven day holding time was up that very day, we asked if we could take him out into the yard for a better look.

We learned the small gray dog was found wandering the streets and was picked up by the dog catcher. Although he seemed in good health, the record indicated he may have been abused. There was no age available for the dog, but the officer estimated him to be between two to three years old. We decided to adopt the dirty, scared little dog and filled out the adoption paperwork.

On the way home we each took turns suggesting names. We quickly rejected all the usual dog names. Before we arrived home we settled on calling him "Biskit." Biskit made himself at home very quickly. He seemed as if he was going to be a great addition to our family. At times though, Ryan became too rough and we had to repeatedly warn him that the dog might bite.

In February of 1990 my first book, *RYAN, A Mother's Story of Her Hyperactive/Tourette Syndrome Child,* was published. Before deciding to publish the book, Jim and I discussed it with Ryan. We wanted to know his feelings about having his story told. We questioned him repeatedly. We wanted to make sure he understood any possible repercussions from having his story made public.

Ryan said he wanted people to know more about TS. He didn't seem at all concerned about the fact that other kids might read the book and laugh or make fun of him.

Shortly after the book was published there was a rash of "publicity." There were several newspaper articles featuring our family and Ryan was extremely cooperative in talking with reporters and allowing pictures. When a TV station came to do a spot for a medical report on their evening news, he happily played with the dog and behaved appropriately. He didn't really enjoy the attention but tolerated it with only slight annoyance.

With all the media attention regarding the book I was concerned about "exploiting" Ryan and his problems with TS in a negative way. I walked a fine line between wanting to get information out to other parents while being careful to protect Ryan's self-esteem and the integrity of our family. I didn't want Ryan's story to become fodder for a "freak of the week" type of tabloidism.

Reaction to the book was overwhelming from the beginning. I began getting phone calls from other parents in response to the news articles. "I can't believe it," they would say. "My son is exactly like Ryan. I felt as if you were writing this book about my child."

Especially rewarding were the letters and calls I received. Several mothers stated that their child was diagnosed with Tourette syndrome because of the book. One woman called to tell me her mother in Oregon had picked up a copy of the book at her library. She recognized her grandson's symptoms and urged her daughter to get a copy. After reading Ryan's story, the mother took her child to a pediatric neurologist who readily made the diagnosis of Tourette syndrome.

Every time a call or letter about the book arrived, I always made sure to tell Ryan about it. He always responded the same way, "Cool, Mom."

One thing Ryan would never do was read the book. Many times I encouraged him to read a chapter or let me read it to him. His response was always the same, "Why do I need to read it? I lived it." I couldn't argue with that.

The Ch.A.D.D. organization (Children and Adults with Attention Deficit Disorder) had recently started a support group in our area and I began to attend the meetings. While many of the problems related by other parents of children with ADHD seemed similar, it always seemed to me that Ryan's problems were much worse. I was invited to speak at a local Ch.A.D.D. meeting and remember the shocked reactions when I related some of my experiences, like the Suburban episode.

My sister Sally, was planning to be married in February of 1990. I was thrilled when she asked Ryan to be the ring bearer at her wedding. Of course, he would have been the natural choice under normal circumstances. But Sally knew we did not live under normal circumstances. She and her fiancee Randy, however, did not hesitate to ask Ryan to play a big part on their special day. This was the first family wedding, or any wedding, that Ryan was invited to attend.

Julie and I were also in the wedding party and things were beginning to get hectic around our house. My Aunt Jane and I hosted a bridal shower for Sally and there were many visits to the bridal shop to choose the gowns and shoes. Ryan was fitted for a tuxedo and before we knew it, the big day arrived.

Ryan behaved extremely well at the rehearsal the night before, but I was nervous anyway. What if he blurted out obscenities while walking down the aisle? What if he had a shrieking episode? What if he threw the ring out into the audience? My mind was in overdrive thinking of all the "what ifs."

Amazingly, there was no disaster. The wedding was beautiful and Ryan was wonderful in his role as ring bearer. He was a gentleman and behaved exceptionally well. He not only made it through the ceremony but also the reception and dinner afterwards. It was another day for Jim and me to be thankful. And we were.

Unfortunately, the successes at the Christmas play and Sally's wedding were the only bright spots. Everything seemed to go mostly downhill after that.

Ryan began having more difficulty with vocal tics. He would have shrieking episodes that were unnerving. The worst part was that the episodes frequently occurred while we were out in public, like at a restaurant or store. The shrieks would start gradually and then build into a very loud high-pitched screech. To make things worse, he always had to make the noise three times. Never just once or twice, but always three times.

It was so humiliating at restaurants. When I heard him begin I would usually try to hurry him outside, but we rarely made it in time. People would stare and make disgusted faces toward us. Sometimes, Ryan would "feel" the urge coming on and we could get outside in time.

Along with the shrieking and other nerve-wracking noisemaking, Ryan was having compulsions. He was constantly kissing me on the cheek— first one cheek, then the other. Even then he wasn't done. He had to do the ritual three times. If I refused to allow him to finish the cycle, he would become so frustrated he would run around in circles saying, "I have to do it, I have to do it. Just let me do it so I can get it over with."

He would approach Jim or me and flip us on the side of the head with his hand. Then he had to flip us on the other side. He was doing this so often we felt as if we were going crazy. We would get angry and scream at him to stop. We tried reasoning with him, threatening him, but nothing worked. He always apologized later. At the time it was happening, though, he would do anything to complete the two flips.

The compulsions also involved Biskit. Ryan would pull one ear and then feel as if he "had" to pull the other. He would kiss the dog on one side of his head and then have to kiss him in exactly the same place on the other side. If he did not get the spot "just right" he had to start again.

Biskit, of course, didn't like all the attention. He would growl fiercely, but that only compelled Ryan to yet another compulsion—making the dog snap at his hand. He would persist in irritating Biskit until the dog snapped at him. Only then could he walk away and feel "satisfied."

Ryan's motor tics were still the same—rubbing his fingers together, wiping his mouth with his shirt (constantly) and adjusting his pants continually. Most disturbing of all, the aggression at home had escalated.

Ryan didn't have to be angry at one of us to become aggressive. Sometimes he could just get angry at himself for some small thing and fly into a rage. It could even be something so simple as accidentally bumping into the corner of the wall or a table and he would begin cursing and screaming. If Jim and I attempted to intervene, he delivered physical and verbal threats.

Other times, Ryan would meet a difficulty with a perfectly normal reaction or no reaction at all. We never knew when he was going to explode at home or in public. We were always trying to anticipate his every move and ward off trouble before it could start.

Dr. Comings had been working at adjusting Ryan's medications. He tried various combinations of Tofranil, Clonidine, Tegretol, Prozac, and Ritalin. He also added Mellaril with the hope of calming the outbursts, but there was no relief. Ryan complained of headaches and being dizzy.

Dr. Comings also tried Anafranil, Norpramin and Prolixin in various combinations with the other medications. By late spring, Ryan's behavior was again spiraling out of control and he was unable to complete even a minimum amount of work at school.

In May, Mrs. Lewis sent home a note that read:

> Mrs. Hughes,
>
> Can we meet sometime next week to discuss Ryan's program and curriculum? Ryan has missed class time due to feeling tired or agitated. Mrs. Berg spoke to him today because he recorded some dirty words on Todd's oral book report tape. He spent time in the office finishing his journal pages that are done each morning from 8:30 to 8:40. He had completed only two out of twelve by 8:30 this morning. Let's find some time to talk.
>
> Mrs. Lewis

By this time Jim and I had learned much more about Tourette syndrome but we still did not know what to do. It seemed clear that much of Ryan's difficult behavior was due to ADHD, OCD and TS; however, we wondered if part of what we were dealing with was side effects from the medications.

I had always agonized over Ryan having to take any medication, much less three or four. Yet, I knew we didn't really have a choice. Ryan was not able to function at all without medication. What was so very difficult to accept, however, was that even with the medications, there were still times he was not able to behave normally.

Sometimes it seemed like such a futile battle. Just when Dr. Comings added a new medication or tried a new combination, Ryan would show improvement for a while. It was almost like a remission of some sort— then wham! Everything would fall apart and we found ourselves starting again.

Mrs. Lewis had done a remarkable job throughout the year, but she, too, was reaching the end of her rope. She felt that Ryan would not be able to handle a regular classroom the following year and suggested that we visit the "Special Day Class" to observe. I couldn't argue with her reasoning.

I wasn't ready for what I saw in the Special Day Class. The teacher, Mrs. Franco, was so "low-key" I knew after a minute of observing she wasn't the teacher for Ryan. The classroom looked dirty and very disorganized. The class was small—only about ten students—which was good. What struck me was the disorder and confusion in the classroom. Students got up and moved around at will. One student was cleaning out her desk. Another student was rolling paper into long tubes while another sat staring out the window.

Mrs. Franco and her aide were helping one student when two others walked up to ask for help. Another student was nibbling on a cookie while taking a test. Several others were eating sunflower seeds. I noticed they also left to go to the rest room without asking permission. Most of the students seemed well enough behaved, although there was quite a bit of talking. I noticed one boy making inappropriate gestures toward his crotch as he returned from the restroom.

After observing the classroom and speaking with Mrs. Franco, I was certain Ryan was not a good candidate for the class. Most of them were slow learners, below average in intelligence, and considerably behind Ryan in their ability to learn. I knew Ryan could not handle a classroom that had such little structure or firm limits. I didn't know where he would attend fifth grade, but I knew it would not be in Mrs. Franco's Special Day Class.

Chapter 15

At Wit's End

"When you get to the end of your rope,
tie a knot, hang on and swing."[1]
Leo Buscaglia

Gordon Miller was the program specialist and school psychologist for our local district, Pacific View Unified. When I told him I didn't think Mrs. Franco's class was appropriate for Ryan, he suggested another program for our consideration.

The Superintendent of Schools' office in our county operated several specialized programs for special education students. One of the programs was a class for children with severe emotional or behavior disorders. The school was called the Landmark Elementary School and was about twenty miles from our home.

When Gordon first told us about the school I immediately had two strong reservations. My first concern was that it was a school for students considered to be "Severely Emotionally Disturbed" (SED). Although Ryan had very significant behavior problems, I didn't consider him to be emotionally disturbed. It was a label I didn't like and didn't feel appropriately described Ryan.

When I managed to look beyond the SED label, I faced the matter of distance. The school was a long way from home. I knew how difficult it was to contain Ryan in the car at times, and I did not relish the thought of having to drive him such a long distance each day. Gordon did some checking, though, and was able to get more information about the school that piqued my interest.

The County Superintendent of Schools' office and the Department of County Mental Health jointly operated the Landmark Elementary School. There were two classes with six boys in each room. Each class had a teacher

93

and two aides. In addition, there was a full-time mental health worker who counseled with the boys each day.

The mental health worker was there to troubleshoot if there were any behavior or acting-out difficulties. She was also there to counsel individually with each of the students at least once a week. In addition, the social worker would make home visits once or twice a week to keep the student's family involved in the treatment program.

The Landmark Elementary School was a "day treatment" program. It was specifically for special education students who had a history of emotional or behavioral problems that adversely affected their educational development. Students at Landmark would typically attend for nine to twelve months, with the goal being the ability to return to their neighborhood schools.

I could see there were definitely strong advantages to the Landmark program. The individualized attention, combined with the mental health interventions, seemed to be just what Ryan needed.

In addition, the county would provide transportation by bus. That alleviated my worry about having to drive Ryan to and from school each day. I still felt terrible about him having to go to school so far from home, but decided that it was a small trade-off for being able to participate in such a wonderful program.

Unfortunately, openings in the Landmark program were few. Even though a local district referred a student to Landmark, it did not guarantee that child's placement in the school. There was a screening process that involved several interviews to determine each student's suitability for the program. After initially being unsure about wanting Ryan to attend Landmark, we now were hoping he was "bad" enough to be accepted.

The first step was the referral by our local district. There was no problem there. Our district was small and offered no SED classes. Gordon wrote the referral to County Mental Health so they could begin their evaluation. It read:

> Ryan requires a great deal of one-to-one teacher involvement and redirection to remain on task and to complete assignments. He is very distractible, excitable and frequently escalates verbal, motor, and physically intrusive (aggressive) behavior during group activities. He most often tries to cooperate with his teacher and do what is expected of him.

> Ryan has been counseled by the school counselor,
> resource specialist, health aide, principal, assistant
> principal, and regular education teacher. He requires
> a smaller, more coordinated, more therapeutic envi-
> ronment.

Once Gordon sent the referral to County Mental Health, they assigned a case manager to come to our home and evaluate Ryan and our family for suitability for the Landmark program. Not only did Ryan need to be suitable but so did our family. Family cooperation, support, and participation were considered to be important elements to a student's success at Landmark.

On the day the case manager, Abby Stevens, was to arrive, Ryan was in rare form. He was very hyper and talk about the new school seemed to fuel his anxiety.

When the doorbell rang, Ryan raced to answer it. When he opened the door and saw Abby standing there, he slammed the door in her face. I immediately opened it, apologizing for Ryan's behavior.

Abby came in, introduced herself, and assured us that she understood. Instead of coming to meet Abby, Ryan ran up to the top of the stairs.

"What does that butt fungus want?" he yelled down the steps. He then climbed on top of the banister, stood straight up and raised both hands to touch the ceiling.

"Ryan, get down from there immediately!" I shouted up at him.

It really scared me. I knew he was in an extremely dangerous position. I was afraid if I climbed the steps to stop him that he might lose his balance and fall. I was also afraid his behavior in front of Abby would disqualify him for consideration in the Landmark program.

I decided to ignore Ryan, hoping that our inattention would discourage him from further acting-out behavior. As Abby and I walked away from the stairs and into the family room, I heard him hit the wood floor. Ryan had jumped from a standing position on top of the banister, over twelve feet to the floor below. He immediately ran into the family room, beating us to the sofa.

I felt embarrassed and unsure of exactly what to do. I didn't know if I should intervene or allow Ryan to continue so Abby could see the behavior we were struggling to control. Abby stayed calm and continued on with the visit as if nothing unusual had happened. While we were talking, Ryan broke into our conversation.

"Ya wanna see my hamster Daisy? I'll go get her," he said, without waiting for Abby to reply.

Abby seemed quite comfortable holding Daisy. She stroked her fur and asked Ryan some questions about his new pet. When she suggested that Ryan put Daisy back in her cage so we could finish our talk, he became hyper again. He started tossing Daisy into the air and then threw her across the room and onto the floor. Again, I was horrified.

What should I do? I wondered. What was Abby expecting me to do? I hoped she wasn't judging me too harshly.

It surprised me to see Ryan's deliberate aggression with Daisy and his apparent lack of concern for her safety. Ryan and Jeff had made parachutes for their hamsters when they first brought them home. I had caught them "parachuting" the hamsters off the tall block wall on the side of the house one day. I had convinced Ryan that Daisy was much too fragile for parachuting and he seemed genuinely sorry he had done something that might have hurt her.

I was finally able to retrieve Daisy and put her away before she became airborn again. Eventually, Abby was able to engage Ryan in conversation about the Landmark School.

"Do you really get to go swimming?" Ryan asked excitedly.

Abby told him the pool was next door at the Easter Seals Society building. Students from Landmark were able to swim there every Friday, Abby explained. There were also other fun outings such as beach trips, field trips and even a year-end trip to Disneyland. That was all Ryan needed to hear.

"I want to go!" he exclaimed. "Am I going to go? When can I start?"

Abby explained that if they selected Ryan for the program, he would probably be able to start in time for summer school. That possibility excited me. I had already started to worry about what to do with Ryan all summer. Our community pool was no longer an option and his problems in the neighborhood made possibilities for summer activities rather limited.

When Abby was ready to leave, she informed us she would definitely be recommending Ryan for placement at Landmark. There were, however, two more steps before they could accept Ryan.

The first step was for the social worker at the Landmark School to interview us. Sylvia Dammon was the mental health liaison who worked with the students and Abby would arrange for her to visit our home. The final step was for Ryan to visit the school and meet the teacher and two classroom aides.

I was very nervous about the idea of another home visit, especially after what had happened with Abby. The prospect of Ryan being able to attend the Landmark School seemed good though. We liked Abby a lot and thought she was excellent in the way she handled Ryan.

When Sylvia arrived for our interview appointment, Ryan behaved much the same as he had with Abby. He was very hyperactive and there was a lot of attention-seeking behavior. Again, I felt uneasy about what to do.

When Sylvia entered our home I sensed a definite "coolness" in her demeanor. While Abby had been warm and understanding, Sylvia seemed annoyed by Ryan's behavior. She was very businesslike in her manner and immediately set the tone for our interview. It was apparent from the beginning that she considered herself to be "in charge" of the decision to accept Ryan into the program. She made it clear she had not yet decided and that there were other students who might be selected instead of Ryan.

All of a sudden, I was nervous that Sylvia would not allow Ryan into the Landmark program. I had not even seriously considered what we might do if the Landmark School did not select him. Our interview with Sylvia made me uncomfortable. I felt the sharp sting of her scrutiny with each question we answered. I could never tell from her responses or her expression what she was thinking or how we were scoring.

With Ryan, Sylvia was just as distant in her responses. When he asked about the pool and the trip to Disneyland, she answered, but was quick to remind Ryan he was not yet "selected" for the program. When she finally left, Ryan began to worry that he would not be able to go to the Landmark School. He obsessed about it, asking us over and over if he was going to be able to go. Unfortunately, we were just as unclear as he was.

I did not like the way Sylvia made any of us feel during her visit. I wished she would have found a better way to explain the process to Ryan without increasing his anxiety. It also upset me that she had "set him up" for an emotional collapse. Ryan knew his behavior was not good. He also knew that the Landmark School was a program for boys with behavioral problems.

How would he feel, I wondered, if they did not accept him? I was sure he would feel that he was so bad that he couldn't even get into a school for bad kids! This, on top of being accused of being "sick in the brain" and his constant fear of going to hell, might be just enough to make him think of suicide again. I knew his poor impulse control could make suicide a reality in one brief moment. It concerned me that a rejection by the Landmark program would be another major blow to his fragile self-esteem.

When we received a call to bring Ryan in to meet the teacher, I felt as if my prayers were answered. The teacher, Mr. Peterson, and the two aides, Berta and Sheila, were very cordial. They seemed to like Ryan, and after our meeting I felt more encouraged about his prospects of being accepted. I was ecstatic when Abby called a few days later to let us know that Ryan could start summer school at Landmark just one week after the end of the regular school year.

The last few weeks of fourth grade were busy with end-of-the-year activities. Ryan was playing Little League again and became excited each time he had a chance to pitch. His behavior on the field was erratic as always—some days good, some days not so good.

I had read in a newsletter from the national Tourette Syndrome Association about a major league ballplayer named Jim Eisenreich who had Tourette syndrome. His story about his battle with TS was interesting and I decided that meeting Jim Eisenreich might be inspirational for Ryan.

I impulsively wrote a letter to the public relations director of the Kansas City Royals and asked if it would be possible to set up a meeting for Ryan to meet the major leaguer the next time the Royals came to California. It pleased me when a few months later I received a letter inviting us to Anaheim Stadium to meet Jim Eisenreich.

Ryan was thrilled that he was going to meet a major league ballplayer. I don't think he really cared too much that Jim Eisenreich had Tourette syndrome. He was more interested in the fact that he was meeting a "real" ballplayer.

Being from the Los Angeles area, we were true-blue Dodger fans. We had never attended an Angels game before, but that day we were ready to root for the Kansas City Royals. Ryan insisted on wearing his "Angels" Little League uniform and took along his glove, just in case there was a foul ball to catch.

While we were waiting for Eisenreich to appear, we became aware of Brett Saberhagen standing next to us, talking to a woman behind the counter. Just a few seconds later, Jim Eisenreich approached from behind a metal door.

"Hi, are you Ryan?" Jim asked. Ryan stood there silently, finally giving a short nod.

"I'm Jim," he said softly, reaching out his hand. "Nice to meet you."

I waited for the major leaguer to say more but he just stood there, awkwardly looking at Ryan and then at us. I spent the next several minutes making small talk, leaving plenty of time in between in case anyone else wanted to talk. No one did.

It was awkward at first. Jim (Ryan's dad) is painfully shy when first meeting someone and he was no help at all. Ryan, who usually never shuts up, was also speechless. What I did not expect was for Jim Eisenreich to also be so shy.

He was very warm though. He just didn't talk much except to answer my questions. I asked him about his childhood and what it was like having TS. He told Ryan not to let Tourette syndrome get him down, that he could do anything he wanted if he just put his mind to it.

We talked for about half an hour before he had to leave for the game. Before he left, I handed him a copy of the *RYAN* book and I also gave him a copy of *Tourette Syndrome and Human Behavior* by Dr. David Comings. He thanked me for the books and then disappeared behind the door.

I was hoping that Jim Eisenreich's encouraging words to Ryan would not fall on deaf ears. That message, delivered from a successful adult with TS was worth the drive to hear. I think perhaps I needed to hear it as much as Ryan did.

Mrs. Lewis was busy with end-of-the-year activities and was making final arrangements for a field trip to the Los Angeles Zoo. There had been other field trips during the year and I had always volunteered to help. I had even, at Mrs. Lewis's request, driven Ryan separately so that he would not create a problem during the bus ride.

This time I received a call from Mrs. Lewis saying that Ryan could not go on the zoo trip. At first I thought the reason was that I was unable to help because of a commitment at work. Jim then made plans to take a personal day off work so that he could chaperone Ryan on the trip. When I called to tell Mrs. Lewis of our plans I was stunned when she insisted that Ryan could not go to the zoo with his class.

"Why not?" I asked in disbelief. "He's never been a problem on any of the other field trips and his dad will be there with him."

"It's not that," Mrs. Lewis explained. "Ryan has really fallen behind in his work. I told him if he didn't get his work done he could not go on the field trip. I have to stick by my word to set an example for the other kids.

He won't be able to go with us tomorrow. He will have to go to Mr. Craft's classroom for the day and do his work."

I was crushed by Mrs. Lewis's words. Didn't she know how much Ryan had been looking forward to the zoo trip? Didn't she know that he couldn't finish his work because his ADHD interfered with his ability to concentrate?

I was upset the rest of the evening. I knew Mrs. Lewis wasn't right in her decision to exclude Ryan from the trip. A few months earlier, I had taken a parent's training course in Basic Rights given by TASK (Team Advocates for Special Kids.) At the training I learned that children in special education had the right to participate in extracurricular activities the same as other students. They could not be excluded from activities by reason of their handicapping condition.

In this situation, the inability to complete his work was due to his handicapping conditions of ADHD and Tourette syndrome. His inappropriate behavior was affecting his ability to learn and was also due to his handicapping conditions of ADHD and TS. It was clearly wrong for Mrs. Lewis to exclude him. I called Mrs. Berg for an appointment.

Sitting across from the principal's desk, I was aware of my nervousness. When she closed the door to her office I could again feel a familiar knot developing in my throat.

I began my conversation with the principal by informing her of Mrs. Lewis's decision to exclude Ryan from the field trip. Mrs. Berg told me she was aware of the situation and that she had fully supported Mrs. Lewis's decision.

"I'm sorry to hear that, Mrs. Berg," I began. "As much as I hate the idea, I'm afraid I must seriously consider filing a discrimination complaint with the U.S. Department of Education's Office of Civil Rights."

Mrs. Berg looked stunned.

"But Mrs. Hughes," she began, "we have other students we need to consider. Ryan did not complete all of his work and we cannot make an exception for him."

The lump in my throat disappeared and I continued with firm resolve.

"I can certainly appreciate the problems you have with the other students Mrs. Berg. I truly can. However, those are your problems, not mine. I have to be concerned about Ryan and his right to an appropriate education. Under the law, that includes the right to participate in all school activities, including field trips."

Mrs. Berg was silent for a few seconds. She then asked what I would like her to do. I asked if she was familiar with Section 504 of the Rehabilitation Act; she said she was not. I then showed her a brochure from the Office of Civil Rights. I had highlighted the areas pertaining to handicapped children having the right to participate in field trips and other extracurricular activities. She read it with interest, then handed the copy back to me.

"I am so sorry about this, Mrs. Hughes," she said. "I was not aware of this, but I will definitely learn more about it."

As I stood to leave she said, "I certainly admire the way that you advocate for Ryan," she said. "He is very lucky to have a mother like you to stand up for him."

I left Mrs. Berg's office with a new sense of empowerment. I realized, perhaps for the first time, that I could not just sit back and "let" educators tell us what was right for Ryan. Just as we were forced to question the "wisdom" of the psychiatrist years before who had missed the diagnosis of Tourette syndrome, we now needed to scrutinize decisions affecting his education. No longer would we be passive participants in the decisions affecting Ryan's education or medical treatment.

A few days later I received a handwritten note from Mrs. Berg. It read:

> Dear Mrs. Hughes,
>
> It has been a pleasure to know you and work with you this year. I think Ryan has made many gains. I admire both you and your husband for maintaining such a positive outlook. Ryan is so fortunate to have parents who care so much and give of themselves. You have helped not only Ryan, but also many other children and parents who deal with the same situation. I wish Ryan all the best. I hope we will be able to work together cooperatively in the future.

Mrs. Berg's note meant a lot to me. I was not used to challenging the authority of "professionals." It was difficult for me to question a doctor, a teacher or a principal. Yet, my love and concern for Ryan compelled me to challenge any decision that was not in his best interest.

Love was not always enough though. We were at our wit's end in trying to manage Ryan's behavior. We had made it through fourth grade. Our confidence was now resting with the Landmark Elementary School and our ever-present hope for a miracle.

Chapter 16

Touch and Go

"Children need love,
especially when they do not deserve it."[1]
Harold S. Hulbert

Problems with our dog, Biskit, continued. Ryan loved the dog but he became "obsessed" about touching him. He was still provoking the dog to snap and I was starting to worry that Biskit might bite Ryan in the face.

One day while I was getting ready to go to the store, Ryan came into my bedroom and began "demanding" that we take him to McDonald's. I had, through the years, learned a thousand ways to say no without using the two-letter word. I tried to explain that we couldn't go right then but that most likely we could go the next day. Ryan, however, was determined he had to go to McDonald's that very moment.

When I refused to submit to his demands, he started hitting and kicking me. I tried to grab his arms but he fought even harder and began shouting obscenities.

Biskit became agitated with all the commotion and started barking and snapping at our legs. The next thing I knew I was lying on the floor with Ryan still kicking at me. I looked up and saw Jim rushing into the room to help just when I felt the pain. Biskit had bitten my leg!

I screamed. Jim grabbed Ryan and dragged him away. I looked down at my leg and saw blood. Jim started yelling at Ryan to stop and Ryan shouted obscenities at Jim. I sat there sobbing, wondering how in the world things could have gotten so out of control—just because I wouldn't agree to go to McDonald's.

As much as we all loved Biskit, Jim and I decided it would be in his best interest and ours if we would find him a new home. I felt terrible about it, especially since we had done the same with Blacky a couple of years before. Julie loved Biskit, but I felt I just couldn't take the risk of having him bite any of us again. Ryan was constantly taunting the dog. I felt I just couldn't risk having Ryan's face permanently scarred because of his impulsivity or compulsivity.

We decided to put an ad in the local paper—"Cock-a-poo, free to a good home." We ran the ad several weeks with no response. Poor Biskit. No one seemed to want him. We didn't want to take him back to the pound so we decided to keep him a little longer. Fortunately, Ryan's compulsions with the dog improved.

Ryan was both excited and apprehensive about beginning summer school at Landmark. He had never ridden on a school bus and that, combined with it being a considerable distance from home, was cause for his concern. Yet, the excitement of going to a school where you could go swimming, take jaunts to the beach, and other fun field trips motivated him to put aside his worries about riding the bus.

On the first day of school, Ryan bounded out the door and enthusiastically jumped on the small yellow bus. There was another student named Steven, who was already on the bus. The driver explained she would also be picking up a third boy before going to the school. According to her, the whole trip should take no more than forty-five minutes.

Ryan had undergone many medication changes and was then taking Tegretol, Prolixin, Catapres and Norpramine. I scheduled his medications with the bus trip in mind, then kept my fingers crossed that nothing bad would happen.

Every thing at Landmark seemed to get off to a smooth start. Ryan adapted well to riding the bus and I don't remember any egregious episodes. We had all anticipated he might have a "honeymoon" period, as often happens in new situations. Ryan was definitely honeymooning at Landmark and we hoped it would last.

Having Ryan doing well at school was a huge relief because he wasn't doing so well at home. Practically every day he would get off the bus in a very hyper and irritated state. He was constantly breaking the rules, refusing consequences and challenging our authority. If I tried to invoke a consequence of any kind, Ryan would run out of the house. If I tried to follow, he would run farther away. If I ignored him and didn't follow, he would do something provocative to get my attention. Although we never allowed him to go outdoors unsupervised he would dart out the door every time he became upset.

One time I chose to wait inside, refusing to be drawn into Ryan's game of cat and mouse. When he saw that I was not going to chase him, he started throwing rocks at the neighbor's car. It was only a matter of minutes until the neighbor was at our door yelling and screaming to keep our rotten kid inside. Another time he jumped on his bike and rode through the bushes in another neighbor's yard. The man became irate and stormed down to our door demanding that we keep Ryan away from his house or else he would physically hurt him.

Rita, the lady who told Ryan he was "sick in the brain," had also been at our house numerous times. Each time I answered the door she would start yelling and cursing at me, demanding that I make Ryan stop giving her and her son "the finger."

The times we did attempt to chase after Ryan he would dash out in front of cars or pick up rocks and throw them at us when we got close. I knew there was no way we could keep him inside the house, short of tying him up, if he really wanted to go outside. Our experience of trying to keep him inside the "quiet room" had taught us that. When we tried to physically contain Ryan he would become abusive—hitting, kicking and butting his head into ours. It was a lose/lose situation with every approach we tried.

I knew that it was not untypical for children with TS to "hold it in" during the day at school and then "let it all out" when they arrived home. The reason for this seems to be that children with TS sense they are in a "safe" place at home. Thus, they feel free to exhibit or express their "pent-up" stresses and frustrations.

I understood that justification to some extent, but I also felt if he could control himself at school, then he should likewise be able to control himself at home. We were constantly trying to judge which behaviors he could control and which ones he could not, which were TS-related and which were purely manipulative.

Sylvia, our social worker, seemed to think that *all* of Ryan's behaviors were manipulative. Part of her duties as the family liaison was to conduct bi-weekly family education and counseling meetings at our home. It was difficult for Jim and me to communicate with Sylvia in the beginning. Her cool demeanor, combined with a "you don't know anything and I know everything" attitude, made it difficult for us to talk with her, let alone like her. That Ryan was doing well at school only added strength to Sylvia's attitude problem.

Although we were still hoping, Jim and I were pretty sure the honeymoon at school wouldn't last. After all, it was Ryan's difficulties at school with Mrs. Terry that had originally gotten him referred to the Landmark program. In the meantime, we knew we had to endure Sylvia's implications that Ryan's behavior could easily change if only *we* would change whatever we were doing wrong. We began to feel as if she was scrutinizing every word we said.

When Sylvia visited our home I was never sure how I should respond to Ryan. He always behaved poorly and acted out when she came. I thought it was probably because he felt he was the focus of the conversation and it made him nervous. Usually by the end of the visits with Sylvia, Jim and I were more nervous and upset than Ryan. She always sat with a yellow pad taking notes. What was she writing? I wondered. How could we be sure she was not misjudging us? The constant scrutiny was difficult.

There had been a few instances at Landmark when the nurse forgot to give Ryan his medications. One day, I arrived at the school for a meeting and Ryan met me in the parking lot. He immediately became overexcited and started acting out. He picked up a handful of gravel and started throwing it toward the parked cars. He was laughing loudly, had a "wild" look in his eyes and was shouting nonsensical words.

I was finally able to settle Ryan down and we started inside the building for the meeting. Sylvia was standing at the door and had seen the parking lot episode. As we were walking down the hall, I asked her if Ryan had received his medication that afternoon.

Clearly annoyed, Sylvia snapped at me, "Why do you want to give him the impression that he only acts bad if he doesn't get his medication?"

I explained that I had only asked about it because Ryan had missed his medications several times that week. I wanted her to know that if he didn't get his pills, or got them later than the usual time, it was important for me to know. Otherwise, I might give him the next dose too early. Sylvia seemed to soften her attitude. She said she was unaware Ryan hadn't been getting his medications on time and she promised she would check on it.

After Ryan and I left school that day we decided to go shopping for a new pair of tennis shoes. He was great as we dragged through several stores at the mall, looking for Nikes that were "on sale." Because he behaved so well at the stores I allowed Ryan to talk me into going to the place with the golden arches for a burger.

As luck would have it, the only seating available was on the small mushroom-shaped stools, next to the window in the heavily congested out-door playground area. Ryan waited patiently while I ordered our food and made my way outside, stepping over a spilled soda and the remains of what had once been a "Happy Meal."

Ryan seemed especially jovial and in good spirits. As we chatted and ate our food I privately relished each moment, thoroughly enjoying our "quality" time together. Then it happened.

From out of nowhere a huge, mean-looking woman appeared at our table and shouted in my face, "Are you just going to sit there and *let* him do that?"

She caught me totally unaware with a mouthful of greasy fries. Confused, I gulped down my food and asked sheepishly, "What exactly is he doing?"

"He's flipping me off with his finger under the table," she bellowed.

I instantly became aware that everyone on the playground was staring at us. My cheeks began to burn with embarrassment as I felt the glare of everyone waiting to see what I was going to do to "whip" my rotten kid into shape. To make matters worse, Ryan had started flashing the finger sign to everyone on the playground who was watching us.

"Ryan, you need to apologize to this woman," I demanded.

Ryan looked up with that "dazed" look in his eyes and replied, "Fuck you, bitch."

"I'm sorry," I offered to the irate woman. He has a neurological disorder called Tourette syndrome. I'm sorry if he offended you."

I stood and quickly gathered up what was left of our lunch and placed it on the tray. Ryan had his "goofy" look and laugh going on. I grabbed his arm and led him to the car. Luckily, he didn't resist.

I had been through similar types of humiliation dozens of times before but it never got any easier. Just when it seemed he was doing well, "something" would set Ryan off. We would then be at the mercy of his disinhibitions until they eventually subsided, at which time he would again return to behaving normally.

Because of all the difficulties in the neighborhood, Jim and I considered moving to an area where the homes weren't so close together and where Ryan would have more freedom to move around. In California, especially in our county, homes with any considerable amount of land are extremely expensive and difficult to find. Although we loved our house and had invested much money and labor in fixing it up the way we wanted, we decided go house-browsing.

One Sunday, while out for a drive, we spotted a brand new two-story home sitting halfway up a hill. It was light blue (my favorite color), had a huge front porch and a "for sale" sign in the front yard. When we drove up the gravel drive, the builder met us and invited us in to take a look. Jim only had to look at the huge garage.

Although there were some features we would have changed, the big blue house seemed to be perfect for our family—especially because it was on nearly three quarters of an acre of land. It seemed to be the answer for our problems with Ryan and the neighbors.

The house was more money than we wanted to pay, but I was able to negotiate a good contract with the builder and he accepted our contingent offer to buy his home. The contingency was our ability to sell our present home. Selling homes was my profession and I was confident we could sell within the time of the contract. I immediately listed our home and put a sign in the front yard.

Moving seemed to make much sense, but we didn't really want to move. Even though we couldn't take advantage of the community pool or parks with Ryan, our neighborhood was a great place to live, and Jim and I really didn't want to leave. Even so, we were afraid each time the doorbell rang that another neighbor would be at our throats. We felt we had no other choice but to find a home that would be more suitable for Ryan.

Over the next few weeks I hosted an Open House every weekend. We had many lookers but no serious offers. It was difficult keeping things in order and keeping Ryan away when someone wanted to look at the house. He always made inappropriate comments whenever someone came, so we relied on Grandma Polly to keep him whenever a prospect came through the house.

Several weeks later Jim and I attended a party at the home of one of the few neighbors who was kind enough to still include us. While we were at the party, someone asked why we were moving. Jim and I explained about Ryan and the difficulties we were experiencing.

Several of the couples seemed upset to hear that we were planning to move only because some of the other neighbors were upset about Ryan. Before we knew it there were several other couples joining in, encouraging us to stay in the neighborhood and to not let just a few make us feel forced to move. Jim and I left the party that evening feeling encouraged. For the first time in many months we felt an outpouring of compassion and understanding about our struggles in trying to raise Ryan.

A few days later Robin, one of the women who had been at the party, called and invited Jim and me to go out for pie and coffee with her and her husband Craig. The four of us talked for hours, almost as if we had been friends for years.

I had always felt too self-conscious about our family situation to be very social. Robin took care of that in short order. Before long I was bowling in the ladies bowling league, was a member of the ladies cross stitch group, and a member of the ladies' bunco club. Jim and I also joined a "couples" bunco group, along with five other couples. After keeping myself sheltered for so long, I was finally able to enjoy the company of other people without the fear of being criticized or judged because of Ryan's difficult behavior.

Julie was very active in our church's youth group. Jim and I, however, had stopped attending services for a while because of Ryan's inappropriate behavior. We had actually stopped going *any* place socially. We were like prisoners in our own home. Robin and Craig encouraged us to start going to church again. When the pastor learned of our situation with Ryan, he was compassionate and kind and assured us there would always be a place for us and for Ryan in his church. We felt as if he lifted a heavy load from our shoulders with those words.

When our contingent contract for the blue home in the country expired, we felt relieved our house had not yet sold and that we would not be moving.

Summer was almost over and my real estate sales were booming. Ryan was preparing to return to the Landmark Elementary Program and, based on his success during the summer session, prospects were looking good that he might have a successful school year.

Chapter 17

Actions Speak
Louder Than Words

*"For every problem
there is an opportunity."*[1]
Unknown

Although I had learned a lot about the IEP process through my experiences over the previous five years, I found TASK's "Basic Rights" training to be extremely useful.

TASK is a federally-funded nonprofit organization that serves as a resource for parents needing assistance and support in obtaining educational, medical or support services for their special needs child. Their Basic Rights course was a review of legislative history and a summary of PL 94-142 (IDEA). The presenters reviewed the principles of educational law along with the protections afforded to students and parents.

One of the first things I learned was that the Landmark School, by law, was required to administer Ryan's medications as prescribed by the doctor. I couldn't remember how many times in the past teachers had told me that it was *Ryan's* responsibility to remember to take his medications. Even though he had Attention Deficit Disorder and was unable to read a clock or tell time, the blame for failing to remember to take the medications always fell on Ryan's shoulders.

I also learned valuable information concerning parent's rights. For example:

Parents have the right to participate in all planning meetings regarding the educational needs of their child.

School districts needs to schedule the meetings at a *mutually* convenient time, not just a time that is convenient for them.

Each child diagnosed as a pupil with exceptional needs has the right to be educated with non-disabled students to the maximum extent appropriate.

Parents may request a conference or an IEP meeting with school personnel to review their child's progress at *any* time.

Parents have the right to inspect, review and be provided copies of all school records and have the right to request an amendment to any records on the basis of inaccuracy.

I also learned more about Section 504 of the Rehabilitation Act. This was the same law I cited to the principal in fourth grade when the teacher denied Ryan the opportunity to go on a field trip with the other students. Although I found the training workshops helpful and enlightening, I was soon to realize the importance and relevance of the material to our situation with Ryan.

When Ryan started fifth grade at Landmark, his medications had changed yet again since summer school. He now was taking a combination of Tegretol, Catapres (orally) and Prolixin. As usual, Ryan was eager to start school and he was eager to have all "A" days.

Landmark used a daily report as part of the grading system. During school, each student earned grades for academics, behavior, and personal goals for each class period. The staff graded students based on standards that involved listening when others were talking, raising one's hand to talk, staying in one's seat, staying on task, and keeping hands to ones' self.

The teacher and family liaison helped to set individual personal goals for each student. Home goals, which were established by the student and his family were averaged and became part of the student's personal goals. Parents were then responsible for grading the personal goals and sending the form back to school with the student each day.

Teachers evaluated a student's progress by the grades earned. The teacher would complete the average of behavior, academics, and personal goals each day as well as a weekly average. An A = Excellent, B = Good, C = Average, D = Poor, and F= Unsatisfactory. In addition, students were able to earn special activities and privileges according to their daily and weekly grade levels.

Chapter 17. Actions Speak Louder than Words

The first month of school I kept a daily log of Ryan's behavior.

Tuesday, Sept. 4

Fairly smooth morning. Got onto the bus cheerfully. Seemed happy about going except for a few comments about not being able to go to a "regular" school. Came home in a good mood. Had an "A" day at school. Pestered Biskit and then settled down. Set the table. Complimented my dinner. Had excellent table manners. Commented that he had spit on another student, Anthony, at school. He said that Anthony had Tourette syndrome and "got on his nerves" with his tics. Said that Thomas had threatened to beat him but that they were friends now.

Wednesday, Sept. 5

Hard to wake up. Promised to have another "A" day at school. Came home upset when he only earned a "C" for the day. He lamented he had gotten into trouble for spitting—said he couldn't help it. He had also written "fuck you" on his arm with pen. He insisted he couldn't help the things he had done wrong at school.

Thursday, Sept. 6

A little better getting off for school. Earned another "C" day. Bus driver was quite upset when he arrived. Ryan had been disrespectful and cursed at him. Also, he had thrown Steven's hat out of the bus window on the freeway (Steven had dared him to do it). Driver warned me that he was writing up a report and threatened to discontinue Ryan's transportation if he didn't straighten up. Ryan promised to do better. There was some stuttering. He was quite difficult during homework. Spit on his paper and then stuck his pencil through the wet part, poking a big hole. Then he wadded the paper up and threw it at me. He said that he hates me for sending him to a school with a bunch of retards. He says I'm just getting back at him for being bad.

Friday, September 7

Had a "B" day at school. Came home somewhat hyper. Spit out three large mouthfuls of ice tea and then emptied the glass upside down onto the floor. Said he felt like he "had" to do it—couldn't help it. He cleaned up the mess. Later, he was defiant to Dad and me, and aggravated the dog. When we asked him to do something he responded, "Make me." Refused to take time-out. Jumped over the furniture several times. There was also much spitting.

113

Saturday, September 8

We stopped at a roadside stand to get some corn. While there, a bug jumped on him. He panicked and started crying (real tears) and was shaking uncontrollably. He clung to me until I killed the bug and assured him it was dead. Even then he felt like the bug was still on him.

Sunday, September 9

We took a half-hour walk but Ryan said he was tired and had to rest before we came back. Real antsy. Couldn't or wouldn't focus on anything to do. Made an attempt to do some chores but became angry while trying to do them. Wrote "fuck you" on his arm. Gave the finger sign to us numerous times. Was stuttering a lot.

Monday, September 10

"B" day at school. Sylvia came at 4:30 for our home visit. Numerous acting-out episodes while she was here—threw the dog's toy and hit me in the face. Sylvia showed us how to do the "basket hold" technique to restrain him. Why hadn't anyone (psychiatrists) told us about this before? I went to a new mental health support group called Special Parents. Most of the parents there had put their kids in treatment centers and were talking about how awful they were. I don't think I belong in the group. Ryan's behavior is the same as the other parents are describing but I would never put him away. How can they just give away their child?

Tuesday, September 11

When I arrived home from work at 3:30 I had a message on the machine from Sylvia wanting me to pick Ryan up. He was not allowed to ride the bus home because of his noncompliance at school. I told Sylvia that she would have to find a different consequence than not riding the bus. After all, having me pick him up was no consequence. He would much rather ride home with me than on the bus. Sylvia insisted he would not be allowed to ride the bus if it happened again. I then reminded her that Section 504 states that transportation cannot be denied to a handicapped student and certainly not as a form of punishment for something he had done at school. I made it clear (in a nice way) that I would not be picking him up again. Ryan was horrible on the drive home. I had to stop many times for him to take a time-out before I could continue driving. When I offered to help him start his homework he blew up and ripped up all of his papers.

Wednesday, September 12

He got up early to finish the homework he had ripped up the night before. Had an "F" day at school. He said Adam had rammed his (Ryan's) head into a wall and that Steven had hit him hard and hurt him. He then threw ice tea on Steven and received an in-school suspension. He blew up when he got home because I would not allow him to wait on the corner for Julie's bus. Hit, kicked, and butted his head at me. I restrained him for five minutes and then released him. (I pooped out). He hit me again and I threatened to call the police. We had to use numerous time-outs the rest of the evening.

Thursday, September 13

"B" day at school. Came home and wanted to go down the street to play with friends. When I told him he needed to wait he shoved me backwards into the steps, hitting my spine on the sharp corner of the wood. He then started crying and said, "I'm sorry, I don't want to hurt you, Mommy." Later in the evening, he spit ice tea out on the floor three times in a row, and then dumped the rest of the glass on the floor.

Friday, September 14

Minimum day at school. I picked Ryan up at 11:45 A.M. Sylvia said that Ryan seemed to be turning things around nicely. As we were walking out the door from school Ryan ran through the cars in the parking lot and hid from me. Later, he became upset when the dentist told him he had a small cavity. He called the dentist a liar and then ran out of his office. After leaving the dentist's office we went for his checkup with the pediatrician. He told the doctor everything was going fine. School was fine. Home was fine. Later, while at the store, he started acting up, throwing huge rubber balls down the aisles of the market and cursing loudly. He went to Grandma's to spend the night. Jim and I went to a Ch.A.D.D. meeting.

Sunday, September 16

Got up for Sunday School. Ryan wanted to go, but when we were getting out of the car he began speaking loudly and inappropriately to others who were walking in. Started to use foul language. We got him settled down, however, during Sunday School, he started using bad language again and kept giving other kids the finger. Disobeyed frequently—had several episodes where his dad had to hold him down. A totally miserable night. He was defiant, verbally and physically abusive to all of us.

Chapter 17. Actions Speak Louder than Words

Monday, September 17

Had a "C" day at school. Bus driver had to pull over a few times because of Ryan and Steven. Horrible when Dad came home from work. Dad had to hold him down twice. Jim had a difficult time breathing while trying to hold him. I was scared he was going to have a heart attack and I threatened to call 911 if Ryan didn't stop. He was bothering the dog, was bothering everyone. Was calm during dinner, then he got into another fight with Dad.

Tuesday, September 18

"B" day at school. Bus driver said that Ryan had jumped off the bus at Steven's house and refused to get back on. Ryan said he got off the bus because the bus driver had gotten angry and had hit Steven very hard, making a red mark on his chest. He said he had gotten off the bus because he was afraid the driver was going to hit him too. Steven's dad called and we both agreed the boys should not be riding the bus together without an aide.

Wednesday, September 19

I called the principal, Peggy Merino, and asked if Ryan's bus route could be shortened and if an aide could be provided to assist the boys on the bus. She said she was investigating the incident with Steven and would let me know what happened. I picked Ryan up from school to go to a dentist's appointment. He was nervous on the way but did not act out. When we got inside the dentist's office, he hid on the floor behind the couch. Was very nervous about getting a shot. He wouldn't let the doctor give him Novocain. The dentist was patient and tried several times but Ryan couldn't get a grip. His heart was pounding and he was shaking all over. The dentist finally gave up. Ryan felt horrible when we left. He cried about what a failure he had been, what a "no-good" he was. Then he became angry and threw what was left of his soda across the lobby.

Thursday, September 20

When Frank, the bus driver, arrived to pick up Ryan, he opened the door to the bus, reached under his seat and pulled out a "harness" type of restraint. Ryan stopped on the first step and asked what that "thing" was. Frank responded, "This is for boys that get off the bus when they're not supposed to." Ryan stepped off the bus and I directed him back, assuring him that Frank was not going to use the restraint. Frank said, "Yeah, I'm not going to use it now." I called the principal to tell her about Frank.

116

Chapter 17. *Actions Speak Louder than Words*

Friday, September 21

"A" day at school. Very hyper at home, couldn't sit still.

Monday, September 24

Beautiful morning. Got up and ready on time. Made his bed. He and Dad practiced pitching. They stopped when he complained of being dizzy. Good at dinner. He and Dad washed the car together. Wonderful evening.

Tuesday, September 25

Excellent morning. "A" day at school. Talked with principal. Bus route has been shortened. Staff does not want an aide on the bus because that would make the boys "dependent" on someone else for their behavior. Also, she was inclined to believe that the driver had just been "joking" about using the harness on Ryan. I assured her it was not done jokingly. A few OCD episodes during the evening. He ripped a new prize baseball card in half because he felt like he "had" to. Started flipping the light switches off and on repeatedly.

Wednesday, September 26

Had a good morning. Angry when he got off the bus—screaming and cursing because he had a "B" day at school. Settled down and was excellent. Had one episode at dinner of spitting tea out. Said he had to do it.

Thursday, September 27

Off to a good start in the morning. Started off good at school. Then stole some batteries out of the school's emergency supplies box for his radio. He said that Steven and Anthony had talked him into it. They told him they had stolen things before and never been caught. Adam, another student, told on them. He was truly remorseful when he got home.

Friday, September 28

Had good day at school but was frustrated it wasn't an "A" day. Had a confrontation with Dad when he arrived home from work and hit Dad in the back. Took his time-out and settled down except for being noisy and hyper. Was fairly good at dinner except at the very end when he put both hands in the spaghetti and "ished" it around. Went to Julie's piano recital and sat quietly for forty-five minutes.

Saturday, September 29

Calm when he first got up. Was badgering and irritating while I was on the phone. Flipping the light switches off and on, doing somersaults on the bed, playing with the buttons on the phone, making the dog growl and nip. Went to the mall later. He saw a pair of "Michael Jackson" shoes and started whining because I wouldn't get them. He said I was stupid. A few minutes later he let out a huge shriek. I started walking ahead of him toward the exit and he ran up behind me and hit me, full force, with his fist in the middle of my back. Then he started crying, "I'm sorry, Mommy, I don't want to hit you. I'm no good. I'm going to go to hell. Why does God hate me? Why did he give me this? I couldn't stop myself. Send me to a hospital, Mommy," etc. He apologized many times throughout the evening. We talked about other things he could do when he got angry.

Sunday, September 30

Wonderful day. There were a few minor episodes with Julie and the dog but he regained control quickly. Played with his Nintendo a lot. We went out for dinner and he was perfect. Sat next to Julie with no problems. He communicated well, was witty but serious and appropriate. We talked about family things we could do if he continued with such good behavior. Best day I can remember in a long time.

As time went on, our relationship with Sylvia improved. She had experienced many of Ryan's "behaviors" at school and seemed to be much more sympathetic than she was at the beginning. I still was not sure she had a true understanding about Tourette's though.

About mid-October Sylvia mentioned that Ryan had been acting "differently" for a couple of weeks. She wondered if he was depressed and surmised that maybe he was finally "getting in touch" with his feelings.

I personally thought there was more to it than that. Ryan had been expressing his fears about being with some of the other boys in the school who were threatening each other and acting aggressively. My log for October 9 reflected one example:

Came home looking tired. Later seemed withdrawn and sad. He came into my room and said, "You did a bad thing sending me to that school, Mom." When I asked why he said, "Because someone is going to get hurt." After dinner, he used Christ's name inappropriately in frustration. When I cautioned him about it he said, "What difference does it make? I'm going to go to hell anyway." I asked him why he was talking like that again and he said, "Because I say bad words and hit people."

At bedtime he talked again about being afraid that someone was going to get hurt.

The next day he was nervous about going to school but had an okay day. When Ryan came home after school he had a fairly difficult evening. He "seesawed" back and forth from high to low. There was a long period of good behavior but one very bad spell where I had to use the basket hold. He was verbally and physically abusive and said that I was going to be dead when I got old—that he was going to get me.

Even in the basket hold he tried to kick me and butted me in the face with the back of his head. After about two or three minutes, he finally calmed down. He was later extremely remorseful about the incident and said that he wanted to have a good life.

There had been one incident at Landmark when the staff had to call the police to assist with the students. Several of the boys, including Ryan, had gone outside the school and refused to come back inside. When the boys climbed over the fence and were dangerously close to being on the freeway, the staff called the police to help in getting them back.

It frightened Ryan when the police arrived. The police officers spoke with the boys about the seriousness of what they had done—about how dangerous it was. Ryan was genuinely remorseful and seemed ashamed he had done something that involved the police being called.

Despite the difficulties, there were things about the Landmark School that Ryan liked. He really liked his teacher, Mrs. Masterson. She was an American Indian and Ryan enjoyed hearing her talk of her native culture. He also liked Sheila, one of the teacher's aides. He merely tolerated Berta and Sylvia.

He also enjoyed swimming at the pool, playing Nintendo in class and the weekly field trips. The students had the opportunity to earn a "TGIF" (Thank Goodness It's Friday) award that was usually a trip to the beach, a park or the shopping mall. Earning TGIF was a big deal for the boys. Earning it depended on the combination of their home and school scores for the week. Ryan always looked forward to TGIF and was able to "make" it a good bit of the time. There was one field trip I will never forget.

Ryan and the other boys went on a trip to a large rural park several miles from the school. During the outing, Ryan tripped while crossing a creek and skinned his leg. It wasn't a big scrape, probably about the size of a quarter. It was no big deal to Ryan or to the school, although they did note it on an incident report. When he came home, he didn't even mention it.

He was particularly hyper and demanding that afternoon. He wanted to go outdoors to play and ride his bike. I could tell from his demeanor that he was in no condition to be out of my sight. Trying to put him off, I suggested he instead have a snack and rest awhile before going outdoors.

It soon became a war of words. He insisted he was going to go bike riding right then. I was firm that he could go outside later after taking a short time to rest and settle down.

Ryan began to scream and curse at me. The next thing I knew he walked over to the coffee table and pushed it over. The water in the vase of roses spilled all over the floor and soaked the magazines that had fallen with the table.

"You pick that table up right this instant!" I demanded, grabbing for my crystal vase that was laying on the floor.

"Shut up, you asshole!" he yelled back at me.

I started after him and he ran, laughing at me as he ducked behind the wall in the kitchen. As I came closer he ran into the family room laughing wildly.

I again demanded that he stop and pick up the coffee table. He responded by kicking over another table and a lamp. Then he picked up the magazines and started throwing them at me. He began to knock over the stools and started pushing the dishes off the counter.

"I'm going to call the police if you don't stop!" I screamed at him.

"Go ahead, you motherfucker!" he yelled back.

I had threatened to call the police before but had never followed through. This time, I felt the time had come. Ryan was continuing to knock over or throw anything he could get his hands on. As I reached for the phone I felt something cold hit my face. He had thrown a glass of ice tea at my head.

I grabbed a towel to wipe my face and hair, picked up the phone to dial and Ryan started hitting and beating on me. I tried hitting back at him to keep him away, and he began kicking me.

I tried again to dial the phone and he knocked it out of my hand. I pulled the phone up by the cord, put it back on the hook and yelled at Julie to run upstairs and call the police for me. When I came back into the kitchen, Ryan started knocking more dishes off the counter and onto the floor.

In a minute, Julie was back downstairs. She had called the police and the operator told her they would send someone right out. Then Ryan attacked Julie and started calling her names. He was throwing anything loose that he could get his hands on.

After what seemed like an eternity the phone rang. I lunged for the phone and answered. It was the dispatcher at the sheriff's department wanting to know if we really needed someone to come.

"Yes!" I cried into the phone. "Please hurry!"

Julie and I were in tears and Ryan was watching us closely from across the room. I asked her to call Grandma Polly and she obediently ran into the other room. Ryan had stopped throwing things and seemed to be in a daze, as if he didn't understand what was happening.

A short time later two sheriff's deputies arrived. I hurriedly explained that my eleven-year-old son had Tourette syndrome and had been trashing the house and throwing things at my daughter and me. I asked if they would please try to "scare" him and make him realize that he couldn't do this kind of thing again.

One officer immediately went toward Ryan and the other put his arm on mine and led me into the kitchen. The officer who was with me looked around the house, surveying the damage. "What happened?" he asked. "Did he do all of this?"

I had stopped crying when the officers came but when I looked out of the corner of my eye and saw the other officer talking with Ryan, the tears started again. He looked so scared. He was sitting in Dad's easy chair, stiff as a board. The officer was standing over him and at one point, I saw him kneel down and point at Ryan's leg. I strained to hear what the deputy was saying.

"How did you get that scrape on your leg?" he asked.

"I got it at school today," I heard Ryan say softly.

"Did someone do something to hurt you?" the officer asked.

"No" Ryan answered.

Then, I heard something that sent chills up my spine.

"Did your mother put that scrape on your leg?" the officer asked Ryan.

"No," Ryan replied again. "I hurt it at school, at the park."

I couldn't believe what I was hearing. The officer standing beside me waited as I listened to Ryan and the other deputy.

"How did you hurt your leg at the park?" the officer continued.

"I tripped going across the creek and fell on the rocks," Ryan said.

"Are you sure your mother didn't hurt your leg?" the officer asked again.

"No," Ryan repeated, shaking his head. "I hurt it at the park."

The officer that was standing with me realized what was happening. He called for his partner to come over and they changed places. He went over to Ryan and the other officer came into the kitchen to talk with me.

"How did he get that scrape on his leg?" the officer began.

"I didn't know he had a scrape until just now," I said.

"What park did he go to?" he asked. I told him the name of the park and he seemed satisfied.

I could hear the other deputy talking firmly to Ryan. He warned him if he ever had to come out to our home again because of his destroying his parent's house, he would have to take Ryan back to the station with him. Ryan sat quietly, tears forming in the corner of his eyes.

Just about that time Jim walked in from school, and Grandma Polly arrived. She went over to Ryan and I walked toward the door to let the police officers out. The officer who had been talking with me first said he hoped he had done some good. The other one didn't say anything.

All evening long the thoughts were spinning around in my head. That police officer thought I might have hurt Ryan! Ryan had been hurting Julie and me, throwing furniture at us and destroying the house, yet the police officer thought that *I* may have put that tiny scrape on his leg.

The more I thought about it the angrier I became. I couldn't believe that I called the police for help and instead, one of them suspected, however briefly, that I might have done something to hurt my child.

I was not only angry, I was crushed. It made me sick to think that anyone would suspect me of hurting my son. It was even more devastating knowing how much abuse Jim and I had both endured over the past few years. We were both victims of "parent abuse," not perpetrators of child abuse.

A few days later I called our community police officer and asked for an appointment to meet with him. I decided that the entire county sheriff's department needed to know a lot more about Tourette syndrome and he would be a good place to start. I also thought it might be a good idea for Ryan to go along and have a tour around the facilities. I hoped that by seeing the jail and some of its residents, Ryan might get a clearer picture of what the officer was talking about.

Officer Powell said he would be happy for Ryan and me to come to the station. Because Ryan had left his local school district to go to Landmark, he had missed participating in the D.A.R.E. (Drug Abuse Resistance Education) program with the other fifth graders. I asked Officer Powell if he had any D.A.R.E. materials he could share with Ryan during the visit and he assured me he did.

When we arrived at the county sheriff's station, Officer Powell met us and asked Ryan if he would like to go on a tour. Ryan jumped out of his chair and followed the officer eagerly.

Then, Officer Powell and I began to talk about my awful experience a few days earlier. He explained that police officers have an obligation to investigate any possibilities of child abuse, but agreed that in this instance, the officer had put too much emphasis on the origin of the small scrape. We talked about Tourette syndrome and I offered him a supply of brochures I had brought from the TSA.

"You know, Mrs. Hughes," Officer Powell began. "You may just want us to put you on our 'hazard' screen."

"What's that?" I asked.

Officer Powell explained that he could "flag" our name in their computer system. Then, anytime we dialed 911, the operator would see that we were a "Hazard Call." There would be a note on the screen saying that we had a son with Tourette syndrome that might become violent and aggressive. That way, Officer Powell explained, should we ever need to call again, the officers would have information about Ryan *before* they arrived at our home.

It sounded great to me. I wouldn't have to convince the operator that I really needed them to come and, hopefully, they would have a better understanding of our situation before they arrived.

"Please," I said, "put us on the screen immediately."

Officer Powell then invited me to meet his Watch Commander.

Lt. Strider was on the phone when we walked into his office, but he motioned for me to sit down. I looked around the room as I waited and remembered back to the days when I worked as a dispatcher for the Los Angeles Police Department. It seemed like a hundred years ago.

When the Lieutenant's call was over he stood and reached for my hand. We talked briefly about my incident with his officers and he asked me several questions about Tourette syndrome.

"You know," he said, "it would be great if you could come back during a roll call and give a presentation to the department."

I agreed to call and set up a time. When his phone rang again, I thanked him and stood to leave.

Ryan met me in the hall wearing a new D.A.R.E. T-shirt and hat. One of the other deputies came over to us and said that his wife had read the *RYAN* book. She was a teacher in a nearby district and a parent had given it to her to read. Small world, I thought to myself as Officer Powell opened the metal door to let us out.

I felt pleased I was able to vent and express my concerns about the officers' visit to our home and had also given Ryan an opportunity to learn about drugs and the jail. I had learned about the hazard screen and I was able to share and distribute materials about Tourette syndrome—and, I was invited back. For just a split-second, I was glad the officer had been suspicious of Ryan's scraped leg.

Chapter 18

A Foot In Each World

"Children's talent to endure stems from
their ignorance of alternatives."[1]
Maya Angelou

In November of that year I attended my first national TSA conference. The conference was in McLean, Virginia, just outside Washington, D.C., and it was well-attended with over five hundred participants. The energy among those attending was infectious. I sat in on as many workshops and group discussions as I could and enjoyed every chance to meet with others in the TS family.

Many of the discussions centered on tics and their troublesome effects. I felt frustrated that many of the other behavioral issues in TS were merely skimmed over in the presentations. I had hoped for more information on handling problems with ADHD, OCD and anxiety.

Here, I had my first encounter with adults with Tourette syndrome. Although I had seen adults with TS on the TSA videos, I had never personally met an adult with Tourette syndrome. The conference was a perfect opportunity. They were all over the place and they were not hard to pick out of the crowd.

The adult Touretters seemed to be enjoying a chance to make and renew acquaintances. It was hard not to laugh at times at the pure spontaneity at which they would often respond to another person's vocal tics. Many times during a presentation or speech, one Touretter would bark or make a comment that would "set off" a response in kind from several others. I had never seen anything quite like it before and found the whole thing very fascinating.

During the dinner banquet I had the privilege of sitting with several of the TSA physicians who were speaking at the conference. During dinner, a woman walked up to our table and greeted one of the doctors.

"Hi, Patty," he said. "How are you?"

"I'm fine Doc," she answered, and then quickly kissed him once on each cheek.

I watched with interest as Patty then moved to the next doctor at the table and kissed him on each cheek! There were ten of us at the table and we all waited as Patty made her way around, kissing each one of us. I was used to dealing with this behavior from Ryan, but it felt bizarre to experience this compulsion from a stranger!

I left the conference with a much better understanding of Tourette syndrome. Although many of the things I saw and heard were foreign to my experiences with TS, I gained a greater appreciation for all the variables involved in the disorder.

Ryan continued to have good days and bad days, both at home and at school. The bus continued to be a problem. It was either late in coming or late in dropping him off at home.

The drivers changed frequently and some of them spoke very little English. It disturbed me that the school did not provide the drivers with any information about the students. None of them knew anything about Ryan's disorder. They only knew to pick him up and drop him off at a certain time. For the ones who seemed interested, I shared information about TS. Unfortunately, just when we got a driver "broken in," they would change routes and we would be back to square one again.

There had been many driver changes since the original driver who had slapped Steven and threatened Ryan with the harness. Although he did well on many days, Ryan still had his share of infractions. My file of "Bus Conduct Report to Parents" file began to grow. One driver wrote:

> One day Ryan took his magic rings on the bus. He let Steven play with them and then demanded them back. Steven refused and they started to hit each other. Steven took his seat belt off and crossed the aisle. They continued hitting each other until, finally, I pulled off the road and separated them.

Another driver wrote:

Ryan started playing rough with his toys. Soon he
and Steven were kicking, spitting, and throwing things
at each other.

I had been keeping in close contact with the principal concerning the
bus problems. Despite my suggestions, she steadfastly refused to put an
aide on the bus with Ryan and Steven. One day, after Ryan returned home
from school, I received a call from Sylvia.

"Susan," she said solemnly. "I was calling about what happened on
the bus today."

Oh no, I thought. What has he done now?

"Ryan didn't say anything when he got home, Sylvia. What did he
do?" I asked.

Sylvia began to tell me what she knew of the day's incident. Evi-
dently, Ryan and Steven had again become disruptive and rowdy. The driver,
Joseph, asked them to sit down and be quiet. The boys refused to obey and
Joseph became quite angry.

The bus route ran through an agricultural area. The two lane road was
narrow with a deep gully on either side. Joseph had pulled the bus off the
side of the road and grabbed Steven by the shirt and began shaking him. He
then grabbed Ryan's hand and physically threatened him by raising a chain
high over his head.

According to Sylvia, the driver threatened to kill both of the boys and
toss their bodies into a canal. He threatened to hit them with the chain and
leave them lying there in the ditch.

I was stunned. After her words sunk in, I asked Sylvia what the school
was going to do. She assured me the incident was being investigated. She
said the principal had already called Joseph in for questioning. She also
said that the staff decided that Joseph did not really mean what he said to
the boys. He told them he was frustrated and only wanted to scare the boys
to make them mind. When I questioned Ryan later that evening, he confirmed what Sylvia had told me but offered little else. He didn't want to
talk about it.

Soon after, Sylvia told me the boys had received counseling at school
and that Joseph was reprimanded for the way he handled the situation.
When I think back on it now, I can't believe I stayed so calm. To this day I
think of how Ryan must have felt when he was threatened with being killed
and dumped in a canal by an angry man wielding a metal chain.

Near the end of the school year I received a call on my answering machine from the principal. Mrs. Merino's message warned that if Ryan had one more infraction on the bus, they would not allow him to ride any longer.

We (the school administrators and I) had covered this subject many times before. The school was nineteen miles from our home. There was no way I could transport Ryan to and from school every day and still be able to work. Besides, it was the school district's obligation to provide transportation for Ryan. That was clear in the law protecting special education students.

More importantly, I felt that learning to ride a bus and behave appropriately was part of his education. At the time, it seemed much more important to me than the academic areas.

I expressed my feelings to Mrs. Merino. The next day, I received a letter from the principal, once again threatening to suspend Ryan from riding the bus. I immediately responded:

> Dear Mrs. Merino:
>
> In response to your letter regarding Ryan's bus behavior, I regret that I must go on record with vehement disapproval of your threatened suspension. Although I have been thoroughly supportive of the staff's wonderful efforts to modify Ryan's behavior throughout the year, I cannot in good conscience support this decision for the following reasons:
>
> 1) To deny Ryan transportation services would seem to be in violation of Section 504 of the Rehabilitation Act. You must provide him transportation in such manner as necessary to afford him an equal opportunity for participation. Thus, I suggest an aide if you feel his misbehavior serious enough to warrant an intervention.
>
> 2) Having Ryan to school at 9 A.M. and picked up by 2:30 P.M. would be an undue hardship on my work schedule that is already mandated by Ryan's very serious needs.
>
> 3) A three-day suspension from the bus would, in my opinion (based on my experiences of living with this child for the past twelve years), be totally ineffective in controlling his undesirable bus behav-

ior.

4) Suspension from riding the bus would very likely reinforce the negative behavior and act instead as a reward (getting to ride with Mom).

5) Suspending Ryan from the bus does not address the primary reason for the misbehavior. An example would be his inability to "connect" the denial of transportation to the inhibition of impulsive acts that are a direct result of his disability.

6) Bus suspension would deny Ryan an opportunity to learn appropriate social interactions that will be necessary for him to function as he grows to adulthood.

Instead of denying Ryan transportation services that are afforded to him by law, I would ask you and the Landmark staff to consider the following suggestions:

1) Instruct the bus company to reduce the P.M. bus time to 30 minutes. (It is now running 70-90 minutes or more).

2) Efforts be made to separate Steven and Ryan and perhaps transport them separately.

3) Give Ryan his medications at 2:00 P.M. when it is scheduled, instead of 2:30 when it is more convenient for the staff. Giving the medication earlier will allow sufficient time for the Ritalin to begin its effectiveness. It should peak around 2:30 when he is about to board the bus.

4) Follow Landmark's general premise of rewarding "positive" behavior instead of punishing the negative, possibly by implementing a reward system at school that would recognize the days that he has good bus behavior.

Because Ryan's bus behavior is generally good, and because major incidents have been few, I would hope that you and the staff will agree to the value in considering my suggestions. I will look forward to hearing from you concerning any constructive ideas you may have that would help to improve Ryan's behavior on the bus. Please be assured that we will fully support any efforts that will not result in a denial of Ryan's transportation needs.

I sent a copy of my letter to our local district, the County Superintendent of Schools office, the County Mental Health director and the teacher.

Ryan continued to ride the bus the rest of the year and the staff never brought up the subject of suspending him from transportation again.

Throughout all of this it was becoming increasingly difficult for me to work. When I first started selling real estate, I had envisioned being able to "set my hours" and be at home when Ryan came home from school. As hard as I tried, I could not always schedule clients around my personal calendar and found it was a constant battle to juggle appointments and phone calls.

Ryan had a history of becoming over-stimulated and provoking each time the phone rang or whenever someone came to the door. Although we did not permit Ryan to answer the phone, he often would run to it each time it rang. Although he always received a swift and sometimes stern consequence, it never kept him from trying to grab the phone. His greetings often ranged from an exuberant "Hello" or "Talk to me" to an irritated "Who is it?" and "What do you want?"

One evening while I was fixing dinner, the phone rang and Ryan jumped to answer. When he politely said hello, I felt relieved. Then in a loud voice he yelled, "It's for you, Mom. It's some stupid foreign person."

I was mortified. The caller was a client who was looking for a condo to rent. That week I had a second phone line installed that would ring only in my bedroom.

Even that did not solve the problem. Every time I went to my room to use the phone, Ryan would enter and start screaming or making the dog bark. If I shut the door, he would bang on it with his fists and kick it with his shoes, yelling and screaming or laughing the whole time. If I put the caller on hold to take care of him, he would stop, then immediately start again when I was back on the phone.

I also got a pager so that the office or a client could reach me throughout the day. However, the majority of messages I received were from Ryan's school. They would call frequently, asking me to come and pick him up from school early. I became nervous each time the pager beeped and I dreaded returning home and listening to the messages on the answering machine.

Many times, on the way to the school to get Ryan, I would put in a Linda Ronstadt tape and play the same song repeatedly. Then, I would allow myself to cry freely as I turned up the volume and buried my sorrow in the words of the song. I felt as if I, too, were broken into tiny pieces of glass, beyond any hope of repair. Yet, when I got to the school, I dried my tears and somehow mustered the strength to once again be a competent and assertive advocate for Ryan.

Only Sylvia was aware of my inner struggle to cope. She offered to counsel with me privately and I took her up on the offer. I felt that she, seeing Ryan at school every day, would have a clear idea of what I was dealing with and be in the best position to help.

During this time I could feel myself fighting depression. I resisted any thoughts of taking medication, but not because I didn't believe an antidepressant could be helpful. It was just my own stubborn determination to control my feelings and emotions. There were days, however, when I felt overwhelmed and devastated, and they seemed to be coming more frequently.

My family was becoming concerned for my health. My mother and other family members often suggested I should look into the possibility of finding a hospital or residential facility for Ryan. My mother was very involved in helping us and she was overwhelmingly supportive of all that Jim and I were doing to try to help Ryan. Yet, she knew that I was struggling with monumental obstacles in just getting through each day. She could see that the constant stress and turmoil was taking a toll on my physical and emotional well-being.

Despite my family's good intentions, I could not even consider the idea of "putting" Ryan somewhere. He was my child and I could not imagine that anyone else could (or would) take care of him any better than Jim and I. In fact, I secretly resented any implication that Ryan should be any place but at home with his family.

"What about Julie?" they would ask. "It's not fair for her."

I knew they were right about that. Living with Ryan's difficult behavior had been humiliating and embarrassing for Julie too. She could rarely have friends to sleep over or have dinner. She, too, had put up with much physical and verbal abuse from her younger brother.

I struggled with how to help Julie contend with the difficulties and with ways to help her understand. We had many mother-to-daughter, heart-to-heart talks and cry sessions. It was hard for Julie to see Ryan misbehave so horribly while Jim and I held her behavior to a much higher standard.

Julie was always the opposite of Ryan. She excelled in school, was an honor student, always tried to please everyone, and had many friends. Yet, Ryan got most of our attention.

I did my best to help her understand. I tried to explain it by having her imagine that Ryan had a physical handicap and could not walk or take care of himself. In that condition, I reasoned, he would need all of us to help him do the things that he was not able to do.

If he had a physical disability, I theorized, no one would question that I would have to give so much of my time and energy. No one would fault me for having to bathe and dress him, or to push his wheelchair or lift him into bed. "Even though Ryan appears to be 'normal,' I explained to Julie, "at this time he is not. We hope, pray, and trust that he will get better, but right now, he is just as limited from living a normal life as a person with a physical disability."

"He needs us to help him," I continued. "Even if that may mean a great deal of sacrifice on our part. Some of our sacrifices might include not being able to have friends over when we want. They may also include not being invited to family or social functions, being talked about by other people who do not understand and being embarrassed when he acts out in public."

Julie always agreed that any sacrifice the three of us might need to make was worth it to keep Ryan at home and our family together. As a family, we were resolved, even when we were not sure how we would find the strength to get up and face another day like the one before. Despite everything, all three of us were dedicated to helping Ryan lead a normal life.

I was one of the original members of Special Parents, a support group for children with emotional and behavioral disorders. I had regularly attended the monthly meetings since Ryan began his first summer at Landmark. It was somewhat of a mystery to me why I continued going. After the first two meetings, I decided that I did not really belong in the group. Most of the parents who attended had already placed their child in a residential treatment facility. It surprised me how cavalier some of them seemed when they talked about it.

Some of the stories the parents related about the various residential facilities were shocking. They seldom said anything positive. Many of the parents who attended the meetings had children who had been in trouble with the law or who had been on drugs. I felt like a fish out of water, but something kept compelling me to go back month after month. I began to accumulate a huge file of notes—comments from the parents and from speakers who addressed the group.

What was so interesting about the various stories at the sharing sessions was the striking similarities in the children being discussed. The behaviors were the same—verbal and physical aggression, impulsivity, oppositional defiant behavior, mood swings, and learning difficulties at school. What was confusing was the wide variety of diagnoses for what appeared to be very similar behaviors. Although practically all the children had ADD or ADHD, the other diagnoses ranged from Schizophrenia, Pervasive Developmental Disorder, Schizoid Affective Disorder, Oppositional Defiant Disorder, Obsessive Compulsive Disorder, Tourette syndrome and Bipolar Disorder (manic depression).

Sometimes I would leave the meetings and cry all the way home. It often seemed as if there was more "scaring" than "sharing." It was frightening for me to hear the horror stories. Yet, I felt that by listening to the other parents, I too, could learn something. By hearing their successes and failures I hoped to gain more insight on how I could help Ryan.

Even though I knew his behavior was extreme and abnormal at times, I desperately clung to visions of the "other" Ryan. I hung on to memories of the Ryan we occasionally got a glimpse of when the medications were working just right. Despite my stubborn denials, I knew deep down that Ryan was living with one foot in this world and one foot in another.

Chapter 19

There Is Always Hope

"Hope is the thing with feathers
That perches in the soul
And sings the tunes without the words
And never stops at all."[1]
Emily Dickenson

Sylvia always told me I needed to "take some time" for myself. She stressed the importance of me having a chance to "get away" for a while and to have a break from Ryan and his constant demands. She suggested I set aside one night a week, leave Ryan at home with Jim and do something that I liked to do, like shopping or going to a movie.

It sounded great to me. Sylvia was giving me license to leave home and I could escape without feeling guilty! Jim was supportive of the idea and very cooperative. On my weekly nights of freedom, I wasted no time in speeding away the minute he got home from work.

It was wonderful at first. I ate dinner out and really enjoyed being alone. I window shopped 'til I dropped. One night I went to the library and spent hours just browsing through books and magazines.

I was still attending the monthly ladies' bunco group and the ladies' cross stitch club, or the "Stitch and Bitch Club," as our husbands liked to call it. Jim and I also played bunco monthly with a couples' group. We also participated in church activities whenever possible. I did my best between working and taking care of Ryan to lead an otherwise "normal" life as a wife and mother.

If it had not been for my own mother's love, support and willingness to help, I would never have had a chance to do anything other than stay at home with Ryan. My mom was always there, whenever or wherever I needed her help. If there was an emergency call from the school and I couldn't get away from work, Mom would go. If another couple called to invite us to dinner, Mom was there. She knew how desperately Jim and I needed the break away from all the stress.

I was always aware of how many times she watched Ryan for me and tried to be careful to not abuse her generosity. The sad truth was, Mom was the *only* person we had to help us. We couldn't hire regular babysitters— we were afraid of what might happen.

Although we had other family, friends and neighbors, hardly anyone invited Ryan over or offered to take him along any place or to sit with him. I couldn't blame them, in a way. But even an hour or two of respite a month would have been such a help. Not only did we need time away from Ryan, but we also needed to feel support from those around us. It would have been wonderful if we had been included more often, excluded less often, and not treated as if he (and we) were a leper or misfit.

Ryan usually behaved well for my mom. Every time he went to spend the night, his grandma spoiled him with platefuls of macaroni and cheese, trips to Target to buy music tapes, and extra (unearned) folding money for his pocket. It was Grandma Polly who affectionately nicknamed him "Booger"— a moniker that has stuck with him over the years, much to Ryan's indignation.

Grandma Polly also had her share of escapades with Ryan, including the "Toys R Us" episode. Ryan was going through one of his "cowboy" phases when it happened. During a cowboy phase, Ryan would do little but think about, dress up like, act like, and talk about cowboys. We had been through other phases, like the Ninja phase, the karate phase, and the Indian phase. However, the cowboy phase lasted the longest and occurred more frequently.

One day while shopping, Ryan managed to talk his dad, Grandma Polly and me into "just looking" at Toys R Us at the cowboy stuff. He was ecstatic when he saw a pair of real-looking handcuffs hanging on one of the displays. I was busy looking at something with Julie and didn't pay much attention to Ryan, since Grandma Polly was with him. A few minutes later, when I walked back to the aisle where I last saw them, I was surprised to see my mom bent over in an awkward-looking position. Ryan was standing nearby with one of those "I didn't mean to do it" looks on his face.

Before I could ask what was wrong my mom said, "He's got me handcuffed to this shelf, Susan. I can't get these things unsnapped. See if you can."

I looked at the handcuffs that were strangling my mother's wrists and saw that there was no place to "unsnap" them. There was only an opening for a key on the side of the cuffs.

"Ryan, where's the key?" I asked, assuming he was hiding the key in his hand.

"I dunno," he said sheepishly. "I don't think there is one."

"There must be a key," I said emphatically. "Look around, Ryan, it must be here somewhere."

We checked the area all around Grandma Polly, lifting up package after package in search of the missing key. I looked for other packages of handcuffs thinking I could open one and use its key. But there were no other packages of handcuffs around. Mom and I looked at each other with disbelief. We did not know whether to laugh or cry. She was embarrassed and her wrists were starting to turn red and swollen from the tight cuffs.

"What are we going to do?" she asked helplessly.

"I'll go get someone to help," I offered.

"Hurry up," she said half laughing. "These things are starting to hurt me."

I tracked down a sales clerk who immediately set off to find help.

A few minutes later the intercom blared, "Manager to aisle twelve." Mom and I looked at each other and broke out laughing. The manager arrived just a few minutes later, key in hand, and immediately set Grandma Polly free.

Ryan was baffled by the whole incident. He had only wanted to "try out" the handcuffs to see if they worked. It had not entered his mind that they would require a key to unlock them. The toy ones he had at home didn't need a key. He was relieved when the incident was over and we assured him that his grandma was okay.

That spring we received a letter informing us that Abby, our case manager from County Mental Health, was taking a new job. We hated to lose Abby. She had been a wonderful help to all of us. Her replacement was a woman named Lucy Richards. Although Sylvia would continue to be our family liaison, Lucy would now be in charge of overseeing Ryan's mental health treatment plan. She would also be participating in our IEP meeting at the end of the school year.

As usual, Ryan was eager to play Little League when the spring season began. His behavior was still quite erratic and we weren't sure if he could handle being on the team. The coach was a good one, a man from our church who knew a little about Ryan and his difficulties and seemed to have patience and compassion.

Although Coach Grady knew about Ryan's problems, the coaches on the other teams did not. Before opening day, Coach Grady informed the other coaches and umpires that Ryan had Tourette syndrome and cautioned that he might, at times, shout out inappropriate words.

Jim and I usually approached the games with trepidation. We were never quite sure how Ryan would behave or how he would react in any given situation, yet we felt that playing baseball and being part of a team was a valuable experience for him. For us it was worth any risk of humiliation and embarrassment we might face.

Ryan was a pitcher for the Angels and was proud to finally be old enough to play on the "major" field. One Saturday, he was scheduled to start the game and he was eager to try out a new technique he had learned.

"I'm going to strike out every single batter," he said with total confidence as he jumped into the truck to head out for the game.

"You can't strike out everybody, Ryan," I cautioned. "Just do your best, that's all."

"Yes, I can," he insisted. "I am going to strike out every single one."

I didn't argue, but I secretly worried that he was beginning to obsess on being "perfect."

He was having the same problem at school. When he had a good day and earned a "B," he often could not enjoy his success because he had wanted an "A" day. It looked as if he was again setting himself up for disappointment by expecting all strike outs, but I knew better than to argue.

The game got off to a good start and Ryan was throwing "smoke." He threw several really good strikes and a few balls, and things were going well. As I watched him standing on the mound, throwing the baseball in a straight, almost perfect line across the plate, I thought of how amazing it was. How could anyone take so much medication and still throw with such precision?

I looked around at the other parents and wished they, too, could realize what a miracle it was that he was playing on the team. So many of them took their sons' activities for granted. Going camping and being in Boy Scouts were activities that other boys could enjoy, but not Ryan. Baseball was the only thing he had and he loved it.

The umpire that day was a big guy, named Duke. We did not know him personally but had seen him around at many of the games. Ryan, who was still pitching well, wound up and released a fastball that dropped right over the plate.

"Striiiike one!" the umpire bellowed.

Ryan beamed and the bleacher full of Angel parents applauded.

"Way to go, Ryan!" they screamed.

"Two more times!" another dad yelled.

Jim and I were on the edge of our seats. Winding up again, Ryan threw another hard fastball.

"Ball one!" Duke barked.

Ryan shook his head and looked up at Jim and me. I flashed him a "thumbs up" sign and he began his wind-up again.

"Ball two!" Duke roared as the fastball crashed into the catcher's mitt. The crowd moaned. It looked like a strike from where we were sitting but the umpire had the better view. It must have been a little inside.

Again, Ryan glanced up toward his dad and me.

"It's okay, Ryan!" I shouted.

"Just throw it to the catcher's mitt!" Jim yelled.

Ryan took a deep breath and began his wind-up. Another fastball sailed across the plate and smacked into the catcher's waiting glove.

"Ball three!" shouted the umpire as he dusted off the plate.

I had my eyes on Ryan, hoping and praying he could hold it together. None of us expected what happened next.

Ryan threw down his glove and screamed at the umpire, "Shut up, you asshole!"

He then ran off the field and went behind a big tree behind the bleachers. Jim and I were speechless. Coach Grady ran over to comfort him but Ryan waved him away.

The rest of the Angel parents were watching us to see what we were going to do. I was not sure what to do. I felt it was best to let the coach handle the situation, but I was also afraid that things might escalate quickly and get entirely out of hand. I was certain the umpire was going to kick Ryan out of the game.

I waited as Coach Grady tried again to talk with Ryan. Duke, the umpire, also walked over and spoke with him. Jim went too, but Ryan refused to talk to anyone. I could see he was crying.

Then the coach from the opposing team walked over to where the others were standing. I was dying to know what they were saying. The game was in time-out while the four men attempted to reason with him. Finally, Ryan motioned for me to come.

"I'm sorry, Mommy," he said, "but I can't go back out there. Everybody will laugh at me."

I was shocked to hear that the coaches and umpire were encouraging Ryan to go back onto the field. I had been sure that they were going to eject him from the game after swearing at the umpire. I went along, encouraging him to apologize and then go out and finish the game. "No one's going to laugh, Ryan," I said. "I think everyone will understand."

It seemed like an eternity until Ryan walked back to the pitcher's mound and picked up his glove. The other players and everyone in the stands were quiet. I was scared, afraid that something might happen again. It did.

Ryan finished pitching the entire game and led the Angels to victory by striking out a total of twenty-one batters!

At the end of the game the coach presented Ryan with the game ball. The rest of the boys hoisted Ryan on their shoulders in celebration. I will never forget the smile on his face as his teammates carried him around the field, still clutching the game ball tightly with both hands.

I do not think the coaches or the umpire will ever understand the magnitude of what they did that day. They could have continued the game and left Ryan crouching in humiliation behind the tree. Instead, they gave him another chance and with it an opportunity to restore confidence in himself. It was the valuable lesson I had hoped he would learn from playing ball. I never imagined it would happen the way it did.

Summer was drawing near and we began to make plans for Ryan's imminent transfer out of the Landmark School. Although he had experienced some difficulties, Ryan had definitely made progress while at Landmark.

Everyone involved in planning his IEP expressed concern about where Ryan would attend sixth grade. I thought it would be best for him to continue at Landmark a little longer—after all, he was making progress. However, we were not given that option.

The staff had told us before Ryan even entered Landmark that it was only a "one year" program. The whole idea was to give students very intense treatment for a year that would prepare them to return to a school in their home district.

Our local district still did not have classes suitable for Ryan. He was definitely not ready to attend a "regular" sixth grade class and our district did not have an SED class.

Sylvia and the rest of the Landmark staff suggested we investigate

SED classes in other nearby cities. They told us our local district, Pacific View, would provide transportation or, if I preferred, we could drive him to class and the district would reimburse us.

One idea that came to mind was to have Ryan attend an SED class in the district where Jim was teaching. One of the benefits offered to teachers was the ability to have their children attend any of the district's schools, despite where they lived. Jim had heard good things about the SED class at one of his district's middle schools and we decided to find out more.

I called the district's special education director, Dick Engle, and asked if Jim and I could visit the class and meet the teacher. It surprised me when he refused.

"You need to send your son to the district closest to your own," Mr. Engle told me firmly. "Our program is not a viable option for your son. Besides, we have no room available in any of our SED classes."

I explained again that we only wanted to come for a visit, to have a chance to "look" at their program, but I could tell I was making no progress.

"We don't encourage parents to 'window shop' for programs, Mrs. Hughes," he said in a patronizing tone. Mr. Engle insisted there was no place for Ryan in his district and that it would not be possible for Jim and me to visit.

It was confusing to Jim and he was more than a little hurt by the ill treatment from the special education director whom he had never met. He decided to call the principal of the school directly and request an appointment for us to visit. When the principal called back, he explained that he had talked with Mr. Engle and because there were no openings, we could not visit the class.

When I heard that I became furious. I called Mr. Engle again and reminded him that Jim was a teacher in the district, and that we were entitled to transfer our children into the district should we choose to do so. Mr. Engle insisted that the situation was "different" with Ryan. He was in special education, he argued, and there was just no room for him.

I told the special education director that I thought he was discriminating against Ryan and against Jim by not allowing us an opportunity to visit the SED class. Mr. Engle continued like a broken record, "There is no place for your son in this district."

The district's superintendent, Dr. Charles Hansen, had always been friendly and very supportive of Jim. That very day, Jim called his office and requested an appointment. Later that afternoon, Jim and I arrived at Dr. Hansen's office armed with literature about TS. When the secretary ushered us into his office, I was nervous but compelled to right an injustice.

Dr. Hansen was very attentive as we explained what had happened with Mr. Engle. I respectfully suggested it was wrong and possibly illegal of Mr. Engle to deny Ryan access to any program within the district. I told him our interpretation of the teacher's contract allowed *all* teachers the benefit of enrolling their children in the district. It would be a civil rights violation, I argued, to deny Ryan access to a suitable program in the district just because he had a disability and would require special services.

It took Dr. Hansen less than a few seconds to agree. When I finished speaking, he immediately picked up the phone and started dialing.

"What day would you like to visit the school?" he asked.

As we left his office, the superintendent put his arm on Jim's shoulder and apologized repeatedly for what had happened. He assured Jim he was a valued employee and that he hoped Jim would accept his apology. He promised us he would take care of the matter immediately.

Mr. Engle called me early the next day. He apologized that we had "gotten off to a bad start," as he called it, and asked when it would be convenient for Jim and me to visit the SED class. We eagerly set the appointment within the next few days. We were both hopeful that the class might turn out to be a good option for Ryan.

When we arrived at the middle school for our visit, I was disappointed to see the classroom was inside a huge building set far away from the main campus. I wondered why the class was not closer to the regular classrooms.

Jim and I went inside to meet the teacher and her aides. They were friendly and the room was okay, but I just did not like the feeling. It was not anything specific, and nothing I could put a finger on. I just did not feel it was the best place for Ryan.

In the meantime, I learned from Lucy, our new case manager, about an SED class that was forming at a school called Sierra Vista. This class would be "enhanced" by having an on-site mental health worker.

Jim and I felt much more encouraged when we learned about the new class. It would be closer to home than the Landmark School, which in our minds was a big positive. Maybe, just maybe, Ryan wouldn't have so many bus difficulties if the trip was shorter.

When we convened the IEP to discuss the transfer, everyone there seemed to feel that the SED class at Sierra Vista was a good choice. I voiced my concern that Ryan had not had a chance to "transition" out of Landmark. I wasn't entirely comfortable that they were sending him directly to a class on a regular campus.

The Landmark staff explained that even though Ryan was not quite ready to "transition," he had already completed a year in their program. They maintained there was no other choice but to transfer him out of the school. They assured me repeatedly that Ryan would do well at Sierra Vista.

I wanted to believe that too, but I wasn't so sure. We were still having quite a few serious problems at home. I explained to the IEP team about difficulties I had when taking Ryan shopping—how he would run underneath the racks of clothes and knock things on the floor, how he would throw tantrums if I didn't buy what he wanted, and how he physically attacked his dad and me in public.

Lucy, our case manager, was an older woman who wore her hair pulled tightly in a bun that sat on top of her head. She looked down at me through a small pair of half-glasses that sat perched on the end of her nose.

"Really, Mrs. Hughes," she began, with a sigh of annoyance, "Are you sure that you have made your expectations perfectly clear to Ryan concerning his behavior at the store?"

I looked at her in amazement. Despite all she had read of Ryan's history, despite all the difficulties at school, she still believed that he behaved inappropriately because I had not been making my expectations clear. I knew then that she did not have a clue about Tourette syndrome or ADHD.

That summer we took a vacation to Jackson Hole, Wyoming with Robin and Craig. Ryan was still in his "cowboy phase" and Jackson Hole was the perfect place for a "wanna-be" cowboy.

Weeks before the trip Ryan started to "obsess" on what he was going to buy when he got to Wyoming. He had also been experiencing other OCD types of symptoms. He was still flipping the light switches off and on, repeatedly. Worse than that, he started feeling as if he had to open the car door while we were driving. That one really made us "freak out." It was dangerous and it made both of us nervous wrecks. When he wasn't feeling compelled to open the car door, he seemed driven to put the car window up and down repeatedly. It was maddening for all of us, including Ryan.

When we left on vacation that summer, he was taking a combination of Clonidine, Prolixin, Tegretol and Ritalin. The medications seemed to help his behavior considerably, but he was still having the OCD problems and seemed to be having a side effect of periodic drowsiness. Many times he really had to struggle to stay awake.

One of the highlights of our trip was going to the local rodeo. Ryan was eager to see the real cowboys up close. In preparation for the night, he got all dressed up in his cowboy costume and put on his new hat, ready to meet his heroes.

During the first ten or fifteen minutes of the show he was wide-eyed with excitement. The next thing I knew he was leaning his head on my shoulder to watch. In a matter of minutes he was dozing. I tried several times to wake him by shaking him and trying to move him around. He would rouse for a short time and then fall back to sleep. I finally gave up and allowed him to lie across my lap.

As everyone else sat and cheered for the bull riders and the cattle ropers, I stroked his hair and privately mourned for Ryan's lost childhood. So many things that other "normal" children could enjoy were escaping him.

We did our best to have a good vacation, but even between the sleepy spells, Ryan had difficulty with all his compulsions. When we went into town to eat, he would feel the urge to shriek. Several times he turned glasses of water or ice tea upside down because he felt like he "had" to. It was as if he could not resist the forbidden. During the episodes he would laugh. Afterward, he cried.

We tried to make the most of the time we had in Wyoming. We some-how made it through the tough times and found pleasure in the little things. We enjoyed going out each night looking for wildlife. All four of us got excited when someone spotted a moose or a herd of elk. Deer sightings were frequent and Ryan enjoyed seeing the wildlife as much as we did.

By the time we came home from the trip we were exhausted. Dr. Comings advised adding Anafranil to help with the OCD symptoms that had become so unbearable. As we were leaving the City of Hope Medical Center that day my eyes were drawn to a large concrete sign that read; "There Is Always Hope."

I knew the sign was right. There was always hope. I knew if I lost hope that Ryan would get better, I would, in effect, lose the battle. Although I had seen it many times before, the words on the sign helped to renew my faith that someday, Ryan would have a normal life.

Chapter 20

The People vs. Ryan

"Pain nourishes courage. You can't be brave
if you've only had wonderful things happen to you."[1]
Mary Tyler Moore

Toward the end of summer, we started seeing a new family therapist from County Mental Health. Her name was Laura Galen and we saw her on an outpatient basis. Because Ryan had previously qualified for mental health services under the AB3632 (California Assembly Bill) funding, there was no charge to us for the visits.

As usual, Jim and I were apprehensive about meeting a new therapist. We always felt we needed to prove our credibility with each new professional. Our first meeting with Laura went very well. When we entered her office she handed me a copy of the *RYAN* book that someone had given her to read and she asked me to sign it. I was pleased that she had taken the time and initiative to acquaint herself with Ryan's history before our first visit.

Jim and I were both impressed with her ability to establish a good rapport with Ryan. After the first visit we left feeling very optimistic that the sessions would be helpful.

After the insensitive comment by Lucy at the last IEP meeting, I phoned the director at County Mental Health and requested a change in case managers. I didn't know if it was even possible to change case managers but I knew that working with someone like Lucy was a waste of time—hers and ours.

The director asked if I had discussed my complaints with Lucy and I confessed that I had not. I was sure, I explained to him, that even after speaking with her, Lucy would not have the slightest clue why we thought she was not doing a good job.

He agreed that we could change case managers but not until I talked to Lucy to let her know of my complaint. As much as I hated the idea, I knew he was right. At the very least, I owed her the courtesy of speaking with her face to face. I called her right away and scheduled an appointment.

I am sure someone briefed Lucy before I arrived. She was barely cordial and her behavior was perfunctory at best. I was nervous to be facing Lucy. Despite the many times I had found myself advocating for Ryan's needs, it was never easy for me to openly challenge a professional's advice or conduct.

Although Lucy did not make it easy, I bravely expressed my concern that she did not have an adequate knowledge of Tourette syndrome and ADHD. I explained that to help Ryan, it was critically important that she understand what was wrong with him and be familiar with the symptoms and behaviors associated with the disorders.

As I left her office, Lucy quipped that the next time she would have to do a better job of at least "acting" as if she knew about the child's disorder. I was glad that I had requested the change. I didn't know who we would get, but I was sure the person could not be any worse than Lucy.

Our second meeting with Laura also went well. Ryan was still not very stable, but we had experienced worse times. As we were leaving, Laura told us that our next appointment would be at 1:30 the following Thursday. I reminded her that school would be back in session by then and asked if we could schedule a different time.

"I'm sorry, Mrs. Hughes," she said, "but I am very busy. Along with individual appointments, I run groups every day and my schedule is completely full. If you don't take the 1:30 appointment on Thursday, I won't be able to see Ryan for six weeks."

Six weeks! I was bewildered. I felt it was important to maintain the good start with Laura, but I also felt it would be a mistake to pull Ryan out of class to go to counseling appointments.

Later that day I talked with Janice from Special Parents. As leader of that parent group Janice had established close contacts with many of the administrators at County Mental Health. It only took my mentioning the problem for her to offer to help.

She called me back a short time later to say that the director of outpatient mental health services would be checking into our problem and would give me a call. Several days later he called and said that he had resolved the situation and that Ryan could have all future appointments with Laura scheduled after school hours.

Ryan was eager to begin sixth grade at Sierra Vista. I was hopeful too, but cautiously optimistic that he would be able to function on a regular school campus. The classroom itself did not concern me as much; his SED class would be small. I worried more about him being around the other students during lunch breaks, recess and before and after school.

The Sweetwater School District received a complete information packet from Landmark concerning Ryan. Toward the end of August, I scheduled an appointment with the district's special education director and the classroom teacher. The program specialist from our home district, Gordon Miller, also attended the meeting.

The new special education director was cordial but not especially friendly. She told us it would not be necessary to conduct another IEP since she already had all of Ryan's files from our home district. She introduced us to the teacher, Mrs. Kling, who I immediately liked.

Mrs. Kling was soft-spoken and sweet-natured. She was also very enthusiastic and upbeat. She told Gordon and me that she had never taught an SED class before but that she did have experience as a special education teacher. Gordon began to fill her in on Ryan's academic background.

I tried to encourage Mrs. Kling and the special education director by describing Ryan as being very bright, inquisitive, sensitive, charming, and humorous. I was sure they were apprehensive after meeting Ryan on paper. I wanted to make sure they realized that there was more to him than just the labels that followed him to Sierra Vista.

I cautioned the new staff there might be a "honeymoon" period at the start of school. I also explained some of the behaviors typically associated with TS and I left some brochures.

I was a little nervous about Ryan's potential difficulties in riding the bus so I expressed my concerns to the director. I asked if the staff would inform the bus drivers regarding Ryan's situation and they agreed it was a good idea. The special education director assured me she would arrange for Ryan's bus transportation so that the route would be in place before the start of school.

Ryan's class schedule was from 8:25 A.M.-2:03 P.M. each day. Alan McCarthy, a social worker from County Mental Health would be at school on Thursdays for counseling. There would be seven students in Ryan's class—two sixth-graders, two seventh-graders, and three eighth-graders, all boys.

I asked Mrs. Kling if I could bring Ryan to school for a brief tour of the campus. I wanted him to have a chance to see the school before boarding the bus to a strange place. Mrs. Kling said we could come the following afternoon.

After seeing the campus and meeting his new teacher, Ryan was even more enthusiastic to start sixth grade. He was happy that he was getting away from Landmark and would finally be going to a "regular" school.

On the first day of school Ryan was eager and ready to go. Unfortunately, his bus did not show up. The district had failed to make the transportation arrangements as promised. I ended up driving him to school and we played his country western tapes on the way.

Ryan had a good day until shortly after lunch time. He had some problems with inappropriate language, but according to Mrs. Kling, he was able to "turn it around."

When I picked him up that afternoon, Ryan said that he had a good day. He expressed his fear, however, that he would never have a girlfriend at that school. He thought because there were only boys in his class he would never have a chance to even talk to any girls.

The second day of school I received a call at work from the assistant principal, Mr. Eastwood, asking if I would come to pick up Ryan. He said that Ryan had a good morning but had "lost it" after lunch and began acting up in class—farting, spitting, etc. He also said that he had urinated on the carpet, crawled around on the furniture and then started throwing chairs around the room.

Mrs. Kling had summoned Mr. Eastwood and Ryan had gone to the office willingly. After he calmed down, he waited in the outer office for me to come. After waiting a short time, Ryan began shouting out and Mr. Eastwood had to take him back inside his office until I arrived. Mrs. Kling commented that it was interesting that both days were fine until after lunch. She asked if it could have been "something" he ate.

I was a bit disappointed at Mrs. Kling's assumption that something in his lunch may have "set him off." For years I had battled suggestions that too much sugar, or too many additives had caused or contributed to his behavioral problems. I had seen the talk shows myself. Unfortunately, the myth of hyperactivity being caused by sugar or additives continues today, much like an old wive's tale and despite all scientific evidence to the contrary.

I couldn't speak for other children, but I knew in Ryan's case that sugar and additives did not cause or worsen his behavior. We had observed Ryan eat candy with no ill effects and had tried various elimination diets when he was younger—all to no avail. Mrs. Kling, I was sure, was wrong about diet playing a part, but I, too, noticed there seemed to be a pattern emerging—good in the morning, difficulty in the afternoon.

Around 3:30 that afternoon, our new case manager, Ted Simmons came to our home for a family meeting. As was his custom whenever anyone came to our door, Ryan began to behave badly. Ted walked in and sat on the sofa, closely observing Ryan and my many attempts to calm him.

Usually, Ryan would act out briefly and calm down at least some of the time. This day, however, was different. It may have been due in part to the difficulties at school that day or perhaps the anxiety of meeting another mental health worker. I am not sure why, but Ryan was completely wild. Several times during Ted's visit I had to physically restrain him using the basket hold.

Soon, I was weak and exhausted from trying to control him. I was also nervous about how Ted was perceiving Ryan's behavior. He had only been in our home a short while when he brought up the subject of group homes and residential treatment centers. I was struggling to comprehend what he was saying while at the same time trying to subdue Ryan. When I heard him mention the State Hospital, it jolted me.

As I wrestled with Ryan on the floor, Ted sat on the sofa, not moving an inch to intervene or help. Instead of speaking to Ryan, or assisting my sometimes futile attempts to gain control, Ted merely sat by and watched as I suffered both physically and emotionally. When I was able to restrain Ryan and he finally regained control, Ted asked, "Have you ever considered what you are going to do two years from now when he is bigger and stronger?"

When he left at 4:30 I was glad. I was also mad that he had just sat and watched me struggle. Wasn't he a mental health professional? Didn't he have training to work with people who were out of control? Why didn't he help me? I wondered.

It also upset me that he talked of nothing but residential facilities and group homes. He even mentioned the State Hospital. How dare he? He didn't even know Ryan. He didn't know anything about him as a person, what a great kid he was or about his many successes.

For the first time ever I felt a fear I had never felt before. If Ted Simmons thought Ryan should be in an institution, I feared he might do or say something that could force us to send Ryan away. Could he do that? I wondered. Could anyone *make* us do that? The questions swirled through my mind.

I knew Ryan had serious problems, yet we still clung to our visions of the "other" Ryan. Despite the behavioral problems, there was still a wonderful little boy in that body. We were committed to the hope that Ryan would get better. We were willing to do anything we needed to do to make that happen, except for one thing. We were not willing to get rid of him or send him away—even if it killed us. There were days we thought it might.

The following Monday Ryan had a great day at school. There was "just a little" trouble in the afternoon but he turned things around nicely and did well. It was the kind of normal day that we strove for and fought to have.

The next day, his bus was forty-five minutes late. Ryan was very anxious while waiting for the bus to come. At school, he got into trouble for calling a campus aide an inappropriate name. According to Ryan, he called her a name and she threatened to "wash his mouth out with soap." She also told him that she didn't care what class he was from, that no one was going to call her names and get away with it.

Mr. Eastwood later told me that Ryan had actually had a run-in with two of the aides. He had run out of the classroom, onto the street, and then stopped in front of an oncoming car. He then taunted the driver to "hit him" before going back into the office.

Mr. Eastwood was obviously distressed over the incident. In fact, each time he called me he seemed astounded and totally overwhelmed with Ryan's misconduct. He told me he had never before seen the kinds of problems he was having with Ryan. He also told me he would be speaking with the mental health social worker and that the whole staff would be meeting very soon to decide what to do.

Later that evening, Mrs. Kling called to discuss what had happened that day. She also warned me that she was going to document Ryan's episode of urinating in the classroom on the second day of school as "sexually inappropriate behavior." She asked if anything like that had ever happened before.

I assured her it had not, that we were just as surprised as she was. As a possible explanation I reminded Mrs. Kling that inappropriate sexual behavior is an associated behavior in some children with Tourette syndrome.

At bedtime I asked Ryan what he thought had set him off, wondering if he might have some insight into what was happening. Ryan said he was feeling mad about having TS. He said he was upset that he was the only one in the class with a "problem."

I asked why he felt so upset about having TS on that particular day and he began crying. "I'm the only one that can't stay in my seat or pay attention, Mom, and I'm the only one that can't do the stupid math."

When I went to bed that night I thought again how Mrs. Kling had surmised that something he ate must be causing Ryan's behavior problems. Not only did Ryan have to battle the impulses of TS, he also had to suffer because no one understood how he felt about what was going on in his life. It only took a minute for me to ask the question. I wondered why the professionals could not look beyond the behavior and just ask the questions.

The next day was better. Surprisingly, no one from school called but Mrs. Kling sent home a note that read:

> Ryan had a good morning. He took his pill at 12:45 instead of 12:00 noon. He had one incident of spitting but got in control. He felt like he needed to walk around outside a lot. Ryan needs to write an apology to the campus supervisor because he called her a name while walking to the bus.

The next day, Mr. Eastwood called me at 9:40 A.M. to say that he was suspending Ryan from school for running out of class. He asked that I come immediately to get him.

Before leaving to pick up Ryan, I called Gordon Miller at our local district. I knew we had to do something. This was an SED class. The staff should know how to handle these kinds of behaviors. Instead, they were "freaking out" every time something happened. I feared they were reacting inappropriately and escalating instead of defusing the behavior. Gordon agreed to call the special education director right away.

When I picked up Ryan, Mr. Eastwood informed me he was suspending Ryan for two days. I pleaded with Mr. Eastwood to not suspend Ryan on the second day because that was the day he was to meet with his mental health counselor, Alan McCarthy. He only came once a week on Thursdays, I explained, and Ryan really needed the mental health intervention. Mr. Eastwood said he would decide later and let me know.

That afternoon Gordon called to say that the Sweetwater staff would like to meet with Jim and me the next morning. A short time later, Mr. Eastwood called to tell me that the staff had made a final decision. They would not allow Ryan to return to school on Thursday, even for the appointment with his counselor.

We also had our third "outpatient" session with Laura that day. Soon after entering her office, Ryan started to act inappropriately. He began crawling on the floor and chanting the words "Mr. Eastwood, Mr. Eastwood" repeatedly. Another boy was walking out of an adjoining office when Ryan suddenly shouted at him and then jumped up and slugged him hard three times.

Seeing him that way really frightened me. Even after all we had been through with Ryan, I had never seen him behave this way. Something was different. Laura brought up the possibility of a brief hospitalization to stabilize Ryan and evaluate the medications he was taking. She recommended University Hospital and said she would call Dr. Comings about it soon. She also suggested that we take him out of Sierra Vista immediately and return him to the Landmark School. Jim and I agreed that sounded appropriate.

Although the mention of a psychiatric hospital had surfaced several times over the years, Jim and I had decided we would only consider it as a final alternative. We worried about any stigma Ryan might face when older about having been in a "mental" hospital.

This time, however, was different. After seeing Ryan crawling on the floor, drooling and acting in such a primitive way, I knew he needed more help than he was getting. Dr. Comings had always supported our decision not to hospitalize Ryan, but I felt certain that this time he, too, would feel it was unavoidable.

The emergency IEP meeting the next day was one for the history books. It was truly the "mother" of all IEPs, at least any in our county. When Jim and I arrived, the secretary ushered us into the principal's office. The small room was full of people. They all sat crowded around a big round table with a mixture of large and small chairs. Those attending were:

Connie Kennedy, special ed. director, Sweetwater District
Mrs. Kling, classroom teacher
Mr. Eastwood, assistant principal
Mr. Dorsey, principal
Alan McCarthy, social worker, County Mental Health
Ted Simmons, case manager, County Mental Health
Paul Rhodes, director of children's services, County
     Mental Health
Linda Orwell, school psychologist, Sweetwater District
Gordon Miller, program specialist, Pacific View District

For some reason I felt as if we were entering a courtroom instead of a school meeting. It only took a second for me to figure out that the school staff outnumbered Jim and me by more than four to one.

By this time I had been through many IEPs. Although I was somewhat nervous, I had always felt confident in my ability to speak effectively about Ryan's concerns and to advocate for his needs. This one, however, was different. When I walked into the claustrophobic room, the enormity of the administrative staff overwhelmed me and I felt vulnerable and powerless.

The meeting began with the principal, Mr. Dorsey, reciting a litany of offenses Ryan had committed. He started with the first day of school. He had documented everything:

> being generally disruptive to the rest of the class with his
> "noises" and "action"
> running out of class
> shouting obscenities
> urinating on the carpet
> spitting
> climbing on tables
> walking on desktops
> throwing chairs
> not staying in the time-out room
> running around the campus
> running into the street
> running in front of cars
> provoking a driver on the street
> climbing a tree
> getting on the wrong bus
> flipping off the bus driver
> sticking his rear end up at the bus driver
> throwing dirt rocks at the bus

About halfway through the list I felt the sting of tears rolling down my cheeks. Jim and I held hands tightly as the principal described every shocking, embarrassing detail of each incident.

My heart was breaking. It seemed as if Ryan were an accused felon and the judge was reading his "rap" sheet. It seemed like anything but an IEP meeting.

I was aware that there were nine pairs of eyes watching me. Thank goodness Gordon was there. He was somehow able to bring some dignity to the proceedings and intervened for us. With his help we were able to focus on constructing a new IEP and behavior plan, pending a referral to University Hospital.

I felt demoralized after leaving the meeting. Except for Gordon, I knew that the others were looking at Jim and me to change Ryan's awful behavior.

Ryan had stayed with Grandma Polly while we attended the IEP. He had been very hyper all day and complained of having a headache. When he returned home from Grandma's house he was very agitated. He kept running outside saying that he needed fresh air. He was irritable, spitting a lot, and doing weird things. When it was time for dinner, he ran out the front door and threw himself face down on the curb. I watched from the window as he lay there with his head hanging in the gutter. He began to dip his finger into the dirty water and then lick it. My stomach was in knots seeing him do such bizarre things. I was more convinced than ever that he needed to be in the hospital.

The following day at school, Ryan was fidgety. He attempted to do his work and was able to complete two assignments. There were some inappropriate verbalizations and he referred himself to the time-out room two times.

When I picked him up, we went shopping at Price Club. He had one brief out-of-control episode at the store—shrieking and giving the finger sign, etc. He didn't feel like having lunch so we returned home.

He complained again of a headache and stomachache. The headache was very bad at times. Dr. Comings was still trying to stabilize Ryan by altering the doses of the various medications. He was taking Tegretol, Prolixin, Ritalin and Anafranil.

After a fairly good weekend, Ryan went to school the following Monday and ended up with an A+ day. He finished his work, was on task, and was very respectful. Mrs. Kling and the aide observed some extraneous movements and noticed that he also seemed to be quite sleepy.

On Tuesday, Ryan was very upbeat in the morning. He was very talkative, loud and animated. Then, he fell asleep during second period at school. After snack break he began making noises, and shouted mild obscenities. He went into the time-out room willingly and regained control. His teacher noted more stuttering than usual.

That evening at home he was good but hyper and restless. He confronted an adult neighbor when he overheard the man scolding his daughter. He gave the man the finger sign and cussed at him for yelling at his child.

During dinner he had difficulty staying seated. Once, he came up to me and started licking my face. He persisted and when I finally pushed him out of the way, he hit me in the head twice with his fist.

The next day, after having a good morning at home, Ryan started to say foul words at school. Throughout the rest of the morning he either slept or was off task, swearing or trying to disrupt others. He ran around the room yelling "shit." During the flag salute he held his left hand up and every other word was "fart." In the time-out room he chanted foul words. Finally, he quieted down, then promptly fell asleep at his desk.

The next day at school was wonderful. There was some sleepiness, but an overall good day.

The following day it started to rain. During class Ryan blurted out, "It's raining, it's pouring, the old fart is snoring." He then laughed and threw sunflower seeds at another student. Mrs. Kling placed him in time-out but he kept opening the door and disrupting the class. He tore up his folder and papers and threw his books on the floor. Mr. Eastwood arrived and removed him to the office.

The next three days were all good days at school. He was somewhat sleepy but was quiet, calm and respectful. Then, on September 27, Ryan lost it again. He entered school quietly and kept his head down on his desk most of the morning. During snack time the staff observed him talking to a couple of girls and he told them to "go fuck yourself."

When Ryan learned he had lost the privilege of being outside on break for a couple of days, he began shouting, "Go fuck yourself, honk, honk penis, honk, honk vagina and fuck you bitch." He began moving his desk, acting as if it were a train and making a "choo choo" sound. Mrs. Kling attempted to hold onto his shoulder, trying to get him under control. She was unable to calm him.

Mrs. Kling placed Ryan into the time-out room with assistance from an aide. He came outside the room and they put him back inside. This time he began kicking at the aide and swung at Mrs. Kling, scratching her. He grabbed hold of a table leg, and Mrs. Kling and her aide had to pry him loose. He opened a cupboard, removed a yard stick and began swinging it. Mr. Eastwood came in and Ryan swung the ruler at him.

Mr. Eastwood then called me to come get him. Ryan was suspended for "causing, attempting to cause, or threatening physical injury to another person."

I felt so discouraged at the time that I couldn't think clearly. Dr. Comings was confident he could eventually stabilize Ryan with medication and avoid hospitalization. We had, in fact, had days that were very good. One thing that was clear, however, was the SED class at Sierra Vista was not an appropriate placement. I called Gordon Miller and we agreed to set up another IEP meeting to discuss possible alternative placements.

Because the last IEP had been so horrific for Jim and me, I decided we would not suffer a repeat. I knew that as Ryan's parents we were *equal* participants in decisions regarding his education. We had felt anything but equal at the last IEP and I was determined we would not be victims again.

I had no doubt that all the teaching staff and administrators were very decent and caring people. I knew they were laboring under a very difficult situation in trying to manage Ryan. Yet, I felt strongly that we needed to talk about what Ryan could do and would do—not just concentrate on all the horrible things he had done.

The staff quickly scheduled an IEP meeting for October 1. Instead of meeting in the small, cramped principal's office, we assembled in a conference room that had a much larger table. Anticipating what might happen, I stayed up the night before and drafted a letter that I planned to read at the IEP. This was one time I did not want my emotions to interfere with what we wanted to accomplish—an appropriate educational placement for Ryan.

When the special education director opened the meeting, I respectfully asked the indulgence of the IEP team in allowing me to read my prepared letter. I explained my hope that the letter would expedite the meeting and clarify Jim's and my position. Those sitting around the table nodded their permission for me to begin.

> I would like to start this morning by expressing our views and position and hopefully save all of us some time. It is obvious that Sierra Vista School is not the appropriate placement for Ryan at this time. The reason we have come to this conclusion is twofold. The first reason involves Ryan. He very obviously does not possess the maturity or self-control necessary to function in a class that is structured like the SED class here. Because of his behavioral problems and the related consequences, Ryan has suffered academically. So far this year he has received virtually no education, although he is a very bright little

boy who wants to learn and wants to come to school.

The second reason we feel this is not an appropriate placement involves the staff. Mrs. Kling, her aides and Mr. Eastwood have diligently and patiently tried to do their best and their efforts to help Ryan have been sincere. However, Mrs. Kling has had no experience in teaching an SED class. I am sure that Ryan's impulsive and attention-seeking behaviors have been more challenging than any she has dealt with.

As we have discussed before, Ryan does not respond well to direct commands or threats. His usual response to those types of disciplines will usually be to do something impulsive—like shouting an obscenity. Then, depending on the response to that, it can and does, escalate beyond his control. The key to controlling this behavior is and always has been in the approach. Ryan, like other behavior-disordered children, can accept discipline when they do not feel threatened, but are able to walk away from the incident without feeling demoralized. This staff has reacted to Ryan's behavior with shock and at times with overwhelming frustration. It is important to remember that it was because of these very behaviors that he came to this SED class. Ryan has not changed. The behaviors are not new. They are the same behaviors the staff at Landmark were able to handle in a calm, nonthreatening way—a way that allowed Ryan a chance to learn from his mistakes in a positive way.

By expressing shock, outrage and frustration in front of Ryan, this staff, despite their wonderful intentions, have empowered Ryan by allowing him to become the manipulator. They have reacted to his behavior in only traditional ways, resorting to traditional suspension for this very "nontraditional" special education child.

Now, we all face the difficult decision of placement. At our last IEP meeting we discussed the possibility of hospitalization. However, in speaking with

Dr. Comings, we have learned that he is not considering that option at this time and we are in agreement with his decision. It has become apparent in the past few weeks that medication changes have made a marked improvement in Ryan's behavior. Although it is not perfect, or even at times acceptable, we still have many options available regarding medications and will be changing and fine-tuning as necessary.

After Ryan was suspended from school on Friday he spent an enjoyable afternoon with me. He then went to a high school football game with his dad and had a friend spend the night — all with no incidents. On Saturday, he played all day with two friends, attended his sister's volleyball game (with one incident of shouting obscenities). He ate dinner with us and another family and then visited the home of some friends until 9:00 P.M. — all with no incidents. On Sunday he went shopping at Kmart and had lunch at McDonald's (no incidents). He spent the afternoon playing with friends and in the evening went with us to a neighbor's home for dinner — all with no incidents.

Yes, he is loud at times. Yes, he is hyper at times and yes, he needs to be reminded to settle down more than the average kid. However, a child who is able to interact and function socially at the level that Ryan has demonstrated is not a child who needs to be rushed off to a psychiatric hospital. He should not be hospitalized solely because the local school has not provided him with an adequate educational setting that will meet his individual needs.

The possibility of a group home or the residential treatment center that Ted Simmons mentioned to us is also not, in our opinion, appropriate for Ryan at this time. Unlike many other SED children who are less fortunate, Ryan has two devoted parents who love him unconditionally and are not only willing, but committed and determined, to care for him and nurture him. Yes, it would be easier for us to send him away.

We are not naive enough to believe that at some time in the future this may be inevitable. But, as long as we have the physical, emotional, and spiritual strength to care for Ryan, we will continue to keep him at home with the support of his family, neighbors and friends.

Another possibility for placement would be to return Ryan to the Landmark School. That program seems to be the best-suited to meet his needs at this time and he has proved that he is able to function in that environment and achieve academically. We can understand the reservations the Landmark staff may have, given it is intended to be a one-year program. It is unconscionable to us, however, that a child could be "kicked out" of a program that was working successfully just because twelve months have passed. Unfortunately, children with severe disabilities like Ryan do not always magically get better in one year.

We feel it would be in Ryan's best interest for him to return to the Landmark program. We feel he should stay until he is able to demonstrate the ability to mainstream into another SED classroom on a regular campus or into the older Landmark program. Because he is familiar with the staff and the expectations at Landmark, it would seem apparent that he could successfully transition back into the program and not lose any more valuable class time.

There was a collective and audible sigh when I finished reading. The staff from Sierra Vista seemed relieved that we wanted Ryan to leave their district and return to Landmark .

The IEP team quickly agreed to make a "high priority" referral back to Landmark Elementary's day treatment program. The meeting ended after a short time with Gordon from our home district assuring us he would initiate the new referral immediately. Unfortunately, Gordon had heard there were no immediate openings at Landmark and he was unclear when Ryan would be able to return. Hearing that made me uneasy.

In the meantime, Gordon proposed that our local district would provide Ryan with home schooling for one hour per day.

Only one hour a day? I thought to myself. What about the rest of the day?

Not quite sure what to do, I agreed to home schooling, but wrote on the IEP form that we would only agree to that placement for a maximum of fourteen days.

I knew Gordon would do his best to work things out; however, I wanted to be sure that no one else would drag their feet in effecting a quick transfer back into Landmark .

Chapter 21

Ryan vs. the School District

"Better build schoolrooms for 'the boy'
Than cells and gibbets for 'the man'."[1]
Eliza Cook

Gordon Miller was true to his word. The very next day, he initiated the paperwork to begin the process of getting Ryan transferred back to the Landmark Elementary program.

I was also busy that day, making phone calls to various people at the County Schools and County Mental Health offices. By mid-afternoon, I had a sick feeling that getting Ryan back into Landmark soon was not going to be easy. Everyone I talked with offered the same sympathetic reply, "We agree, Ryan needs to be at Landmark, but there are no openings."

When I asked when, they told me there might be an opening sometime after the first of the year but, of course, there were no guarantees.

It troubled me that Ryan was only going to have one hour a day of home schooling. As always, I felt strongly that being at school, socializing with the other students and learning "life" skills were more important for Ryan's future success than any of the academics. Those could always come later.

Meanwhile, Gordon was getting the same response to his inquiries. I felt sorry for Gordon. He was doing his best to help us and Ryan. But even he was finding it difficult to convince County Mental Health and the county school officials to make a place at Landmark for Ryan. He suggested that we wait a while and possibly consider another SED class in a neighboring district if the Landmark opening did not develop.

As much as I respected Gordon's opinion and advice, I was convinced that Ryan needed to be back in school and that the school should be Landmark. I struggled to think of a solution. I called Protection and Advocacy in Los Angeles. I also called Mental Health Advocacy in Los Angeles, and several private educational advocates to inquire about their charges.

Finally, it hit me. I remembered the class on Basic Rights I had taken at TASK the year before. I thought back to what I had learned—that Ryan (and every other child) has the right under federal law (IDEA) to a free and appropriate education in the least restrictive environment.

I knew that one hour a day of home schooling was not appropriate or the least restrictive placement. Because there was evidence Ryan had made positive gains while at Landmark, it proved there was an educational setting in which he could successfully function.

I felt sure that Landmark School had violated a Section 504 regulation by not "transitioning" him out of the program slowly, but merely "dumping" him at the end of twelve months. I was sure we had some legal ground to stand on, but I was unclear about some of the gray areas. With County Mental Health involved in the funding of the program, I wasn't sure if that entity fell under the same guidelines as local public school districts.

Another thing I remembered from my TASK training was that parents had the right to file for a "Fair Hearing" if they did not agree with their child's placement. One positive thing about filing for a Fair Hearing was that it would immediately put the local school district on a "timeline" and force them to act.

At the training I learned that once the State Department of Education receives a request from a parent for a Fair Hearing, the "clock" immediately starts to tick. According to the State's guidelines, a mediation hearing would be scheduled within fifteen days after a request was received.

Fifteen days seemed much more acceptable to me than waiting until after the first of the year for an opening that might or might not happen. That evening, I stayed up late drafting the following letter to the State Department of Education:

> Dear Mr. Honig, State Supt. of Schools,
>
> Our purpose in writing is to respectfully request your assistance in initiating, on behalf of our son, Ryan, the Due Process and Procedural Safeguards authorized under California Education Code Chapter 5, Section 56502. The reason for our request concerns the inappropriate placement or, at this time, the lack

of placement for Ryan in our local district, Pacific View.

Ryan has been a special education student since kindergarten due to learning disabilities and associated behavioral problems related to Tourette syndrome and ADHD. He qualifies for special education services under the "Other Health Impaired" category.

Ryan was able to remain in a regular classroom through fourth grade when the IEP team determined his educational needs required placement in a day treatment program. This program, called Landmark, is operated through an interagency agreement with our County Schools Office and County Mental Health. Ryan entered into this program through an AB3632 referral. It was our understanding that this program lasted only one year and that the goal of the program was to gradually transition students back into classes in their local district.

Ryan functioned well in this highly structured, intense SED class and especially benefited from the mental health services provided. At the end of the twelve month period the staff informed us that Ryan's time in the program was over. Although he did not have an opportunity to be "transitioned out," as originally proposed, we were forced to look for other placement options.

Because Ryan did not have a chance to transition out of the Landmark program, he immediately began to have difficulties adapting on the regular school campus. His behavior problems escalated and the staff, although very caring, sincere and gracious, seemed overwhelmed and frustrated with Ryan's unique needs. In just the first few weeks of school, Ryan was suspended numerous times. After two lengthy meetings, the IEP team agreed that the most appropriate placement for Ryan would be at the Landmark School. That school, however, is reluctant to admit Ryan because he has already completed twelve months in the program.

Because this is a difficult situation, we have agreed for Pacific View to provide home teaching, not to exceed fourteen days, while they attempt to pursue a referral back to the Landmark program. Even though everyone agrees that this program is the most suitable for Ryan, our district's program specialist has had indications that they will not readmit Ryan without a decision from a fair-hearing officer.

As of today, Ryan has not been in school for five full days. At this point, he does not have a school or a program to attend. The district has not yet arranged for home teaching; however, I have been informed that the job has been "posted" and the district is waiting for someone to respond. In the meantime, I have a very bright, energetic child that is becoming depressed because he wants to go to school. I fear that this depression may cause other symptoms to appear, behavioral problems to escalate and his academic achievements to suffer a severe regression.

We feel it is the duty of our local district, Pacific View, to provide Ryan with an appropriate education. We request that the district place Ryan back into Landmark, or that they create a similar program. It has been proven that he is able to function and achieve in that kind of educational setting.

Because Ryan is not presently able to attend school because of our district's failure to provide an appropriate program, we would appreciate your assistance in helping us to resolve this issue promptly.

Instead of dropping my letter in the mailbox, I drove to the post office and mailed it "Overnight Mail." I knew the sooner the State Department of Education received my letter, the sooner the fifteen day time-line would begin.

Just four days later I received a legal-looking notice from the Special Education Hearing Office, Institute for Administrative Justice. The formality of the letter surprised me. There at the top in bold it read: *RYAN HUGHES VS. PACIFIC VIEW SCHOOL DISTRICT.* The notice informed us they had received our letter and that a mediation conference was scheduled for October 16. It also stated that in the event we were unable to reach an agreement during the mediation, our Due Process Hearing would be on October 31.

Jim and I were eager for the mediation hearing, but also a little nervous. It seemed a shame to have to go through such a cold and unfriendly process just to get educational services that state and federal laws guaranteed for Ryan. I also felt troubled that the negotiations had forced an "us" against "them" situation. I did not feel that we were against anyone. We only wanted what was best for Ryan.

I genuinely liked and respected the special education staff in our district. Gordon and the special education coordinator, Mary Barnes, had worked cooperatively with us over the years to formulate creative IEPs that would give Ryan every chance to succeed. Nevertheless, I was willing to do whatever was necessary to see Ryan in the appropriate placement.

Although I was confident in my knowledge about many areas of the law, there were still some questions of which I was unsure. Jim and I contemplated hiring a special education advocate to attend the mediation hearing with us but decided against it. Instead, we consulted a special education attorney with our questions. Through my associations with other parents on committees and support groups, I learned of an attorney in Los Angeles who had a reputation of being very competent and aggressive in special education matters.

After spending an hour with Beverly Schmidt, Jim and I felt good about our decision to file for a Due Process Hearing. We were also confident about our legal right in having Ryan returned to the Landmark program.

In short order, Beverly cited several areas in which the involved districts were out of compliance with the law. First, we learned there is no "waiting list." School districts are notorious for using that excuse. It is illegal, however, for them to have a waiting list for any type of special education service.

Children are entitled to an appropriate education *now*, not when one is available. If the program does not exist, the district has the responsibility to *make* a program. Actually, I already knew that. I had learned it at TASK, but it helped to hear Beverly affirm it.

Furthermore, the district was wrong in offering Ryan only one hour of home schooling per day. Beverly explained that Ryan (and every other special education student) is entitled to six hours per day of instruction, just like every other student in the state. She advised us to immediately send a letter to the school revoking our permission for the one hour per day of home schooling and ask for six hours. Knowing the district would find it difficult to provide six hours per day of home schooling, she felt certain it would help speed up the process of getting Ryan returned to Landmark .

Beverly also told us that the district was out of compliance by "dumping" Ryan at the end of twelve months. It is illegal, she explained, for the district to have a time limit on a program in which a child is functioning successfully and one that the IEP team agrees is an appropriate placement. It was also wrong, she explained, for them to dismiss Ryan from the program without giving him time to slowly transition into the new program.

Beverly also armed us with other good information. Jim and I left her office feeling empowered and very confident we could be good advocates for Ryan during the mediation hearing. The visit cost one hundred dollars and was worth every penny.

The morning of the mediation hearing, Jim and I arrived at the district office sharply at 10:00 A.M. Gordon was already there, along with Mary Barnes and Paul Rhodes, the Director of Children's Services from County Mental Health. After some friendly chitchat, they led us into a large conference room where we met the Special Hearing Officer, Mr. Garrison.

Mr. Garrison was an older gentleman who seemed warm and friendly. We had received a brief description about his qualifications from the Department of Education. He was a former teacher and principal and had also served as a director of special education in Illinois. Mr. Garrison held several degrees, including a Ph.D. He was married with ten stepchildren.

The hearing officer took control of the meeting immediately. He started by describing the events that led us to the mediation hearing and then asked Jim and me to explain our position.

Mr. Garrison listened to our request that Ryan be returned immediately to the Landmark program. Then he turned to the representatives from the district and asked for their response.

Paul Rhodes from County Mental Health agreed that Landmark was the appropriate placement for Ryan. He regretted, however, that there were no openings. He explained that the Landmark program was successful partly because of the limited number of students in the program. He maintained that adding an additional student would jeopardize that success. He assured us Ryan was at the top of the waiting list but until there was an opening, he would have to wait.

At that point, Mr. Garrison requested that Jim and I go into another room. He directed the school administrators to stay in the larger conference room. The mediation was about to begin.

For the next several hours, Mr. Garrison went back and forth between the two rooms. After hearing the district's offer of more hours of home schooling, we refused. We maintained that Ryan needed to return to Landmark and we cited the law that supported our request. The hearing officer nodded in agreement and then left the room to speak with the school representatives. Back and forth he went. Each time the mediator returned with a new offer from the district concerning a different program option, Jim and I stood firm. We would not agree to anything but having Ryan returned to the Landmark Elementary School immediately.

Late in the afternoon we started to sense a small degree of progress. Paul and the district representatives had been busy making phone calls to other people. They finally decided there might be an opening at Landmark for Ryan after all. After a few more back-and-forth dialogues with Mr. Garrison, we finally got word that Ryan would be able to begin classes at Landmark on November 1, which was just two weeks away. The placement was not immediate, as we had wanted, but it was only two weeks away. And, it was guaranteed.

That offer was certainly workable, in our opinion. After seeing an imminent end to the mediation, Mr. Garrison asked both sides to come together again in the larger conference room.

By this time we were all exhausted by the length of the proceeding. Mr. Garrison was busy with the paperwork, trying to reduce the day's events into a format that would fit on one page. While we were sitting around, making small talk and waiting for him to finish, Paul from County Mental Health spoke.

"You know, Susan," he said, "I just had an idea."

I wasn't sure I was ready to hear another idea. We had just reached an agreement and were waiting to sign the papers.

"I know we just agreed that Ryan can start back to Landmark on November 1, and he can," Paul said. "I was just thinking about the older Landmark program, and wondered if that might be something for us all to consider."

I had not even considered the older Landmark program. I was a bit skeptical but listened anyway. Paul explained that the older Landmark program was originally for older high school students; however, the ages of the students attending had gradually been getting lower. Most of the students, he said, were not that much older than Ryan.

Paul wondered if going into the older program might be a better option for him. Going to the older Landmark School, he reasoned, might not make Ryan feel as if he had "failed." By attending the high school program, Ryan might feel as if he was "moving up."

Although the other students would be slightly older, the other Landmark program offered some enhancements and advantages. Paul explained that the older Landmark students were able to have pets at school. After earning the privilege of getting a pet, each student would get to go to the pet store and select a pet of their choice. The pets remained at the school, but students had the responsibility of taking care of their pet. In addition, they had access to their pets all day, even during class. The reason, Paul explained, was that pets were comforting and soothing for kids with emotional and behavioral disorders.

I had to admit the idea intrigued me. I was not entirely comfortable about making a change of plans so quickly though. We had just fought over seven hours to get Ryan returned to Landmark Elementary. I needed some time to think.

Mr. Garrison offered a suggestion—he would extend the mediation hearing until the following week. In the meantime, Jim and I would have the opportunity to visit the older Landmark program and decide if it would be an appropriate placement for Ryan. If we approved of the program, Ryan could start by October 28. If we did not like the program, Ryan would start back at the Landmark Elementary program on November 1.

We agreed that County Mental Health officials could contact Dr. Comings and request that he participate in the next IEP by telephone or be available to answer the staff's questions about managing Ryan. We also agreed that our local district would make a good faith effort to seek an interim home teacher quickly. Also, the district agreed to provide two hours of home teaching per day instead of one.

I knew Ryan was entitled to six hours a day, but I also knew he was not capable of sitting through six hours of tutoring. Besides, I felt it was important to compromise whenever possible and I did not want to make a big deal of the issue.

I had raised concerns about transportation, so Mr. Garrison added a clause to the mediation agreement—our local district, Pacific View, acknowledged its responsibility to provide Ryan with transportation to and from the Landmark School, which ever one we chose.

Finally, at 5:30 P.M., seven-and-a-half hours after we began, we all signed the agreement. The mediation had been an ordeal for all of us. At the end, everyone felt relieved it was over and happy we were able to avoid

a Due Process Hearing. I felt no ill will toward any of the school administrators. All of us had come to the meeting with the sincere intention of
doing what was best for Ryan. We each did what we had to do. Fortunately,
we were able to come to an amicable agreement. Paul arranged for us to
visit the older Landmark program just a few days later.

One of the first advantages I could see was the distance to the school.
It was quite a few miles closer to home than the elementary program. That
meant a shorter bus ride that, I hoped, would mean fewer problems on the
bus.

Abby Stevens met us at the school—the same Abby who had originally been Ryan's case manager before he started at the Landmark Elementary School. She had transferred and was now a family liaison at Landmark
High School. We had always liked Abby and I knew Ryan would be happy
about seeing her again.

The school was near a small airport. The program consisted of two
classrooms of nine students each. The office and the classrooms were both
located in a renovated airplane hanger. The facilities were certainly not
aesthetically appealing, but any reservations I had disappeared when I met
the teacher.

Marlene, as the students called her, was totally "cool." I knew immediately that Ryan would like her. As I watched her interact with the other
students, I felt totally confident that she would be a good teacher for Ryan.
Marlene definitely had a nontraditional style of teaching. She was very
low-key, but she was also very direct and firm in her instructions. I could
sense that she was a "learn by the seat of your pants" type of teacher—not
the kind that followed the book chapter by chapter. She seemed to patiently
handle the many interruptions during our visit. She was very firm and structured, yet she also seemed to be flexible. Most of all, she seemed experienced. I felt sure that she would not succumb to Ryan's manipulations or
be shocked by his outrageous behavior.

The students all seemed "normal"-looking. We did not notice any severe acting-out behavior during our visit. All the kids were friendly and
several were eager to show us their pets. As we walked around the classroom I cringed when I saw one student with a small snake wrapped around
his neck.

"He won't hurt anybody," the boy explained. "Ya wanna hold him?"

Before I could answer, another boy jumped up and politely offered,

"Here, you can hold my rat."

Marlene saw my discomfort and rescued me by taking me outdoors to see their new litter of bunnies. The class menagerie also included several guinea pigs, some hamsters and a chinchilla.

We also met Wayne, the full-time "time-in" counselor. (They called it "time-in" instead of time-out.)

I wasn't as sure about Wayne. He seemed to have that "I know everything about your kid and you know nothing" attitude that we had seen before. We were all sitting around the conference table when I asked Wayne if he had much experience working with children with Tourette syndrome.

"Oh yeah," he replied with confidence. "I know all about Tourette's. I used to work at a psychiatric hospital."

For some reason, Wayne's declaration that he "knew all about" Tourette's did not convince me. I had met many professionals who told me they understood Tourette syndrome but didn't. I decided if Ryan was going to be attending Landmark High School, I should provide some up-to-date literature.

After visiting the school, Jim and I decided that Landmark High School would be a good placement for Ryan. We discussed it with Ryan too, and he was enthusiastic about going. He was especially excited about the prospect of getting a new pet.

Landmark High School worked on the same model as the elementary program. Emphasis was on helping students develop coping skills, social skills, problem-solving strategies, family living and classroom skills.

A "time-in" counselor was always available when students were having trouble in the classroom. Additional mental health support was to be provided by two family liaisons. In our case, the liaison was Abby.

The school also had a psychiatrist on staff for consultations, a principal and a mental health supervisor to provide administrative support. A daily point sheet, much the same as the one at the elementary school, would communicate Ryan's performance as to academic, personal and home goals.

After notifying Mr. Garrison of our decision to send Ryan to the Landmark High School program, we received notice that our Due Process Hearing was postponed until January 1992. This was to ensure that in case the Landmark High School placement was not satisfactory, we would still have the option of a hearing. If the placement proved satisfactory, we could cancel the scheduled hearing at any time.

On the morning of October 28, Jim and I accompanied Ryan to Landmark High School for his first day of classes. We wanted to do our best to help him avoid any further "transfer trauma." Together with Marlene, Gordon Miller, Abby and the other mental health staff, we wrote an IEP that was challenging, yet one with realistic goals we felt Ryan could accomplish.

At the close of the meeting I offered a collection of materials I had brought on Tourette syndrome. Wayne seemed uninterested, but Marlene and the principal eagerly picked up the pamphlets and quickly sorted through them. Along with the publications, I also brought a form that I asked the staff to sign acknowledging they had received the information about TS and its associated behaviors. Several at the table looked at me quizzically. I could tell it was the first time a parent had asked *them* to sign a form. Marlene picked up my form and readily signed it.

I decided, after my disappointing experiences with Lucy and the inexperienced staff at Sierra Vista, that any teacher or service provider working with Ryan should and would be knowledgeable about TS. Yet, I knew from experience that my grandfather was right—you can lead a horse to water, but you can't make him drink. Or, you can tell people about Tourette syndrome, but you can't make them understand—not unless they really want to.

Chapter 22

Ignorance Is Not Bliss

"There's nothing like a little experience
to upset a theory."[1]
Unknown

The next two months at Landmark were very rocky. Despite the efforts of the staff, Ryan had much difficulty. When it became imminent that Ryan was going to be removed from school unless hospitalized, Dr. Comings helped me get the process started. Because he is not a psychiatrist and City of Hope Medical Center is not a psychiatric facility, it was necessary that we find a doctor with admitting privileges to University Hospital.

Dr. Comings offered to call a colleague of his, Dr. Michael Curtis, for direction. I had met Dr. Curtis, a pediatric neurologist, on several previous occasions. He had been very complimentary about the RYAN book and told me he recommended it to all the mothers of his TS patients. Each time I had seen Dr. Curtis he always inquired about Ryan and seemed genuinely interested in how he was doing. I felt confident he would be very helpful.

Upon receiving the call, Dr. Curtis was very receptive to following Ryan's case. There was one problem, however. He only had admitting privileges to the regular medical center, not to the psychiatric unit.

After investigating further, Jim and I learned we did not need a private admitting physician. We only needed to check Ryan into University Hospital ourselves. Upon admission, the hospital would assign Ryan a staff psychiatrist who would serve as the admitting physician. At the time it seemed logical to us. We were totally unaware that we were making a horrible mistake.

I was nervous about how Ryan would react to our decision to admit him to the hospital. He had never been away from home except to spend the night at Grandma Polly's. I was also nervous about how frightened he would be at being away from us, sleeping in a strange place, and being with strange people.

Surprisingly, though, Ryan was not at all opposed to going to the hospital.

"I need help, Mommy," he insisted. "They'll help me at the hospital."

He was full of optimism and, despite our reservations, Jim and I were optimistic too.

The night before Ryan left, I was busy packing his suitcase. He was full of questions. Could he bring his radio, his Walkman, his Game Gear? He was eager to take all of his "goodies" and it was hard for me to say no.

I helped him pack his bag of toys and after he had gone to bed, I began to pack his clothes. One by one, I marked his name inside each item with a black permanent marker. I stacked the clothes into neat piles inside a large suitcase. With each shirt I folded it became more difficult to hold back the tears.

What was I doing? I asked myself. He is just a baby, I thought. How can I send him away like this? I fought hard to make sense of what was happening. I became overwhelmed with pity. Pity for Ryan and for myself. How could this be happening? I sat next to the suitcase, crying silently until I felt Jim's arms around me.

As he pulled me up, I thought of one last thing. Pictures! Ryan should have pictures of his family in case he gets homesick. It was getting very late but I had a mission. I began scouring the house for pictures. I found an empty photo album in the dresser and slowly began filling the plastic sheets.

He needed a picture of me, Dad, Julie and, of course, our dog Biskit; also, one of Grandma Polly, Aunt Sally, Uncle Randy and Dorian and one of Great-Grandma Purkey and all the other relatives. I soon had the album full. I was satisfied that if Ryan got the least bit homesick, he only needed to pull out his album and we would all be there in the hospital with him.

The next morning we arrived on time at the huge modern-looking administration building. After filling out reams of insurance forms and signing paperwork, a clerk told us that Anne, the admissions coordinator, would meet with us soon.

Ryan was doing fine, but I felt emotionally and physically drained. It seemed like forever before Anne finally came out to greet us in the small waiting area.

"Hi, Ryan," she said in a cheery tone. "Follow me and I'll take you across the street to the hospital."

I glanced at one of the admitting forms and noticed that the attending physician was Dr. Pamela Mazzuchi.

"Who is Dr. Mazzuchi?" I asked Anne. "Is she the doctor who will be seeing Ryan?"

"Yes," Anne explained. "She is the director of the adolescent unit." Hearing that Ryan's doctor was the director of the unit gave me confidence that he would be in good hands. You can't get much better than the director of the unit, I thought to myself.

Ryan followed her eagerly and Jim and I hurried to keep up with their quick pace.

"Do I have to get any shots?" Ryan asked. "Are they going to help me at this hospital?" He was full of questions for Anne.

The huge brick hospital loomed before us as we crossed the street. It looked old, not at all like the new administration building we had just left.

Once inside we started down a long corridor, bustling with people. Suddenly, we were at the elevators. I was getting increasingly nervous. Ryan took my hand as the elevator door opened and we stepped inside the crowded car.

When we left the elevator we were facing a huge metal door with a big glass window. A bright red sign on the glass read, "A-South, AWOL Risk, Keep Door Locked At All Times." Anne stepped up to the door and pushed a small button that was on the adjacent wall. Immediately there was a loud buzzing sound. Anne turned the handle and pulled open the heavy metal door to the unit.

She asked us to wait just inside the door as she carried Ryan's paperwork to the person sitting at a desk behind another glass window.

I began to look around. I strained to see every nook and cranny of the place that Ryan would stay—the place that would keep him away from his home and away from his dad and me.

What I saw stunned me. It was nothing like I expected.

I knew the hospital had a good reputation. It had a reputation of being one of the best. But it was so *old*. The walls were all a yucky-looking green color and looked as if they needed a fresh coat of paint. The flooring was old and cold-looking. I peered inside a set of double doors and spotted a Ping-Pong table and a piano. The furniture inside the room was dark brown and not in very good condition.

To my right was another set of double doors with glass windows. Inside that room were several round tables with chairs and some steel serving carts. There was an accordion curtain partially raised which revealed that the room was a cafeteria.

After just a few minutes, Anne returned and led us into the empty cafeteria area. A nurse carrying a folder of papers also appeared. Anne then bid us farewell and we sat, anxiously waiting for information from the nurse.

"I'm Lila," she said, not showing much expression. "I'm going to do your intake."

She began sorting through the stack of papers as we sat expectantly. She asked why we were bringing Ryan to the hospital. She also wanted a thorough history, so we obediently supplied all the details. About halfway through the long and labored interrogation, a younger-looking woman joined us. She, too, was carrying a stack of papers and she introduced herself as Dr. Donna Mills.

I was glad when Dr. Mills joined us. She smiled at us and shook my hand with a weak grasp. It was comforting to see a friendly face. Shortly after the doctor sat down, Lila stood to leave. I didn't know if she was planning to return or not, she didn't say.

Jim and I were still anxiously waiting to learn what was going to happen to Ryan and what we could expect from the hospitalization. I wanted to hear someone say that they were going to make him better. Maybe Dr. Mills was going to tell us.

When Lila left, Dr. Mills opened her folder and began shuffling papers.

"I'm sorry," she said, "but I'm afraid I'm going to have to ask you some of the same questions you have already answered for Lila."

We answered questions, mostly the same questions we had answered for Lila for the next hour and one half. Finally, at 1:00 P.M., weak from a bad case of nerves and from skipping breakfast, I asked if we could break for lunch. Dr. Mills agreed and directed us to the cafeteria. When we returned, there were more papers, more questions, and more forms to sign.

When are we going to meet Dr. Mazzuchi? I wondered.

During her questioning, Dr. Mills asked what medications Ryan was taking. I was careful to give her the names of each and the exact dosages. I reached inside my purse and offered her the brown paper bag holding the four prescription bottles. Dr. Mills removed and inspected each bottle, making notes for her file before handing them back to me.

When she finished her paperwork, Dr. Mills told us she planned to taper Ryan off all his medications and observe him "baseline" as she called it. She wanted to do this before making any determinations. She also said she would like to do an EEG; Jim and I agreed. Then, Dr. Mills stood, extended her hand and thanked us, saying she would be in touch.

It surprised me that she was leaving and I asked, "When will we meet Dr. Mazzuchi?"

"I don't believe she is here right now," Dr. Mills said. "Actually, I'm the doctor who will be working most closely with Ryan. Dr. Mazzuchi is the head of the unit."

"What about the tour?" I asked, confused that she was dismissing us so abruptly. "We thought we could have a tour of the unit. Also, we would like to see Ryan's room. Will he be sharing a room or will he have a room-mate?" I was full of unanswered questions.

Dr. Mills said she would try to find Lila and see if anyone had time to give us a quick tour.

I was beginning to feel as if we were "bothering" Dr. Mills and the staff. I did not understand how they expected us to bring our child to a strange and scary place and then just hand him over to complete strangers. I needed some encouragement from someone, some reassurance that we were doing the right thing. All Jim and I got was a feeling that we needed to hurry and take a quick look because everyone was busy.

Lila eventually appeared at the door of the cafeteria and said she could give us a "mini" tour.

As we left the cafeteria and turned right we approached a glassed-in area that seemed to be the "nerve" center of the unit. Behind the walls of glass I saw many people milling around, who I assumed to be doctors and nurses.

No one seemed to take notice as we passed the room until Lila tapped on the glass and motioned with her hand. I heard a loud buzz and she opened another door that led us into a long narrow hallway.

As we made our way down the hallway I cringed and grabbed Jim's hand. The whole place was so drab and dreary, so depressing. On our right was a row of metal doors, each with a small glass window. The door to the first room was open and I saw a worn-out brown sofa, a couple of chairs and a television set. After we passed a few more rooms, Lila opened one of the doors and motioned for us to enter. The appearance of the room startled me. A narrow mattress sat on top of a twin bed that hugged the floor. The walls were dingy and there were black marks and holes that were evidence of what had occurred with the previous occupant. A small beat-up nightstand with drawers and a desk that showed signs of prior abuse stood beside each other, pushed up against a dirty-looking, gray wall.

Sitting close to the door was an empty plastic crate that Lila explained was a hamper for dirty clothes. I walked to the window and for the first time became aware that there were metal grates that obscured a clear view. Seeing the metal bars jolted me into the stark reality. The room seemed just like a prison cell. I felt sick to my stomach.

Lila continued with the tour and led us across the hall to a community bathroom that the boys would share. I reminded her that Ryan was afraid of using the bathroom because of his fear of bugs. She assured me that someone would help him whenever he needed to shower or use the restroom.

The tour was over quickly and too soon it was time for Jim and me to leave. One of the nurses asked us to bring Ryan's suitcase to the front desk. She explained that the staff must inspect all personal items brought from home before the child could take his things into his room.

As we prepared to say our good-byes, one of the staff members challenged Ryan to a game of Ping-Pong. We hugged him briefly and made promises to talk to each other later that night. Then he was off to the day room to play. Lila walked us to the metal door that would allow us to leave the unit. As the door buzzed and then slammed shut behind us, I broke into tears.

Jim and I walked slowly and forlornly to the parking lot. I looked up at the tall, red brick building, trying desperately to identify which floor and which room held our little boy.

Why? Why? I asked the question over and over in my head. Why does this have to be happening? Why can't Ryan just be okay?

Later that evening he called us collect from the pay phone. It was then we learned for the first time that he would not be sleeping in a regular room that night. According to Ryan, the nurse told him he was going to be on "observation." When we hung up, I called the nurses' station to find out why.

"It's routine, Mrs. Hughes," the nurse explained. "We keep all the kids on a 'suicide watch' the first night." She explained that Ryan would be sleeping in the TV room located right across the hall from the nurse's station. This was so they could keep a close watch on him.

I understood their policy, but I didn't like it. It would have been helpful to know about the policy in advance. Perhaps we could have helped Ryan understand it a little better. I hoped that sleeping close to the nurses' station the first night would be comforting for him. I hoped it would ease his fear of being away from home and in a strange place.

That night, as we held each other close, Jim and I grieved for our son. We were also grieving for our lost dream—the dream of having a perfect family. Admitting Ryan to a psychiatric hospital meant admitting that things were beyond our control. It was a fact we could never erase. I knew that Ryan's life and ours would be different from that day forward—for better or for worse. It was hours before I finally drifted off to a restless sleep.

The next morning I called the nurse's station and learned that Ryan had fared well his first night. Even so, I was still eager to see him, to hug him, and to reassure him how much we all loved him.

Visiting hours at the hospital were terribly inconvenient. Parents could only visit from 5:30 P.M. until 6:30 P.M. each evening, Monday through Saturday. On Sundays, the visiting hours were from 1:30 P.M. until 3:00 P.M. and then again from 5:30 P.M. until 6:30 P.M.

It was forty-three miles one way from our house to the hospital. On a good traffic day, we figured it would take at least an hour to get there. It would take even longer to get there in late afternoon rush-hour traffic. Nevertheless, when Jim got off work at 3:00 P.M., he rushed thirty miles home to get me. We then jumped on the freeway and drove fast to make it to the hospital, find a place to park, and get up to the unit by 5:30 P.M.

During our visit the first night we learned just how strictly the staff would enforce the visiting schedule. There were two other parents besides Jim and me waiting to enter. One father was from England. He was there to see his daughter who was being treated for anorexia. Another woman told us she was from Hawaii and had brought her daughter to the mainland for treatment of severe Obsessive Compulsive Disorder.

The door to the unit opened promptly at 5:30. A nurse led all of us into the empty cafeteria to wait for our children to join us.

Ryan came in quietly and sat down in the chair beside me. He seemed happy to see us and asked if we wanted to play cards. The sixty minutes seemed to fly by as we played Gin Rummy and Go Fish. I was sad when it was time to leave. As I passed through the big metal door I flashed Ryan our "I love you" sign and he flashed it back. Then he was gone.

One of the nurses told us there was a parent's "support group" meeting we were required to attend on Thursday evenings. As the staff explained it to us, we could not visit with our child on that evening if we did not attend the meeting.

I remember walking into the room that first night. There were chairs arranged in a large circle. By the time the meeting started there were maybe six or eight parents besides Jim and me.

The facilitator, Neil, was one of the staff members from the adolescent unit. He started the meeting by asking each of us to introduce ourselves and to tell a little about our child. By the time it was my turn, I could barely speak my name.

I silently cried through the whole session. I felt so empty inside. As I listened to the other parents talking about their children, I wondered how they could be so calm. Weren't they hurting inside like Jim and me?

During the meeting we learned that several parents had brought their children to the hospital because of problems with anorexia. A few of the others seemed to be having severe conduct and discipline problems, although it was unclear to me if there was any particular diagnosis. It surprised me to see how angry some of the parents were—angry at their children and angry that they would be returning home soon. As far as I could tell, Ryan was the only child with Tourette syndrome.

The third night Ryan called home again in tears.

"They're going to make me sleep in that room again, Mommy" he cried. "I'm not going to kill myself—tell them I'm not. They won't believe me."

I, too, was unclear why Ryan had to sleep in the TV room again, but I did my best to calm him.

"Just sleep there again tonight, honey," I encouraged him. "Tomorrow we will get it straightened out with Dr. Mills," I promised.

When we hung up, I phoned the nurse and asked why Ryan had to sleep in the TV room again. She said she wasn't sure but would check on it. A short time later she called back and said that they would be assigning Ryan to a room right away. He would not have to sleep in the day room after all.

In the beginning, Dr. Mills was good about calling us. After just a few days, she called and told us she would like to call in a neurologist to do an evaluation. I readily agreed and asked if she would call Dr. Curtis. Dr. Mills said they preferred to use "one of their own" neurologists, as she put it—someone they were used to working with. I told her I would talk it over with Jim and get back with her.

I was unclear why Dr. Mills did not want to consult with Dr. Curtis. After all, he knew us and he knew something about Ryan. Dr. Comings had also recommended him, yet Dr. Mills was reluctant. I called Dr. Comings to ask for his advice.

"Susan, you have every right to use Michael Curtis if that's who you want," he advised.

That was all I needed to hear. I called Dr. Mills and told her that Jim and I did not want to use a staff neurologist. We politely insisted that she call Dr. Curtis to do the neurological evaluation. Dr. Mills told us she did not know if that would be possible. She said she would have to check with Dr. Mazzuchi and would get back to us later. When she called us back, she said they would call Dr. Curtis.

Dr. Mills kept us informed about the changes they were making in Ryan's medications. Just a few days after his admission I noticed he was taking more Ritalin than he was before he entered the hospital. It confused me because Dr. Mills had told us she was planning to taper Ryan off all his medications. When I called her to ask about the increase, I was shocked to find out what had happened.

At the time of our intake questioning, Dr. Mills had looked at the dosage on the bottle of Ritalin I had brought with me. She copied those directions instead of writing down what I *told* her he was taking. The dosage written on the bottle label was wrong. By not listening to me, Dr. Mills had inadvertently increased the Ritalin when the intent of the treatment plan was to discontinue the medication.

I didn't want to show my annoyance to Dr. Mills but I was secretly steamed that she had not paid attention to what I had told her. Not only had I told her and Lila, I had given them a paper with the correct dosages written. I certainly did not expect they would discount what I was telling them and rely on the outdated directions on the bottle.

As part of Ryan's treatment plan, we were to see a social worker for weekly therapy sessions. Our therapist's name was Marilyn. Of all the staff we met, she seemed to be the warmest and most empathetic.

Our first visit with Marilyn was more of the same—answering dozens of questions about Ryan's history. As always, Jim and I were very open and up front about sharing everything we knew. We disclosed even the most embarrassing details of our family life for Marilyn, Dr. Mills or anyone who asked. We knew that to help Ryan, we could neither embellish nor conceal any aspect of our family dynamics. Although I liked Marilyn, I was still dubious, based on our past experience with Lucy.

During his stay, Ryan was attending a school located inside the hospital. In addition, he spent time in recreational therapy (RT) and occupational therapy (OT). He really enjoyed his RT time, playing basketball, volleyball and other sports. In OT he made each of us a beautiful handmade gift. He crafted a ceramic vase for me and painted it with colorful stripes. He made his dad a handsome leather keychain. For Julie, Ryan made a pair of earrings and for Grandma Polly, a necklace of hand-strung beads. Besides these activities, there was also group and individual therapy with Dr. Mills and Marilyn.

During our brief evening visits with Ryan I became more aware of things happening on the unit. One evening, when Ryan hugged me, I bent over to kiss his head and noticed his hair reeked of smoke.

"Where have you been where people are smoking, Ryan?" I asked.

"Mom," he said excitedly, "you are allowed to smoke in here! A lot of the kids do it."

Later I asked one of the nurses about the smoking policy. She said that adolescent patients could smoke inside the day room. She explained that many of them had acquired the habit before entering the hospital and they would find it too hard to quit. That explanation did not set well with me at all. There were signs all through the hospital that smoking was prohibited in the facility, yet they were allowing kids to smoke on the unit and around other patients.

Another problem was the kind of music the staff allowed the kids to play in the day room. Ryan had told us early on about some of the tapes the kids were playing. He was eager to let us know that the staff was allowing him to listen to groups like "Metallica" and "Megadeath"—music we would never permit him to listen to at home.

The music concerned me for several reasons. We had worked hard over the years to provide Ryan with positive role models. Ozzie Osbourne and Alice Cooper were not what we considered to be good role models.

I also felt that exposing a child with Ryan's history of behavioral problems and suicidal thoughts to such outrageous music was irresponsible on the hospital's part. By allowing that kind of music, they were indirectly condoning the messages it conveyed and were promoting the musicians and their propaganda.

The hospital's unwillingness to screen the patient's music and to confine smoking to an area away from the other kids disturbed me. Even so, I did not voice my complaints, at least at the beginning. I worried that my grumbling might affect Ryan's relationship with the other patients and staff members.

During one of our early visits with Marilyn, Dr. Mills joined us toward the end of the session. I was happy to see her because I was curious about an orange colored pill I saw one of the staff members give to Ryan.

When I asked Dr. Mills about the pill she seemed a little unsure but speculated that it was Prolixin. I told her that the 5 mg. Prolixin we used at home was green. I wondered if the pill may have been a generic one.

"I really can't be sure," Dr. Mills said. "Maybe it was a vitamin."

That seemed odd to me.

"Are you giving Ryan vitamin therapy?" I asked. Dr. Mills replied that she was not.

When I persisted in knowing what the orange pill was, Dr. Mills said she would call the unit and find out about it. This, along with the Ritalin mistake, left me uneasy about Dr. Mills' expertise. I didn't understand how a doctor could be "unsure" of what medications her patient was taking.

Despite a few reservations about Dr. Mills I still felt that Ryan was in good hands. After all, I reminded myself, this hospital was supposed to be "one of the best."

Ryan had been in the hospital a little over a week when Dr. Mills notified Jim and me that they had finally determined what was "wrong" with him. The way she said it led us to believe they had discovered something new. It amazed us when she announced that Ryan had Tourette syndrome and Attention Deficit Hyperactivity Disorder—as if we did not already know.

Dr. Mills also told us that Ryan did not have Obsessive Compulsive Disorder and that she had seen nothing to indicate Oppositional Defiant Disorder. Also, she had seen no evidence of any phobias, despite what we had told her during the intake questioning. I found her observations concerning OCD to be particularly ironic.

One evening during a previous visit we had followed Dr. Mills and Ryan into his room. As he entered the room, Ryan stooped over and picked up his shoes. He then set them down, arranging them perfectly next to each other. After lining up the shoes, he picked them up and repeated the procedure two more times. Dr. Mills paid no notice. I wondered how many other OCD symptoms were going unnoticed.

During our talks with Dr. Mills and Marilyn, Jim and I were beginning to get "the feeling." The feeling we were getting was that Dr. Mills and Marilyn just did not get it. They just did not have a clue what we were going through with Ryan. Everything we had been trying to tell them was falling on deaf ears.

Since being admitted to the hospital Ryan had not exhibited any aggressive behavior. In fact, he was acting downright next to perfect. Despite his history and all of our complaints, it was becoming obvious, although done in a subtle way, that Dr. Mills and Marilyn thought that we were the ones with the problem. Their message was becoming clear. If Jim and I changed whatever we were doing wrong, Ryan would be perfectly fine.

After all, they hinted, if he was truly as bad as we had said, they would surely be seeing it at the hospital.

Marilyn even suggested that maybe I was "making Ryan my whole life" and that I should become involved in "other" things. She suggested that maybe I should get out more.

I wondered how that could be possible. I explained to her that I was working a full-time job. I also took care of Jim and Julie and attended each of their activities. In addition, I advocated with the school district, negotiated with the insurance company, picked up prescriptions and kept all the medical appointments. I bowled in a women's league once a week. I played in a ladies' and a couples' bunco group and cross-stitched with the sewing club. I did volunteer work for the school and church, and assumed a large responsibility in visiting and caring for my elderly grandmother. I also attended various support groups and a weekly prayer group for parents of teenagers.

I really did not know what Marilyn expected, but I knew that I was doing everything within my means *not* to make Ryan my whole life. Unfortunately, she offered no advice—only the inaccurate observations and criticisms.

During many of our visits with Ryan, he complained of being afraid of going to the bathroom and the shower alone. Although we had told her about the problem when we admitted Ryan, Dr. Mills still denied the presence of any phobias. We asked Ryan if he had told his doctor he was afraid to go into the bathroom. He assured us he had told Dr. Mills and the nurses about it several different times. He also said that it didn't do any good because no one believed him.

I knew he was having problems because I had found dirty underwear stuffed in his drawer on two separate visits. When I asked why there was soiled underwear in his drawer, Ryan said it was because he was afraid to go down the hall and into the bathroom by himself. It upset me to think that Ryan had clearly been expressing his fears to his doctor and that she was not listening. It was also upsetting that he could keep dirty underwear in his drawer with it going unnoticed by the staff.

While playing cards during one of our nightly visits, I noticed Ryan was not wearing his watch.

"Where is your watch, Ryan?" I asked, afraid that he had lost it.

He pushed up the long sleeve of his shirt to show me his watch and I noticed bite marks on his arm. He quickly pushed his sleeve back.

I asked him if he had been biting himself and he said, "Yeah, sometimes."

As we were leaving that evening, I told the nurse about the bite marks and asked if she knew he had been biting himself. She said that none of the staff was aware of it, but she would mention it to Dr. Mills and they would observe him more closely. During our next weekly meeting with Dr. Mills, I asked about the problem with Ryan biting his arms.

"Oh, we checked into that," she said. "We determined he was just doing it to get attention. It's clearly an 'attention-seeking' behavior."

I could not believe it. The bite marks had gone completely unnoticed by the staff, and we had discovered them by accident when looking for his watch. Even so, Dr. Mills concluded that Ryan was biting himself to "get attention."

By this time alarms and bells were going off in my head signaling that "something" was not right. When results from a routine EKG came back, I lost what little confidence I had left in Dr. Mills' capabilities.

The results from the routine heart exam showed a first degree AV block, an irregularity in the electrical current that causes the heart to beat. When Dr. Mills received the test results, she called to tell us about the irregularity. She also said she would be having the test evaluated by a pediatric cardiologist.

Several weeks passed and we still had not heard anything regarding the cardiologist's findings, so I asked Dr. Mills about it during our next weekly session. She told us she thought the AV block was due to the Anafranil Ryan was taking.

I reminded her that a similar test done six years earlier had also demonstrated the very same AV block—long before Ryan ever took Anafranil. Dr. Mills shrugged her shoulders and seemed annoyed that I had questioned her. She offered no further explanation.

By this time I was also concerned about Dr. Curtis' lack of involvement in Ryan's treatment. Despite our repeated requests, Dr. Mills did not invite him to participate in the many staff meetings regarding Ryan. Dr. Curtis assured us he was eager to attend, but that Dr. Mills was not informing him about the meetings or inviting him to come.

After several weeks of hospitalization, Dr. Mills informed us they were ready for a "feedback" session. It surprised me that they were ready to offer us "feedback" when they had not even discussed many of the issues and behaviors pertinent to the hospitalization.

Exasperated, I compiled a letter and a list of Ryan's behaviors that were the most difficult and distressing for Jim and me to deal with—ones that Dr. Mills had never even discussed with us. I felt strongly that she needed to explore these areas before she could come to any conclusions about Ryan's diagnosis or prognosis. I drafted a letter and delivered it to Dr. Mills the following day.

I also attached a list of the behaviors (and examples of each) that Dr. Mills had never considered:

RAGE ATTACKS

Short temper (very irritable and flies off the handle easily). Sometimes he can just sense that someone is looking at him and he blows a fuse.

Temper tantrums (when he can't do something when he wants to do it, he yells, screams, and stomps his feet).

Can't take "no" for an answer—gets very verbal, loud, accusatory, and may hit walls with his fist or slam doors.

Examples of Rage Episodes

These behaviors have happened in response to a variety of situations, all unpredictably, some in response to inward frustration, some in response to external triggers and stimuli.

While playing Nintendo, Ryan "lost" a game and became so angry that he started throwing things in his room, to the point of breaking objects and putting holes in his door and walls. These types of episodes have happened frequently.

When facing a disappointment such as a friend not being able to come over at the exact time Ryan had planned, he begins to vent the rage or frustration on the nearest person. An example would be hitting his mother, sister, or father—with great force— until he is restrained and subdued.

While riding in the car, Ryan has on numerous occasions become frustrated with the conversation. He begins to scream, curse and open the car door—no matter how fast the car is moving. Other times he may just begin to kick the back of the driver's seat or hit the driver in the head repeatedly—no matter who the driver may be.

If Ryan becomes frustrated or angry and the dog is near, he picks up the dog and hurls him full force across the room or yard.

One time Ryan became angry because I asked him to change clothes and he started cursing and calling me names. As I bent over to pick up his shoes, he swung to hit me and busted my lip.

Ryan has had numerous altercations with adult neighbors as a result of becoming angry at something they have said. He would vent his anger by throwing things at them, kicking their cars, throwing rocks at their cars, cursing at them, and kicking their front doors.

On occasions when Ryan has become angry on the bus, he has climbed out of the bus window, while the bus is moving and thrown things out the window.

On many occasions, these rage episodes have involved knocking over large pieces of furniture. He also throws furniture, dishes, and breaks valuables (even his own). He throws water in our faces and pulls our hair. He also engages in biting, spitting, kicking, hitting, or ramming his head into walls and doors. He has also gotten a knife out of the kitchen drawer and threatened to kill us or himself. Any of these types of reactions can result from something as insignificant as his spilling his glass of tea at dinner and becoming violently upset.

There are many times when the rage episodes are not present. It seems that these episodes can be controlled, especially with medication. It is important to note these episodes are not limited to home. There have been reports from the last three schools Ryan has attended as well as from numerous bus drivers, and parents of other children. Episodes have also occurred at his grandmother's house, during Little League games and numerous other public places such as restaurants, parking lots, and even church functions. It does not seem to affect Ryan whether these episodes are in public or private.

OBSESSIVE COMPULSIVE TENDENCIES

Touching or doing things a certain number of times. Most commonly he feels as if he has to do things "three" times, "two" times, etc.

Evening things up (if I kiss him on the cheek, he makes me kiss him on the other cheek so it will "feel" right).

Touching others excessively. He does not seem to be able to resist touching or grabbing other children. It's not always done aggressively.

Biting himself. The times we have noticed this it was discovered inadvertently and not done as an attention-seeking behavior.

Feeling as if he has to hurt himself and not feeling relief unless "it" has been accomplished. Example: When riding his skateboard with friends, he would separate from the others and deliberately smash his body into the curb or concrete to "feel" the pain. Also, he asks (demands) that his friends physically hurt him at times.

Repeating a certain word over and over, such as "fart, fuck, beans." (Not always bad words.)

Mental coprolalia. He says that sometimes the bad words are in his head and he just can't get them out.

Compulsion to write bad words (not done to seek attention!). We have "found" pieces of paper in his room and have discovered foul words written on places like the mini-blind in the bedroom.

Obsessing that something "bad" was going to happen. He was afraid for days that his mother was going to die or was afraid for weeks that a hand would come through his bedroom window. Most recently he has become obsessed that gangs are going to come and kill him.

Unusual attraction to knives. He often feels like running the sharp blade through his finger tips. He can't walk past a knife without picking it up.

Perseveration. He repeats a thought or idea over and over again. This is one of the most annoying and exasperating symptoms he displays and at times it seems more pronounced than others. Example: "We're going to have spaghetti for supper tonight, right, Mom? You promise. Spaghetti. Not tomorrow night—tonight. You PROMISE that we're having spaghetti tonight. We are having spaghetti. You promise. Spaghetti. Tonight. We won't do it. We probably won't have it. You promise? Tonight? This very night. You promise this exact night we are going to have spaghetti, right?" This continues until "something" finally clicks in and he feels satisfied.

Placing objects in just the right place.

Pulling up his socks. This one is very bad at times.

Adjusting his pants. (Tic or compulsion?) This one has lasted for years.

Feeling compelled to annoy or torture the dog. Example: Squeezing the dog's head between his hands too tightly, pulling the dog's ears, throwing rocks, hugging dog until it cries, pulling its legs. During these times Ryan insists that he feels as if he "has" to do it.

Annoying the dog by teasing him until the dog snaps. He does not give up until the dog hurts him or until someone else discovers what is going on and intervenes.

SEXUAL INAPPROPRIATENESS

Pulling his pants down in front of other family members. (This seems to come and go.)

Urinated on the carpet at school, and on the bus.

"Mooning" people out the window of bus.

Hitting people in private areas.

Using very explicit and horrible sexual language. This does not occur frequently, but it is very disturbing when he is going through this stage.

PHOBIAS

Fear of insects—particularly spiders. Even if they are already dead.

Unreasonable fear of going into the downstairs bathroom, even though it is in a very open area and even though family members are close. Once he has "made" it to the bathroom, he has to maintain verbal contact with someone the whole time he's there.

Going up steps to his room. Even though it is light and bright, he is afraid to go up, even with someone watching. Once he has made it upstairs, he is comfortable in his room as long as he makes frequent verbal contact with someone in another part of the house. This seems bizarre because he has no fear about going to bed at night and being left alone in his room, even knowing the rest of the family will be downstairs.

Afraid of being in the shower alone. Even though the shower door is glass, he has to leave it ajar.

After receiving my letter and list of targeted behaviors, Dr. Mills post-poned the feedback session.

Jim and I began to notice a marked change in Ryan's demeanor during our visits. When we arrived in the cafeteria he would barely smile and offered only a limp hug. He seemed to have difficulty holding his head up and at times would just sit and stare with his head leaning on his arm. Sometimes he would even lay his head down on the table and tell us to "keep on talking." He lost interest in playing cards, complaining that he was "too tired."

Of course, I mentioned all of this to the staff and to Dr. Mills. She told us he was fine when we weren't around and that he was just acting that way to "get attention."

Jim and I were at our wit's end.

By this time University Hospital had charged our insurance company close to sixty thousand dollars for Ryan's "treatment." Instead of receiving help for Ryan, they told us he was perfectly able to control his behavior. Dr. Mills implied that if we would just "do as they told us" and follow their new behavior modification program (the same one we had used in the past), Ryan would not behave inappropriately.

After this, we were eager to bring him home and pushed for the feed-back session as soon as possible. This time, Dr. Mills invited Dr. Curtis to attend the session and we were glad to see him. Although she had deliber-ately excluded him from many of the decisions involving Ryan's treat-ment, Dr. Curtis had been seeing Ryan weekly on a private basis and I felt complete confidence in his expertise.

When Jim and I arrived for the meeting, Dr. Mills was present, along with Marilyn, Dr. Curtis, and Dr. Puckett from the hospital's school.

Just as the meeting was about to begin, an older-looking woman rushed into the room. She looked quite disheveled and hurriedly plopped into an empty chair. She did not look at Jim or me but began talking with some of the others in the room.

The woman had a frosty air about her and I sensed she did not want to be there. It was only after the meeting began and everyone introduced them-selves that I learned she was Dr. Mazzuchi, Ryan's attending physician.

During the feedback session, Dr. Mills repeated more of the same we had been hearing for the past six weeks. Ryan, she maintained, responded well to the highly structured behavior modification program they had imple-mented on the unit. After the first few weeks of hospitalization, she noted, there was little record of Ryan being verbally abusive, swearing at the staff or threatening verbal abuse—evidence to her that they had "fixed" the problem.

Dr. Puckett, from the hospital's elementary school, reported on Ryan's behavior in class. Dr. Curtis asked about the results of any testing they had done to identify learning disabilities. "What testing?" Dr. Puckett asked. He seemed confused.

"One of the purposes of the hospitalization was to check for learning disabilities," I added. It was obvious they had done nothing. Dr. Puckett started scribbling some notes in his file and indicated he would look into the situation.

I brought up the subject of Ryan's drowsiness since he was again taking Clonidine. Dr. Mazzuchi hastily said that if he was appearing drowsy, he must be doing it on purpose for our benefit because they certainly were not seeing it on the unit.

Curious about the doctor I had never seen, I asked, "How many sessions have you had with Ryan since he's been here, Dr. Mazzuchi?"

The doctor shot me an icy glare and replied, "I observed your son the day he was admitted, Mrs. Hughes. I also observed him during group one evening and I think I know your son very well."

Before I could reply, Dr. Puckett spoke up and added that they also had observed Ryan in class putting his head down on his desk and drifting off to sleep. The conclusion of the school staff, he said, was that Ryan was deliberately acting drowsy to avoid doing his school work.

I could not believe what I was hearing. Ryan was so drugged when we arrived for our visits that he could not even play cards. He would literally fall asleep during our brief visits. Yet these so-called "professionals" decided that he was falling asleep while with us to "seek attention" and falling asleep in class to "avoid school work."

That was it as far as we were concerned. We had put up with enough. Jim and I informed Dr. Mazzuchi that we were taking Ryan home. She admonished us that we should at least let him stay over the weekend. When we insisted on having him discharged, she scolded us and said that we were not acting in Ryan's best interest.

By the time he left in mid-March, Ryan had been in the hospital over six weeks. Jim and I were both emotionally and physically drained. Driving the eighty-six round-trip miles each night in rush hour traffic had taken its toll. Trying to cope with the painful feelings of having Ryan in the hospital and dealing with Dr. Mills and some of the other staff members had left us emotionally bankrupt.

When Ryan came home we diligently followed the behavior plan the hospital staff had started. Each evening at bedtime I would run a tub of warm water for him and add a few capfuls of bubble bath. Then, after a slow relaxing bath, I would fix him a cup of hot chocolate and we talked about the day's events. There was a copy of the "feelings chart" with the little faces hanging near his bed. I encouraged him to pick a face that best fit his mood each night. Almost always, he picked the happy one.

Ryan returned to school at Landmark where he started on yet another behavior program. Unfortunately, it was not as easy to manage Ryan at home and school as it was in the hospital.

We continued to have difficulty with the side effects from the Clonidine. If Ryan took enough to control his behavior, it would put him to sleep. It seemed there was a very fine line between how much it took to control his behavior and how much was "too much."

Chapter 23

Physician, Heal Thyself

"Cured yesterday of my disease,
I died last night of my physician."[1]

Matthew Prior

Ryan had been home from the hospital less than a month when we left on a family vacation to Oregon. It was spring break and we were anxious for a chance to try out our new motor home with a drive up the beautiful California and Oregon coast.

Ryan was happy to be out of the hospital and excited to be going on the trip. By the third day we were wishing we had never left home.

We were traveling with Robin and Craig and their three children. One afternoon we all stopped for lunch at a restaurant near a shopping mall. Several of us wanted to go to one of the stores in the mall and Ryan, who loves to shop, was ecstatic. When he learned we were only going to one store, he became angry, insisting that we go to *all* the stores. We tried reasoning with him, explaining that we needed to get back on the road. Ryan quickly became verbally abusive and refused to come into the mall with us.

I knew he would not stay outside alone, so I turned and began to walk toward the mall with the others. Ryan then ran up behind me and slugged me in the back of my head. The other family looked on in shocked disbelief. Even though they were aware of Ryan's problems, they had never seen him physically hit us before.

After his five minute "storm" was over, Ryan started crying, repeating that he was sorry he had hit me. I did not want to hear it. My head was hurting from the force of his blow and I felt humiliated in front of our friends. More than that, I was devastated that after six weeks in the hospital, Ryan was still having "rage" attacks. Despite his cries of remorse, I left him with Jim and continued on inside the mall.

How much longer could I endure this kind of behavior? I wondered. Doubts pierced my mind as I walked, feeling half-numb into the store.

Jim was harsh with Ryan, letting him know clearly that he would not tolerate him physically abusing his mother or anyone else. When I arrived back to the motor home Ryan seemed contrite and again was very apologetic. We continued with the trip, assuming we had set a limit for his behavior that he would not violate.

Despite his good intentions and ours, Ryan crossed the line many more times, exploding with rage at barely the slightest provocation. Once, in anger, Ryan kicked the wall of the motor home and tore down the mini-blinds.

Jim had already reached his limit of tolerance with Ryan and he too went "out of control" when he saw his new motor home being damaged. He grabbed Ryan, pulled him off the bed, and away from the blinds. Ryan began kicking and spitting in his dad's face.

It was the first time I was fearful that Jim was going to "lose it" and hurt Ryan. I could see Jim's anger—his face was red and the veins in his neck were bulging. It scared me but all I could do was sit and cry. I felt powerless to move, almost as if a huge weight was holding me down on the chair.

Luckily, Jim did not hit Ryan. Craig came to the door of the motor home, saw me crying and went back into the bedroom to offer his help.

Ryan was nasty to him too. From that day on I saw a change in Craig's attitude with Ryan. He, too, began to talk to us about "placing" him somewhere. Despite the hopelessness we felt at that moment, Jim and I were still not ready to give up on Ryan.

Five months after Ryan came home, I was still furious about our experiences at University Hospital. I requested a copy of the discharge summary from the hospital and after much wrangling, eventually got one. It was upsetting to see so many inaccuracies in the report.

A list of medications Ryan had taken previously was incomplete. The report stated we had only used a behavior modification program for the past one to two years, when we had actually used behavior programs for over ten years.

The report stated Ryan did not have problems with sleep, yet we had reported that he had a history of sleep problems for many years, including night terrors; that Ryan hit and punched the family cat, although we have never owned a cat; that Ryan was right-handed when he is and always has been left-handed.

One of the staff members stated that Ryan "avoids interpersonal closeness." In reality, Ryan has always been very loving and affectionate, except during "rage attacks."

The report stated *we* requested a neurological evaluation when it was Dr. Mill's who requested one. Our only request was that she use Dr. Curtis.

It denied the presence of any rituals or obsessions with Ryan, except for the first week of hospitalization. If we had not persisted in telling Dr. Mills of our problems with OCD at home, she would have certainly continued to deny its existence.

Altogether I noted fourteen misrepresentations in the discharge summary. I carefully documented each mistake in a nine-page letter to the Director of University Hospital. In closing my letter, I conceded that our experience had not been entirely negative. We felt the group sessions and the occupational and recreational therapy programs had all been very helpful. We also felt some of the parent support sessions were helpful.

I also stated that, despite some difficulties, we would consider the services of University Hospital again, but only if Ryan was under the direction of a private or staff physician who was knowledgeable about ADHD, Tourette syndrome and Obsessive Compulsive Disorder.

In response to my letter, I received a brief reply from the director, thanking me for taking the time to share my experiences. He said that he had reviewed my comments and had forwarded them to a multi-disciplinary review committee. By the time Ryan was discharged, University Hospital had billed our insurance company nearly $78,000.

In the meantime, Ryan continued to have difficulty at home and school. At the beginning of summer school we received word that Ryan's teacher, Marlene, would not be returning to Landmark in the fall. The news was a bombshell for Ryan and for us. Marlene had worked wonders. She made learning exciting and fun for Ryan and I did not see how anyone could take her place. Getting a new teacher was yet another transition for him to make—another obstacle in his path of achieving stability.

Sometime that June we received notice from our insurance company that our mental health benefits were changing. Beginning July 1, all mental health visits needed to be pre-approved by a company called American

Behavioral Health. In addition, we now needed to use a psychiatrist who was part of their Preferred Provider (PPO) "network."

Although we were still seeing Dr. Comings for Ryan's medication management, Jim and I worried that Ryan might, at some time, need to go to the hospital again. We decided it would be a good idea to establish a relationship with a new psychiatrist, just in case hospitalization became necessary in the future. I called American Behavioral Health and received a referral to a Dr. Lehrer, whose office was close to home. I scheduled our appointment for July 1, the first day our benefits with the new company were to begin.

A few days before our appointment, I delivered a packet of information to Dr. Lehrer's office that included Ryan's records from University Hospital. I also included a list of all the behaviors we were having trouble with at home. I thought providing the doctor with the materials ahead of time would expedite our consultation visit.

Ryan was not happy about seeing another doctor. He was apprehensive that going to another doctor meant going back into the hospital. We tried to assure him that this was just a "talking" doctor that would be able to help him and us cope with some of the difficulties we were having.

Dr. Lehrer's office was on the upper level of a modern office building. The office was difficult to find and Ryan opened a few wrong doors before I finally guided him to the right one. The doctor's office was small and cramped. The outside waiting area was very narrow and stuffed with a couple of chairs, separated by a glass table and a lamp.

There was a closed door at the end of the waiting area. Ryan immediately ran over and tried the handle. Failing to open it, he pushed a button resembling a door bell that was on the wall to the right of the door. I immediately grabbed his arm and tried to pull him away.

Just then the doctor stuck his head outside the door and said, "I will be with you in just a few minutes."

I looked over and saw the receptionist glaring at us. Ryan saw her too and scowled, "Quit looking at me, bitch." She looked flustered and finally turned away.

Ryan became obsessed with trying to push the button again. He was like an octopus, arms and legs flying all over the place. It was all I could do to control him and keep him away from the lamp, the door and the buzzer. I became aware the receptionist was watching us again.

Finally she said, "Can't you make him stop?"

As I continued to grapple with Ryan, I replied, "*This* is why he is here." She quickly looked down and began typing.

It seemed like forever before the doctor finally opened his door and invited us inside. Despite the small cramped waiting area, the doctor's inner office was spacious and handsomely decorated. He introduced himself and asked us to sit on a plush sofa. Dr. Lehrer began by asking Ryan questions.

I knew Ryan was nervous about seeing a new doctor but even I was unprepared for his behavior. Practically every question the doctor asked, Ryan replied with a lie. This was particularly surprising because Ryan never lied. It was totally out of character for him. After the third or fourth question, when I realized what he was doing, I interrupted and told Dr. Lehrer that Ryan was not being truthful.

The doctor curtly replied that he was talking with Ryan. He told me I would have my turn to speak later. The interrogation then continued.

"Do you have any brothers and sisters?"

"Yeah, a brother," Ryan lied. Dr. Lehrer jotted down the answer.

"He has a sister," I said, concerned that the doctor was believing what Ryan was saying. Dr. Lehrer shot me an annoying glance.

"What is your sister's name, Ryan?" Dr. Lehrer asked.

"Asshole" Ryan replied with a straight face. Dr. Lehrer continued with no reaction.

"Does anyone else live with your family?"

"Yeah, my grandma," Ryan fabricated. The doctor continued writing.

It went on and on. I could see that Ryan was enjoying the game of "stump the doctor."

Before Jim and I even had a chance to tell Dr. Lehrer about our concerns, he was glancing at his watch saying that we would have to continue our visit later.

We hurriedly asked if he would be willing to work with Dr. Comings, as we wanted to continue consulting him for Ryan's medication management. He said he did not see that as a problem.

Jim and I were both disappointed with Dr. Lehrer. It was obvious he had not read any of the materials I had left for him. The entire visit lasted forty-five minutes to the exact second. It disturbed me that he spent all that time jotting down the lies that Ryan was gleefully spewing out at him.

We were not sure if we should call the insurance company and request another doctor or not. We left on summer vacation the next day and decided, despite our reservations, that we would give Dr. Lehrer another chance.

Jim and I were especially looking forward to this vacation. We were planning to return to Jackson Hole, Wyoming in our motor home. What made this trip so exciting was that Ryan was staying at home with Grandma Polly. Because we had such a miserable time on the trip to Oregon, we decided that this time we would just take Julie. We really wanted to get some rest and relaxation. Fortunately, Ryan seemed happy to stay home with his grandma. If he felt disappointed in not going, he didn't let it show.

I worried about staying away for two full weeks. Although my Mom was good with Ryan, I knew he could wear her out quickly. The good part was that he would be in summer school during the daytime and she would just have to deal with him in the evenings.

Jim and I desperately needed the break. Yet, it still weighed heavy on my heart that we were leaving Ryan behind. I knew I would have to work at setting aside my feelings of sadness to have a good time. The first few days of the trip I called home every night. As far as I could tell, things were going okay with Ryan.

Then, Ryan started to have problems at school. Chuck, from Landmark High School, and Abby, his mental health liaison, were calling my Mom daily and requesting that she come to get him. After being gone only a week, Jim and I decided we should cut our vacation short and head home.

We were alarmed to hear Ryan was having so much trouble at school. I knew if he continued to have problems, the subject of residential treatment centers would come up again. That subject, it seemed, was always looming over us.

Even if we could somehow continue to manage Ryan at home, I knew he had to be in school some place. Landmark was the most restrictive placement our county had to offer for children with behavioral problems.

Home schooling was not even an option we would consider. Jim and I felt that there was more to an education than being tutored in reading and math. We wanted Ryan to experience *school*. School to us meant socializing with other kids, learning how to control his behavior, interacting with adults, etc. We knew if he couldn't make it at Landmark, the next option was to go away, somewhere outside our county.

During the parent meetings we attended at University Hospital, we had learned from another couple about two residential treatment facilities in Provo, Utah. They selected Utah for their daughter's placement because laws in that state allow residential facilities to have "locked doors." In California, no facility other than a psychiatric hospital can lock their doors. Thus, juveniles who have a history of running away find it very easy to do so.

Although Ryan did not have a history of running away, I feared what he might do if we placed him in a residential treatment center. Despite our hurry to get back home, we decided to stop and check out the two schools. I was lucky that each of the school's directors allowed us to come without an appointment.

I don't know what I expected a residential treatment center to look like. The first one sat at the foot of a beautiful mountain and offered a separate campus for boys and girls. The inside of the facility seemed similar to the unit at University Hospital, only on a larger scale. It boasted a twenty-year history of treating troubled youth.

The dorms seemed adequate and their recreational facilities included a pool, gymnasium, bowling alley, tennis and basketball courts, playing fields, and a skateboard ramp. The fully accredited school was on the same grounds and their teacher-to-student ratio was low. One of the first things that caught my attention upon entering the school was a huge sign that read, "Swearing will not be tolerated by anyone—no exceptions." I wondered how a child with Tourette syndrome would fit.

The kids were in class during our visit. There seemed to be many small classrooms that were full of well-behaved students. I noticed that all the boys seemed to be much bigger and looked much "tougher" than Ryan. I could not quite picture him fitting in with the ones I saw.

The second residential center was in the same general area but offered more of a homelike environment. Five big six-bedroom houses lined a cul-de-sac on the campus. A huge rectangular swimming pool separated two of the houses. A horseback riding arena, playing fields, bicycle trails, volley-ball pits and a skate board ramp were all close to the dorms. We learned that water skiing and snow skiing were some of the other activities available when weather permitted.

This facility seemed especially proud to offer services for adolescents with "dual diagnoses," i.e., those who have an emotional, behavioral and academic problem along with a substance abuse problem. In speaking with the director we learned that most of the kids were there for substance abuse issues. They, too, looked much bigger and older than Ryan. Some of the boys had tattoos and looked pretty rough. I could not picture Ryan with his stuffed tigers fitting in too well.

Visiting the residential facilities was both comforting and disturbing. I was happy to see they were not horrible-looking mental institutions, yet they definitely were not places that I felt I could send my child.

During the drive back home to California, Jim and I decided we should see Dr. Lehrer again. Perhaps we had misjudged him the first time. We knew Ryan had demonstrated much improvement with medication in the past. If we could just be patient, perhaps Dr. Lehrer would be able to get Ryan stabilized again. We made plans to call for another appointment when we got home.

Our second visit with Dr. Lehrer had a much different tone than the first. When we asked if he had a chance to consult with Dr. Comings, he told us that he was not interested in speaking with Dr. Comings.

"I am not used to working with other doctors," he said. "Quite frankly, I'm kind of a 'take charge' kind of guy," he said firmly.

After grilling Ryan with questions for about thirty minutes, he turned to Jim and me and said, "I notice that you both are rather soft-spoken. Have either of you ever tried using a loud voice with him, or getting up in his face?"

As if that comment were not enough, Dr. Lehrer said, "Sometimes nice people like you make the worst parents for kids like Ryan." Then, ever mindful of the clock, he announced that our time was up. Jim and I left his office feeling exasperated, empty and numb.

My thoughts were spinning. What was this guy's problem? Did he really believe we had managed to raise a child with Tourette syndrome, ADHD, Oppositional Defiant Disorder and Obsessive Compulsive Disorder without ever using a loud voice or getting up in his face? Hadn't he read the reports from County Mental Health?

Jim and I were beginning to have strong suspicions that Dr. Lehrer did not have a clue about what we were trying to tell him or what we needed.

When school started in September, Ryan met his new teacher, Luke Wagner. I worried about how he would treat Luke since he was still upset over losing Marlene.

It was rough the first couple of weeks. Ryan compared everything Luke did with Marlene, and not too favorably either. Fortunately, Luke took the criticisms in stride and made every effort to establish a good relationship with Ryan.

Abby, our mental health liaison from Landmark, was still coming for weekly home visits. We told her about our problems with Dr. Lehrer, and she encouraged us to give him another chance.

Because Ryan's behavior was becoming increasingly unmanageable at school, she offered to go with us to our next appointment. Abby thought that perhaps she could better relate the difficulties they were having at school in managing Ryan. She also wanted to share with Dr. Lehrer their concerns about Ryan's wide mood swings.

Besides Ryan's mood swings, Abby expressed concern that his "affect" was not always appropriate. Sometimes when hurt, Ryan would laugh instead of cry. She and the other staff wondered if perhaps Dr. Lehrer might want to consider a trial of Lithium in hopes of stabilizing his mood.

Jim and I agreed it would be a good idea for Abby to go with us on our next visit. We certainly were not getting through to the doctor. Perhaps she could.

Our third visit with Dr. Lehrer was on November 9. Abby accompanied us to the office (without Ryan) and for the entire forty-five minutes she explained the difficulty they were having at Landmark in trying to manage Ryan's behavior. She explained that Landmark was a highly-structured, very intense day treatment program and that all the staff were mental health professionals with hospital backgrounds.

Abby pointed out that, despite their experience, the staff was unable to handle Ryan. They also felt that a medication change was in order and even possibly, hospitalization.

Before we were able to resolve anything, our forty-five minutes were up and we rescheduled another appointment for two days later.

By the time we arrived for our fourth visit with Dr. Lehrer, Ryan was totally out of control both at home and school. Abby went with us and again spent much time detailing Ryan's difficulties. Finally, it seemed, she was able to get her point across.

Dr. Lehrer agreed that Ryan should go to the hospital, but it was a conditional agreement. "Before hospitalizing him," Dr. Lehrer said, "I would like to gradually get him off the Prolixin he is taking now."

Abby and I both expressed our apprehensions about the safety of trying to manage Ryan at home and school while reducing the medication. But Dr. Lehrer was insistent that we wait a week. He wanted Ryan off Prolixin before admitting him to the hospital.

All three of us were disappointed with his decision and hard-pressed to understand the rationale. Ryan was already unmanageable. Reducing the Prolixin had the potential of making him much worse.

The next morning Ryan went to school but was only able to stay an hour before Abby called for me to get him. By the time I arrived, she had already called Dr. Lehrer. Abby told me that the doctor had decided to hospitalize Ryan right away and that he wanted me to call him at his office to make the arrangements.

Ryan and I arrived home around 10:30 A.M. and I phoned Dr. Lehrer's office the minute I got in the door. His secretary told me he was not available so I left a message that I had phoned and would be at home waiting for his call.

By this time Ryan was wild with anxiety. Before leaving school Abby had told him that he would be going to the hospital right away. He was anxious and ready to go. He said he wanted to go to the hospital because he needed help. Ryan and I waited and waited for Dr. Lehrer to call. As the hours ticked by, he became increasingly anxious. I was totally confused. Dr. Lehrer had told Abby that he was going to hospitalize Ryan right away. After several more hours, I called Abby again to make sure I had not misunderstood. She assured me I was not mistaken.

Finally, at 7:30 PM, Jim and I decided to take Ryan out for an ice cream cone. We hoped getting out of the house would help relieve his anxiety. During the brief time we were away, Dr. Lehrer called. He left a message on our answering machine stating that I could reach him at his office early the next morning. He made no mention of his plan to hospitalize Ryan and we spent the rest of the night trying to cope with a very confused and distraught little boy. We had no answers for him.

I phoned Dr. Lehrer's office at eight o'clock the next morning. A machine answered and I left a message that we were very eager to speak with him. At ten, his secretary called and said that the doctor would call me sometime after twelve-thirty. When Dr. Lehrer finally called, he said he would discuss Ryan's hospitalization at our 4:00 appointment that afternoon. By this time, I was really confused.

When we arrived for the appointment, Ryan was extremely anxious, agitated, irritable and hyperactive. He was speaking so rapidly you could barely understand a word.

Ryan immediately asked the doctor when he would be going to the hospital. Dr. Lehrer told Ryan he wanted him to wait a few more days until he was off Prolixin. I could not believe what I was hearing and neither could Ryan. When he heard that the doctor wanted him to wait longer, Ryan became upset. He started to beg and plead. He told the doctor he needed to go to the hospital, that he needed help *now* and that he couldn't wait much longer. Dr. Lehrer persisted, explaining to Ryan that he had to be off Prolixin first.

As Jim and I continued talking with Dr. Lehrer, Ryan literally began bouncing off the walls. He paced quickly back and forth across the room. He started knocking over the doctor's personal things. He picked up a gold clock, a paperweight, and some pictures and began throwing them up into the air, oblivious to the doctor's demands for him to stop.

Dr. Lehrer finally stated, "You know, Ryan, I think you are right. You need to go now."

Dr. Lehrer said he would meet us at Meadow Grove Hospital at noon the following day. As we were leaving his office he said, "By the way, I will be billing you for a full session today, even though you were here only ten minutes. I've spent a lot of time on the phone with Ryan's school and with your insurance company."

That night Ryan eagerly packed his suitcase. I had to fight back tears again with each pair of jeans I folded. "Don't worry, Mom," he said. "They are going to help me at this hospital," he said confidently. "We're gonna have a good life."

The next afternoon Jim, my mom and I drove Ryan the short distance to Meadow Grove, a local psychiatric hospital. Mom and I remarked how great it would be to have Ryan so close to home. We were happy we would not have to fight the rush hour traffic to University Hospital this time.

The hospital was in a beautiful neighborhood and the building was a newer one. It was certainly a contrast from the old, tall brick building at University Hospital. I was eager to see the children's unit and to see where Ryan would be staying. It seemed like hours before we completed all the paperwork, consent forms, insurance forms, etc. Then, finally, we were on our way upstairs.

Dr. Lehrer met us at the entrance of the unit and confessed his unfamiliarity with hospital procedures. He seemed a bit uneasy and flitted back and forth, making frequent inquiries to the nursing staff and struggling awkwardly to unlock the doors inside the unit. After getting Ryan checked in, we all walked down the hall to his room.

The rooms at Meadow Grove were larger than the ones at University Hospital and seemed much more cheery. Although they were sparse of furniture and decor, the rooms were bright and had less of a "prison cell" feeling than the ones in the older hospital.

Dr. Lehrer chatted with us briefly before leaving us alone with Ryan to unpack his things. I noticed a few of the other patients walking around the hall and wondered why they were there. Most of them were older and larger than Ryan but they all looked nicely dressed and appeared to be doing well.

Ryan liked the looks of the hospital. I think he pictured this to be more like a vacation to "Club Med" or something. He was excited about the swimming pool and tennis court. When we kissed each other good-bye, Ryan was in good spirits and again he encouraged me, "Don't worry, Mommy. I will be fine here."

The next morning Jim and I went to church before going to see Ryan. We arrived shortly after lunch time. He was waiting at the front desk and seemed happy to see us. He immediately led us into his room but once there he became extremely irritable. He did not want to answer any questions and during the visit he vacillated from being happy and eager to being testy and agitated. We tried to play gin rummy but after a short time he folded up his cards, laid his head in my lap, and fell asleep.

The next afternoon, Ryan called to make sure we would be coming during visiting hours from 5:30 P.M.-6:30 P.M. He was happy that Julie and her boyfriend Joe would also be coming. At one point during the visit he took me aside and told me he really loved me and that he was sorry that he had behaved so badly the night before. As we were leaving that evening the nurse reported that he had been really "hyper" all day.

Two days later Ryan called to tell me there was going to be a family meeting that evening. No one from the staff had told us about the meeting but I assured him that his dad and I would come. I learned from the nurse that Ryan acted withdrawn and seemed sad that morning. When I asked if he was eating and sleeping well she replied, "If he wasn't, someone would let you know."

When we arrived for the meeting that evening, Ryan was in the middle of cussing out one of the female staff members and calling her a bitch. She looked at us despairingly and said that he had "just started" behaving that way. Jim and I offered to leave but she asked us to stay. When we entered his room, he was very hyper, jumping from bed to bed. Each time the nurse closed his door, he opened it. He also ran back and forth into the hall frequently.

While I was in Ryan's room, I overheard a girl talking outside his door. She was complaining to her parents about a kid on the unit that was aggravating her. The girl was upset because the staff wasn't doing anything about it. That was all I heard.

The parent meeting that evening was different from the ones we attended at University Hospital. At this meeting, the kids also attended. Everyone sat against the wall, grouped by families. A man, who I later learned was a psychologist, started the meeting by asking the family sitting closest to him to explain why their daughter was in the hospital.

They brought Crystal, they explained, because of her drug addiction and affiliation with gang members. I could feel the mother's pain as she tearfully detailed the difficult experiences that had led them to Meadow Grove. When the mother finished speaking, the therapist turned to the attractive dark-haired girl who sat slumped in her chair.

"How does hearing your mother say these things make you feel, Crystal?" he asked. Crystal shot an icy look toward her mother.

"I don't care what she says," Crystal retorted. "The gang is my family and when I get out of here, I am going back to them and she can't stop me."

Repeatedly, Crystal pledged her allegiance to her gang "family." I was shocked that we were sitting across from a beautiful young girl who was a hard-core gang member. Like a tennis ball being batted back and forth, the therapist took turns asking Crystal and then her mother "how it made them feel" when they heard the other one speak.

This back and forth dialogue went on for close to an hour before the therapist moved on to the next family. Then it was more of the same. The parents would speak, then the therapist would ask the kid how hearing their parents made them feel. The "how does it make you feel" psycho-babble went on ad nauseam. Most of the kids seemed to know the lingo and responded in typical psychology textbook fashion. They seemed to have quickly learned the "right" way to answer.

Another girl named Nikki also had friends in a gang. I recognized her as being the girl I had overheard in the hall. Instead of being upset with her family, Nikki lashed out at the hospital staff. She complained bitterly about how they couldn't "handle" the kids on the unit and that one boy in particular had been annoying her.

"This kid is driving everyone in here nuts," she complained bitterly, "and the staff can't do anything with him." As she spoke, it became obvious who she was talking about. Several of the kids were looking in our direction and Ryan was fidgeting uncomfortably in his chair.

When the therapist finally got Nikki back on track, she began to brag about her gang affiliation. I started to feel sick inside. Obviously, Ryan had done something to upset this girl. Nikki repeatedly insisted that she was a gang member and would *always* be a gang member.

"They would kill me if I tried to leave," she said, "and besides, I don't want to leave them. They are my family."

The more I heard, the more nervous I got. I didn't know much about gangs except that they liked to "retaliate" when someone bothered one of their members. I could not wait for the meeting to be over so that I could talk privately with Ryan.

Except for him, all the teens were in the hospital because of substance abuse or delinquency. Jim and I felt totally out of place at the meeting. The conversation did not seem at all appropriate for Ryan and I worried about what he might be learning from the other kids on the unit. Worse yet, I worried that he might get hurt by one of the other kids. I was dumbfounded by the anger and open hostility displayed between the parents and their children.

By the time the meeting had dragged on for nearly two and a half hours, Ryan had reached his limit and started to move around. The therapist made an off handed comment about how much difficulty Ryan was having sitting still. Then he asked us why we had brought him to the hospital.

I explained that Ryan had Tourette syndrome and that we had brought him to the hospital to adjust his medications. We also, I explained, would like for Ryan to get some help in learning how to control his behavior. The therapist nodded his head and then dismissed the meeting. Jim and I left the hospital feeling very uncomfortable with what was happening.

I got up early the next morning to call the Adolescent Unit. When I asked how Ryan was doing that morning, I received the same pat answer I always did—"He must be doing fine or someone would call you."

"Listen, Karen," I began, "Ryan has been there four days and I have not been able to get anyone to tell me anything. I want to know how he is doing and I will no longer settle for a 'generic' answer." She hastily transferred me to a nurse named Della.

When Della came on the line I could sense a definite edge in her tone. "Ryan is fine," she said, "but he did have difficulty sleeping last night. He was very restless."

I asked if she was aware that Ryan had been provoking Nikki.

Della denied knowledge of any tension between them.

"Our staff keeps an eye on all the kids at all times, Mrs. Hughes," she said. "If anything was going on, we would definitely be aware of it."

I told her about the meeting the night before and how angry Nikki had been with Ryan. Della cut me short and said that it sounded to her as if Nikki was being very appropriate in expressing her feelings. "Besides," she said, "Nikki is not violent."

206

"It's not Nikki that worries me," I said. "It's her gang family. I am also concerned about how Ryan feels about his behavior being so annoying to the other kids. His hyperactivity is not being treated," I explained, "and he really cannot help some of the things he does."

Della said it would be better if I called back at two that afternoon. She said that she was too busy to talk during the morning hours.

Later that day Abby, called to see how *I* was doing. I poured out my concerns and Abby agreed that they were all valid. She suggested we contact Dr. Lehrer right away to find out how long he was planning to keep Ryan in the hospital. She assured me that the Landmark staff wanted to remain very involved and that she would do anything she could to help.

I told her that Jim and I were disappointed that Dr. Lehrer had not called or met with us for several days. We could not get any answers from anyone or find out what was happening. We talked briefly about University Hospital and wondered if we had made a mistake in bringing Ryan to Meadow Grove.

After hanging up with Abby I called Dr. Lehrer's office. He was unavailable but his secretary called an hour later to say that he would like to meet with us at the hospital that evening.

Jim and I met him in Ryan's room around 6:30 P.M. Dr. Lehrer made no attempt to begin the conversation so I asked him to tell us about his treatment plan for Ryan. He said he had no intention of significantly altering Ryan's medication.

That surprised us. Before the hospitalization, Dr. Lehrer had agreed with Abby that a trial of Lithium might be beneficial. Now, the psychiatrist insisted that Clonidine was the *only* medication Ryan needed. Knowing our previous experiences with Clonidine, I was extremely doubtful.

Jim and I told Dr. Lehrer about the parent's meeting the night before. We explained how we felt out of place since all the other patients were there for substance abuse, not neurological problems. We expressed our worry that nothing about the hospital's program seemed related to Ryan's problems. We also underscored our extreme concern that Ryan's hyperactivity was agitating the other patients and that he had alienated Nikki, a hard-core gang member.

I told him that at University Hospital, most of the patients seemed to have neurological instead of psychological problems. Dr. Lehrer seemed surprised at what I said.

"Most parents do not *want* their kids hospitalized with schizophrenics," he remarked sarcastically. Dr. Lehrer then explained that Ryan's difficulties were entirely "fixable" by using behavior modification. He repeated again that if we would just "use a loud voice with Ryan from time to time" or "get up in his face" for a change, he could be controlled. Jim and I looked at each other in amazement.

Then, Dr. Lehrer asked if we had ever read Dr. James Dobson's book The Strong-Willed Child. I was really miffed by that question. I had quoted extensively from Dr. Dobson's book in the *RYAN* book. Didn't Dr. Lehrer even bother to read it? I wondered. It was obvious he had not.

Dr. Lehrer suggested that Ryan was acting out at school because Jim and I had probably said something to "undermine" the teacher's authority. He speculated that we had said something derogatory about the teacher in front of Ryan and that was the reason for his outrageous behavior at school.

That was all we needed to hear. Jim and I realized that Dr. Lehrer had absolutely no knowledge of Tourette syndrome, ADHD or OCD. It was also obvious that he did not have a viable treatment plan.

We left the hospital that evening in despair. We were distraught at what was happening with Ryan. We were also angry that a "professional" could be so unknowledgeable and seemingly incompetent. We had bent over backwards to give Dr. Lehrer the benefit of the doubt, and in doing so, Ryan had paid the price. Instead of helping Ryan, Dr. Lehrer was making him worse. His hyperactivity was going unchecked. I learned from the nurses that he was spending most of his time locked up in the time-out room. He was exhibiting extreme mood swings, at times being giddy and at other times appearing sad and depressed. He was having difficulty sleeping and eating. He was unable to do any work at school. His mouth had a huge red ring around it from licking his lips ever since Dr. Lehrer had discontinued Prolixin. We knew we had to get him out of Meadow Grove and away from Dr. Lehrer as quickly as possible.

The next morning I called Abby and was fortunate to reach her before she left for the meeting with the staff at Meadow Grove. I told her what had happened with Dr. Lehrer and let her know we would like to get Ryan out of Meadow Grove as soon as possible. She agreed it was a good decision.

I wasn't sure what to do at that point. I knew Ryan needed to get away from Dr. Lehrer and from Meadow Grove, yet I did not want to admit him to University Hospital again without having a good doctor. I called Dr. Curtis to ask for recommendations and then tried to match the names he gave me with names on our insurance company's "preferred provider list." I didn't have much luck. Two of the doctors that seemed like possibilities were out of town. After spending most of the day on the phone, I did not find a single possibility.

The next morning I called Anne, the admissions coordinator at University Hospital, and explained our situation. Anne advised me that I needed to make arrangements for a transfer with our insurance company first, but offered to do whatever she could to help.

After calling several numbers, I finally reached our case manager, Luanne Pringle, at American Behavioral Health. I described our situation, outlining the problems we were having with Dr. Lehrer and explained how Ryan was deteriorating while under his care. I was used to dealing with insurance representatives, but Luanne's icy response surprised me.

"We don't do transfers," she said coldly. "If you have a problem with the doctor, you need to work it out with him. We never do transfers."

I continued talking—trying my best to make her understand. As hard as I tried, I could tell I was making no headway. My only choice was to call Dr. Lehrer and get him to agree that a transfer would be in Ryan's best interest. I was amazed when I called his office and got right through to him.

I was very forthright, relaying our concerns that he was not being sensitive to Ryan's needs, and that he seemed to have a vague and ineffective treatment plan. I also told Dr. Lehrer of our concern with his lack of personal contact with Ryan. I suggested it would best for Ryan to transfer to University Hospital and I asked if he would speak with our insurance company's case manager regarding that possibility.

Not surprisingly, my suggestion was met with open hostility by Dr. Lehrer. He insisted that the only medication Ryan needed to control his ADHD was Clonidine. He also insisted we could control the rest of Ryan's behavioral difficulties with behavior modification. He didn't say it outright, but the implication was clear. He thought that Jim and I could not control Ryan because we had not been using an appropriate behavior modification plan.

I reminded Dr. Lehrer that we had been seeking therapy and using behavioral plans for the past *ten* years. I tried to explain that unless Ryan was properly medicated, he would not be able to respond to therapy or behavioral programs.

Dr. Lehrer vehemently disagreed with me and reaffirmed his assertion that Ryan's behavior was our fault. He adamantly declared he would not support a transfer to University Hospital.

I then asked if he would at least call our insurance case manager to discuss the situation, but he stubbornly refused. By the time I hung up, I was angry and more determined than ever to get Ryan away from a doctor who seemed to me to be incompetent. I knew calling Luanne Pringle again would not be easy. She had not left open even the slightest possibility that a transfer would be approved, but I had to try. I silently prayed as I dialed the phone.

When Luanne answered, I explained my dilemma with Dr. Lehrer and told her about his refusal to discuss a transfer. At that point, Luanne offered to allow us a change in doctors but insisted that a transfer was not possible.

I knew I was losing the battle, but I was still not ready to quit. I asked Luanne if she would at least consider speaking with Abby, our case manager at County Mental Health, before making a final determination. Luanne seemed annoyed with me, but she finally agreed to talk with Abby.

I waited all afternoon for her to call me back. Each time the phone rang I jumped, hoping and praying that a miracle would happen. Finally, late in the afternoon, she called. After talking with Abby, Luanne said that American Behavioral Health was now willing to consider a transfer. She cautioned that they could not resolve all the details so late in the day and told me I would have to wait until Monday for an answer. I was ecstatic.

That night, when we visited Ryan at the hospital, he was extremely hyperactive. He also was anxious and agitated. One of the aides told me he had been bouncing around so much they were having difficulty talking to him. I told her that I thought he needed a different medication for the hyperactivity and she enthusiastically agreed.

Ryan told me he had seen Dr. Lehrer at the gym that afternoon. He said that Dr. Lehrer was there to talk with another girl. When Ryan asked him if he was going to see him too, the doctor told him, "No, not today. You are doing good, Ryan. You don't need me to talk with you today."

The next day was Saturday. Jim, my mom and I visited Ryan right after lunch. He was extremely agitated and very hyper. During the whole visit he vacillated between being "up" and "down." The three of us noticed yet another increase in tics such as eye blinking and rubbing his fingers together. He was also widening his face—something new for him.

Later that evening, Ryan called home and said that Dr. Lehrer had come to his room to see him. I asked how long the doctor stayed and Ryan said he was there just a few minutes. He was bubbly and excited because Dr. Lehrer had promised Ryan that if he could be "good" for ten days straight, he could leave the hospital. After we finished our talk, I called the unit and left a request for Dr. Lehrer to call us before he saw Ryan again.

On Monday I was on pins and needles waiting for Luanne's call. When

I had not heard anything by 12:30, I called her. She explained they were still trying to work out the details of the transfer and that two of the medical directors would be discussing Ryan's case that afternoon. She also said that it was unheard of for them to do a transfer and that was why it was taking so long in getting everything arranged. She promised we should hear something in the next day or two.

That night at the hospital, Ryan was still very agitated. He was extremely irritable during the entire visit. He would not look at us and pushed me away, accusing us of not wanting him any more. Then, when we tried to leave, he started to cry and pulled us back inside the room. Jim and I took turns holding Ryan and did our best to comfort him.

I asked Ryan what he thought they were doing to help him at the hospital. He quickly replied, "Nothing."

Just then, Wendy, one of the aides, walked into his room and Ryan asked her, "What are they doing at this hospital to help me?" Wendy told Ryan that the "groups" were the main thing. Ryan told her that no one even talked to him during the groups—that no one ever asked him anything.

Wendy told him that he needed to speak up more. Then she looked at us and explained that the kids "really help each other" during the groups. Before we left, Ryan begged us to take him home and let him leave the hospital. I wanted so badly to tell him that we were working hard to get him out of Meadow Grove and back into University Hospital. Because nothing was certain yet, I could not say a word.

On the way home, Jim and I marveled that our insurance company was paying a huge amount of money for Ryan's hospitalization, especially since the only help he was getting was from the group sessions with kids who were in gangs and had substance abuse problems.

I waited all morning on Monday to hear back from Luanne. Finally, at 11:30 A.M. I called her. She told me everything was progressing nicely and that Dr. Gibson from University Hospital would be calling me later that day to go over a treatment plan.

I told Luanne about Ryan's increase in tics. I wondered if we should consider bringing him home until they could arrange the transfer. She said to just hang on a little longer—that it should happen soon.

Dr. Gibson from University Hospital called early that afternoon. He was very pleasant to talk with—quite a departure from Dr. Lehrer. The doctor said he was calling to review what he and our insurance company had in mind concerning a treatment plan and he wanted to get our view also. He told me our insurance company was leaning strongly toward the possibility of Ryan needing a residential treatment center if this hospitalization was not successful. He asked how I felt about that possibility and I conceded that we would at least be willing to discuss it.

Dr. Gibson also commented on the letter I had sent to the hospital director after Ryan's last visit. He said they had reviewed my letter and that there were definitely some constructive ideas they were able to address. He said he just wanted to make certain that we were on the same wavelength concerning the transfer and, after speaking with me, it seemed that we were.

We discussed which doctor would handle Ryan's case. Dr. Gibson said he had hoped to get Dr. McCracken but that chances were slim that he could take Ryan's case. He offered to assign Ryan to Dr. Marentini, the new director of the adolescent unit. He promised that he would strictly oversee Ryan's treatment and he assured me that Dr. Marentini would be much more involved than Dr. Mazzuchi had been during the previous hospitalization.

He also suggested that Ryan be admitted to the A-West Unit instead of A-South because it tended to be more structured. That unit, he explained, was generally for kids who had developmental delays, but that the current population was kids with behavioral and attention problems.

We also talked about his plan to review Ryan's medications. He asked if I thought Dr. Comings would make his records available and I assured him it would be no problem. He asked when we wanted Ryan to be transferred and I urged him to make the change as soon as possible.

Thanksgiving Day was just a few days away and that in itself was causing much anxiety for Ryan. He wanted to be home for the holidays. Dr. Gibson promised to call the insurance company right back and let them know what we had decided.

On Wednesday morning, November 25, I received the call that our insurance company had approved Ryan's transfer. My mom and I hurriedly jumped in the car to pick him up at Meadow Grove and drive him to University Hospital. When we arrived at Meadow Grove we found Ryan locked in the time-out room. The nurse Della told us he had been there all day because of his hyperactivity.

The ring around his mouth looked fiery red and he was licking his lips frequently. One of the nurses advised me I should "get something" for his dry lips. It was amazing. They still did not recognize a motor tic when it was staring them in the face!

I hastily signed the discharge papers, eager to get my son away from that horrible hospital. When I read the discharge summary, Dr. Lehrer had written that Ryan was "improved" and that he was in "good condition" upon discharge.

Chapter 24

A World of Difference

*"What do we live for if it is not to make
life less difficult for each other?"*[1]
George Eliot

Ryan felt disappointed that he could not come home for Thanksgiving, but he was agreeable about going to University Hospital. On the drive there, we stopped at McDonald's for his favorite "meal deal" and he was in good spirits.

When we arrived at the admissions office, Anne Kattner was there to meet us. After Anne completed the paper work, she handed me a form to sign and I noticed that Dr. McCracken was listed as the admitting doctor.

Anne said that, despite a very heavy schedule, Dr. McCracken had agreed to take Ryan's case. According to her, Dr. McCracken was "curious" about the case. She also said he wanted to meet with us at 6:00 P.M., if that was possible. I felt relieved that for once, things seemed to be moving in the right direction.

The A-West Unit was very similar to the A-South Unit Ryan was in previously. The staff this time was friendly, helpful and very cordial. There were still many forms remaining, but Lynne, the charge nurse, made completing them as painless as possible.

I noticed that one of the other boys on the unit seemed to be ticcing. A different boy, who seemed to be several years older than Ryan, appeared to be mentally "slow." The others showed no outward symptoms.

The unit was bustling with activity. Grandma Polly and I were able to follow Ryan into his new room and help him get settled.

215

Promptly at six, Dr. McCracken arrived on the unit and introduced himself. He had a beard and was younger than I expected. He asked if we would mind meeting in his office upstairs and we followed him into the elevator to the fifth floor. His office was at the end of a long hall. It was very small and seemed more like a closet than a room. Stacks of papers and piles of books lined his desk, shelves and window sill.

Several times on the way upstairs, Dr. McCracken apologized for having to meet with us so late. He was extremely sensitive to my emotional state and treated my mother and me with respect and what seemed to be genuine concern. We spent nearly two hours with the soft-spoken doctor, giving him a detailed history of Ryan and emphasizing the behaviors that were most problematic. Never once did Dr. McCracken glance at his watch or seem preoccupied. He ignored his phone which rang frequently. He gave us his full attention and several times mentioned his regret that he was keeping us so late.

I could tell by the questions he asked that he had an excellent understanding of Tourette syndrome and ADHD.

It was hard not to like Ryan's new psychiatrist. After our horrific experiences with Dr. Lehrer, I was highly suspicious, defensive, and skeptical of meeting a new doctor. After spending time with Dr. McCracken, I was, for the first time in a long time, hopeful that Ryan would get help. Before we left, Dr. McCracken said he thought he would be able to help Ryan and I believed him.

The next day was Thanksgiving. It was the first Thanksgiving Day that our family of four would be apart. Usually, Thanksgiving Day meant getting up early to watch the Macy's parade and putting the turkey in the oven. Instead, Jim, Julie, Grandma Polly and I went to the hospital and spent the afternoon with Ryan.

Ryan was sad about being in the hospital on Thanksgiving Day. He and the other kids had a nice turkey dinner before we arrived, but he didn't have much of an appetite. By the time we left the hospital it was getting late and the four of us were hungry. We stopped at a local coffee shop and had our Thanksgiving Dinner. I almost resented the waitress for being so cheerful and friendly. She didn't know that one of us was missing—that on the inside I was aching because it was Thanksgiving and our son was in the hospital.

During the first five days of hospitalization Dr. McCracken did not make any changes in medication. His plan was to first observe Ryan before making any drastic changes. During this time Ryan was extremely hyperactive and exhibited oppositional and defiant behavior toward the staff. He also was aggressive and even threw a chair in the cafeteria when he became angry.

It was like music to my ears to hear the staff reports. Several times Lynne would meet us at the door and report, "We are seeing *everything* that you see at home." As difficult as it was to see Ryan having so much difficulty, I wanted Dr. McCracken and the staff to experience what we lived with every day. How else could they understand?

Because of the explosive rage attacks, Dr. McCracken started Ryan on a trial of lithium. There seemed to be some improvement in aggressiveness; however, after ten days on lithium and clonidine, Ryan's tics were still quite severe. Dr. McCracken quickly tapered and eventually discontinued the clonidine and started him on Haldol.

I was initially hesitant about using Haldol again. Ryan had taken Haldol several years earlier, and it had definitely altered his personality. It seemed to "blunt" his spirit and although it did control the tics and help with his behavior, I didn't like the way it made him look or act. Dr. McCracken convinced me of the wisdom of giving Haldol another trial and I reluctantly agreed.

Adding Haldol resulted in a dramatic improvement. The frequency and severity of the tics were reduced to less than five tics per minute. Ryan also showed a mild improvement in his ADHD symptoms.

Dr. McCracken and Lynne initiated a behavior plan that charted Ryan's compliance in fifteen-minute increments. Lynne devised a chart and made up some paper "Ryan Bucks." For every fifteen-minute period that Ryan was compliant and behaved appropriately, he received a happy face stamp on the chart. The happy faces could then be converted into "Ryan Bucks" that he could spend.

Some of the things he could spend his dollars on were trips into town to McDonald's (his favorite), trips to the bookstore, candy bars, comic books, etc. Ryan quickly adapted to the new system and was able to attain quite a few short term goals.

Dr. McCracken saw Ryan every day. He would often take him on walks into town or play basketball with him outside on the deck. When he learned Ryan liked to pitch, Dr. McCracken offered to catch with him.

Other times they would meet upstairs in the doctor's office or somewhere on the unit. There was a world of difference between Dr. Lehrer and Dr. McCracken. I made a mental note to file a complaint with our insurance company. I thought if enough people complained, insurance companies might remove doctors like Lehrer from their list of preferred providers.

The time between Thanksgiving and Christmas had always been difficult for Ryan. This year was certainly no exception. As Christmas Day drew closer, he started to perseverate on coming home. As difficult as it would be to have him in the hospital during Christmas, I knew that he was still not ready to come home. Ryan pressed Dr. McCracken to give him an answer. He also wanted Jim and me to promise him he would be out of the hospital in time for Christmas. Each time we met with the doctor, that was all Ryan could think or talk about.

Finally, Dr. McCracken made a decision and broke the news. Ryan would need to stay at the hospital during Christmas. We were able to work out a compromise, however. He could come home on a pass for six hours on Christmas Eve and for six hours on Christmas Day.

Ryan seemed happy enough with the plan, although we had to reassure him numerous times before he really believed it. Still disappointed he couldn't be discharged, Ryan asked Dr. McCracken if *he* was going to be at the hospital on Christmas Day. In a sincere tone, Dr. McCracken replied, "If you are going to be here on Christmas, Ryan, then I will be here too."

Jim and I were happy Ryan would be coming home for Christmas, even though it would only be for a few hours. We were planning to celebrate Christmas Eve at Grandma Polly's house and Christmas Day at our home.

Jim, Julie and I drove to University Hospital on Christmas Eve to get Ryan. He was jubilant but behaving very appropriately. I noticed on the way home that his hands were trembling. He told me they had been shaking a lot lately.

We had a wonderful time together, exchanging gifts and eating lots of food. Ryan's behavior was perfect, but we all noticed something disturbing. Despite the festivities and the excitement of opening presents, there were times Ryan would sit in somewhat of a stupor with a dull look on his face. What disturbed me most was seeing his tongue slightly protruding. Seeing him like that reminded me of my great-grandfather who suffered with Parkinson's, and it scared me.

Around eleven o'clock that evening, we left for the long drive back to the hospital. The freeway traffic was sparse and the four of us were silent as we listened to Christmas carols on the radio.

The usually busy hospital was quiet and empty of visitors. A security guard was sitting at the front door and he stopped us for questioning. We explained we were bringing Ryan back from an evening pass, but he seemed skeptical because we had no identification.

Finally I asked, "Do you really think we would be bringing our son here at midnight on Christmas Eve if we didn't *have* to?"

He put down the phone and waved us by. We walked Ryan up to the unit and kissed him goodnight. He was sleepy but needed us to assure him again that Christmas morning would be "just like it always was." We promised we would be back early the next morning and that Christmas Day would be the same as always.

Jim and I were up early to arrange packages under the tree. We sat out a plate of half-eaten cookies and a glass with a small amount of milk left in the bottom, just as we had done for the past twelve years. Stockings, chock-full of small goodies, were hanging in their usual place on the fireplace, waiting for Julie and Ryan.

We grabbed a quick cup of coffee and again made the long drive to University Hospital. Ryan was ready and eager to come home.

He showed us a new video he received from the hospital staff. The staff gave each of the kids a chance to select something that cost up to twenty-five dollars and Ryan had picked a movie.

I thought it was great that the kids received a gift from the hospital. I felt disappointed, however, that there wasn't more. I had seen on TV where one of the professional basketball players had paid a visit to the children in the medical center to help lift their spirits on Christmas. Also, various companies had donated gifts for all the children that were spending the holiday in the hospital. I wondered why kids in the psychiatric unit could not receive the same attention and consideration.

We had a good Christmas day together. When we first arrived home, I fixed a big breakfast and Grandma Polly came over to join us. Later in the day, we had turkey, stuffing and all the fixings. Ryan said grace as we all held hands around the big dining room table. We read the Christmas story from the Bible and it was a wonderful day.

It was Christmas as usual at the Hughes' until the clock reminded us it was time to go. Again, we made the long drive back to the hospital and kissed Ryan good-bye. When we came back home, Julie was asleep in the chair. I sat down in front of our Christmas tree, mesmerized by the colored lights and shiny ornaments. Tears were coming much too frequently these days.

Although Ryan was showing considerable improvement, he was still having much difficulty at the hospital school. He was very hyper in class and often displayed "giddy" and silly behavior.

A trial of Dexedrine had been disastrous. It actually made the ADHD worse. Because Ryan was also having difficulty falling asleep, Dr. McCracken decided to add Tegretol to the Lithium and Haldol.

There seemed to be some improvement shortly after he started Tegretol. Ryan was calmer and his mood seemed much more stable. Several days after beginning the new medication, however, he started complaining of double vision.

Ryan had taken Tegretol in the past and had never had any side effects. I could only surmise it was the combination of Lithium and Haldol with the Tegretol that was creating the problem. Dr. McCracken continued with Tegretol for a few more days, hoping the double vision would disappear, but it didn't. The initial improvement we had noticed also seemed to disappear.

I had insisted all along that Ritalin had always been the most helpful medication in controlling Ryan's ADHD. Dr. McCracken, however, resisted using Ritalin. He cited the long-held belief that stimulant medications should be avoided in Tourette patients because they might make tics worse.

When Ryan's hyperactivity continued to be unmanageable, despite all the staff's behavioral interventions, I urged Dr. McCracken again to reconsider using Ritalin. I reminded him we had always found that Ritalin seemed to make Ryan's tics better, not worse. What is more important, it had always been wonderfully helpful in controlling the severe ADHD.

Late one evening, not long after Tegretol was discontinued, Dr. McCracken called. He told me he had consulted with another doctor at University Hospital who specialized in ADHD and pharmacology. They had decided to give Ritalin a try. I had to chuckle when Dr. McCracken started the dosage at 5 mg. three times per day. I was positive it wouldn't be enough, yet I respected his conservative approach and I trusted his wisdom. In short order, the Ritalin was increased to 7.5 mg. three times a day. The results were positive and dramatic. Ryan's school performance increased and the unit staff noted a marked improvement.

Although Ryan's hospitalization was originally to be only two to three weeks, it lasted nearly six weeks. Jim and I were very pleased with Dr. McCracken's treatment plan. Both in individual and group therapy, the staff tried to educate Ryan regarding his disorder. Many times he expressed his feelings that he was stupid or retarded and Dr. McCracken helped to reduce the personal blame he put on himself regarding his neurological disorder. The behavior program also seemed to be successful in helping Ryan keep on track and the "Ryan Bucks" provided concrete reinforcement.

Throughout the hospitalization, the staff at Landmark remained very involved. During one of the hospital staff meetings, Ryan's teacher, Luke, along with Abby, and Sherry O'Brien, our mental health case manager drove the long distance to attend. Gordon Miller, our school district's program specialist also attended. It was very encouraging for Jim and me to know that the people at Landmark still cared for Ryan. They were all quick to let us know that Ryan's place at Landmark was still open and that they would welcome his return. Even so, we all had some reservations about their long-term ability to manage him.

One thing that disappointed me during his hospital stay was the staff's decision to use Thorazine to calm Ryan during difficult outbursts. He hated the way Thorazine made him feel and would call home crying after receiving a dose.

Sometimes, a staff member would threaten to give him Thorazine if he didn't "calm" down. This would only hype his anxiety and make him worse. I never quite understood their rationale for using Thorazine. I wondered how Ryan would ever be able to learn how to control his behavior if they "knocked him out" every time he got out of control. On the day he left the hospital, I only half-jokingly asked Dr. McCracken, "Where is *my* thorazine?"

During the time Ryan was in the hospital I found myself fielding many inquiries from other parents of children with Tourette syndrome. I had thought many times about starting a support group in our area but always figured someone else could do a better job. Surprisingly, it seemed therapeutic for me to lend support to other parents, even during times of intense personal crisis. After sensing an urgent need, I enlisted support from two other parents and organized a local county support group of the Tourette Syndrome Association.

There were thirteen parents at our first meeting on February 1, 1993. It was there that Jim and I met Tom and Linda Piersma and Cheryl and Dave Novak. I did not realize it at the time, but starting a TSA support group meant the beginning of many new and wonderful friendships. By extending a helping hand to other parents, I found instead a wealth of support for my family and myself.

When Ryan returned home from University Hospital he was much improved, but still not one hundred percent. We were grateful that the Landmark School was willing to take him back and that they were not pushing us to pursue residential treatment. Unfortunately, while he was in the hospital, Abby took a new position with County Mental Health. Her leaving was one more transition for Ryan to make.

The first day he returned to school we developed an IEP that allowed him to attend school for four-and-a-half hours. This took some negotiation on my part and some sacrifice from his teacher Luke.

His new liaison, Nathalie, felt strongly that Ryan should only stay at school for three hours a day. Jim and I felt it was best to set high expectations for Ryan and pushed for him to stay throughout the lunch break and physical education. As always, we felt that socialization skills were just as important as academics. Luke offered to spend some one-on-one time with Ryan during lunch and I agreed if it did not work out, Ryan would go a shorter time. Also, we agreed to have another IEP in seven weeks to evaluate his progress.

Ryan had no difficulty in handling the four-and-a-half hour days. He was happy to be back at school. A note home from Luke shortly after his return stated:

> It is a pleasure to have Ryan back with us at Landmark. We will continue to work with him so that he can self-monitor his behavior. Most of all, we want Ryan to know that he is a unique and valuable person and we want to support him in attaining his full academic, behavioral and social potential. Also, when Ryan returned, 'Mr. Guinea' sang for the first time in months!

At home we were using the same "15 Minute Happy Face" chart they had used in the hospital. I always tried to remind Ryan every couple of hours how he was doing—also to physically hand him the "Ryan Bucks" he had earned for the period. The constant reinforcement seemed to work best in motivating him to do well.

The first few weeks he was home went fairly well. He had some problems respecting body boundaries and there was some immature "badgering" but nothing too drastic. On one day he missed six of his "happy faces." He impulsively threw orange juice at my face, ignored a request to take his hand off the gear shift in the car and his feet off the dashboard. Also, there were episodes of name calling, frequently burping at the dinner table, and going into Julie's room uninvited.

One of the most disturbing things we had to deal with during his first weeks at home was an increase in fears and phobias. On just the fourth day home he had a "panic attack" in the car over an imagined spider. Also, he was "seeing" (imagining) images of faces, bloody heads and tigers. These fears would strike suddenly and he would jump up and scream in terror. He also complained of hearing noises. Sometimes he would freak out saying that Biskit's eyes looked as if they were bugging out.

There were still many annoying and nerve-twisting behaviors that kept Jim and me on edge, such as farting and other inappropriate noises. These behaviors seemed to improve dramatically when Dr. McCracken increased the Ritalin dosage to ten milligrams. It was a pain, trying to remember to mark the behavior chart every fifteen to thirty minutes, but it soon became habit.

By mid-March the obsessions and fears were so severe that Dr. McCracken decided to try a trial of the antidepressant Paxil. There were times at school he would totally panic when he saw a cricket. He would scream loudly and run out of the classroom.

Sometimes he would describe feeling as if there were "bugs crawling all over him." The feeling was so strong and disturbing that he needed to leave school. Once, he jumped up and screamed with fear because he sensed a cat behind him. The cat turned out to be just a shadow.

He had also started "obsessing" on various themes, like buying something or going somewhere. Luke reported that during group, Ryan became so obsessed with what he was going to be able to buy on a class field trip that he had to leave class to call home. He was not able to engage in any class activities until this "gestalt" was complete.

Despite all the difficulties, Ryan always managed to keep his sense of humor.

Jim had to speak at a teacher's conference in Northern California and wanted Ryan and me to go along. Before leaving, we talked about our expectations for the "mini-vacation" and about the fun things we could do if Ryan behaved well.

Shortly after arriving at the hotel, Ryan became super hyper. He began yelling and jumping up and down on the beds, then jumping back and forth from one to the other. When we tried to grab him, he started throwing things and threatening us. Later on in the evening he began badgering and crying because he couldn't go swimming. When a security guard showed up at our door to check on the commotion, Ryan became frightened. He was afraid the guard was going to take him away from us.

I felt humiliated that a security person had to come to our room. When we finally got Ryan settled down, I took a long hot shower to calm my nerves. When I came back into the bedroom I found a hotel envelope lying on my pillow. Scribbled in large print, it said: *"Secrit Mesige."*

Inside I found a letter, printed in two colors of ink, along with a picture of a face with huge ears which I later learned was supposed to be Ross Perot. The letter read:

> Dear Mom,
>   I'm sorry I was a butt head but I'm going to try to make this vacation the best one you've ever had with me. I love you and I aint slow dancein' with ya either. I love you mom. Your beuteful.
>   Love, Ryan.

Ryan's grades on his April report card were all B's and C's. His teacher Luke reported:

> Toward the end of this five-week period Ryan has demonstrated a decreased ability to engage with his school work. There has also been an increase of brief incidents where Ryan impulsively acts out, including oppositionality to teacher prompts, loud yelling/cursing and three occasions of jumping on tables. After these episodes, Ryan has been able to regain composure and stay in program. These behaviors have been demonstrated with all four Landmark teaching staff. Ryan rarely has insight to his behavior and shows no remorse or embarrassment for his actions.
>   He has made tremendous gains since his hospitalization, yet in the past two weeks there have been more difficulties. We enjoy working with Ryan and hope to work with Ryan's parents, doctor and the Landmark treatment team to provide a continued successful experience for him."

I was impressed with Luke's commitment to help Ryan. Although he was not the only boy at Landmark with severe behavior problems, I was aware that he was, at times, the most challenging.

Although Luke and Rachael, his aide, were calming and stable influences for Ryan, some of the mental health staff presented some problems. Wayne, the time-out counselor often seemed to overreact to some of Ryan's behaviors and that tended to make him "escalate."

Nathalie, his new therapist and family liaison, submitted her resignation after only a few months on the job. After losing Abby and then Nathalie, Ryan seemed very unsettled. He was so dependent on personal relationships that any changes in staff troubled him

Nathalie's replacement was another social worker already on staff at the school, named Chuck. I only knew Chuck from seeing him around the school, but I was glad he would be taking Ryan into his case load. He seemed nice enough, and I was pleased he already knew a little about Ryan.

The first time Chuck came to our home for a family visit he sat on the sofa. That was about it. Jim and I waited for him to set the tone for the meeting, but he just sat there. I attempted to bring up various subjects, areas of concern, etc., but nothing I said elicited much reaction from Chuck. We figured things would get better with future visits, but they didn't.

Chuck was having much difficulty dealing with Ryan's problems at school. He was at a loss on how to help him with his obsessions and fears. Whenever Ryan started to act out, Chuck would zone out. During our home visits we would ask his opinion about what to do in various situations and he would just sigh heavily and then shake his head. I could tell he knew very little about Tourette syndrome or OCD.

Throughout April and May, Ryan's difficulty with obsessional thinking increased. Although he had his hamster, Daisy, at home and his guinea pig, Mr. Guinea, at school, Ryan determined that one of his goals would be to earn a second hamster. Of course, during the time he was "earning" the hamster, he was also obsessing—talking about it nonstop and badgering us to stop at the pet store every time we left home.

During one of his trips to the pet store a clerk informed Ryan that Daisy was really a male, not a female. He immediately changed the hamster's name to Harvey and decided that his *new* hamster would be a female so that he could have babies and sell them to make money to buy Nintendo games. It was all he could think or talk about for a week.

When he finally earned the money for the new hamster, he brought "Annie" home and introduced her to Harvey. They hated each other. It was soon evident that one of them was going to kill the other if we didn't get a second cage. Hamster cages had already cost me a small fortune. I had originally (and mistakenly) bought Daisy an inexpensive cage. I didn't realize that hamsters really required the very expensive ones—the ones with the colored tubes that twist and turn.

Spending money on an expensive rodent motel was only one of my problems. Daisy had a propensity to "escape" frequently. One time I found her inside a dresser drawer where she had chewed up a hand-knitted baby blanket I was saving for Julie. Many nights I stayed up late with a piece of carrot tied to a string trying to coax her out of a kitchen cabinet. By the time Annie came on the scene, I'd had my fill of hamsters.

A new pet store had just opened in town and I was able to get a new metal cage for Annie. Not too long after buying the new cage, Ryan decided to give her away to his friend Jeff. Jeff's hamster had died and Ryan thought that giving him Annie would make him feel better. In the meantime, Mr. Guinea needed a new cage. The one he was living in at school belonged to someone else, who now wanted it back. I had no idea that guinea pig cages were so expensive. I shopped all over trying to find a cheap one, but I couldn't.

Not too long after getting a new cage, the staff decided that Mr. Guinea and all the other pets at Landmark had to go. I truly believe that Ryan and his obsessions over the pets had something to do with the school's decision to eliminate the pet program. For several months he could do nothing but talk about and obsess over hamsters, guinea pigs and cages. It was impossible for him to concentrate on even a minimum of school work because of the perseveration over the pets.

At home, we were going equally bonkers. One morning, in an act of utter desperation, I wrote the following note and sent it to school with Ryan:

> Dear Luke, Rachael, Abby and any other poor soul
> who has had his life unduly chaotic for the past week
> due to hamster mania,
>
> Harvey the Hamster, a.k.a."Daisy," is now our
> only resident rodent and will continue until infinity
> to be our only resident rodent until he/she? expires.
> At that time, and only at that time, will we entertain
> the discussion of replacing him or her.
>
> Annie, the newest hamster, now resides with
> Ryan's best bud Jeff. She will not be returning.

Harvey is now living in the new $20 cage that I bought for Annie. The $60 cage I bought for Daisy is now in the trash, along with the $25 cage I bought when I first lost my sanity and agreed to buy a hamster in the first place. The $45 cage I bought for Mr. Guinea is now vacant and will remain that way until our next garage sale, at which time it will be sold with glee to the first person who glances in its direction. The cage that Ryan brought home from school that used to belong to Chris is coming back to school today and I trust I will never see it again in this lifetime.

The topic of hamsters and/or any other pets is totally PROHIBITED in this house until I have had the opportunity to regain what little sanity I had before all of this nonsense began. You may not be aware but I suffered from this same scenario a few years ago with a Kuli loach and some Chinese fighting fish.

If anyone has any questions about any of this hamster information, please do not call. I will be in my closet in the fetal position for the first few hours after Ryan leaves this morning and will be unavailable.

Sincerely,
Susan Hughes,
Victim of "Hamster Mania"

Several of the staff called to say they loved the note!

I always tried to keep a sense of humor, but it sure was not easy. The manic episodes Ryan sometimes experienced were horrible. During these times he would speak so rapidly that we could not understand him. He was tormented by hamsters, Halloween, his birthday, Christmas or whatever happened to come into his mind.

By the end of summer school, Ryan was still seesawing between good and bad behavior, and up-and-down mood swings. Problems with fears and obsessions were paramount, but the Landmark staff was still hanging in there with us. The July report card noted:

Ryan has averaged two episodes per day where he would become loud, rude and require time-out. On most occasions he would turn it around within twenty minutes. Ryan continues to have difficulties with obsessional thinking that gets in the way of academic achievement. Ryan also has periodic outbursts of obscenities. His fear of insects has seemed to diminish over the month. Ryan has a wonderful curiosity about life and we hope that we can continue to foster that at Landmark. We look forward to seeing him in the fall.

That summer we took another trip up the beautiful Oregon coast. Ryan was manageable but not particularly pleasant. We stopped at Lake Shasta on the way and Ryan had fun running his remote control car between the campground spaces. We celebrated his fourteenth birthday at a beautiful spot right on the beach. Coming home we drove through the Giant Redwood forest and picnicked beside beautiful rivers.

It seemed our family was always the center of attraction for other travelers. Ryan was always being too loud or doing or yelling something inappropriate. Even so, we still enjoyed each moment of "normalcy" we could grab. Jim and Julie and I were more determined than ever that Ryan would have the opportunity to enjoy the same things we did—even if that meant much sacrifice on our part.

Chapter 25

To Err is Human,
To Forgive Divine

*"Sending a child home in response to misbehavior delivers conflicting
messages. It says to the child that he can express anger,
but not too much; that he is accepted, but only on condition,
that classroom learning is important, but he can be moved from it.
A delinquent child may respond positively to suspension,
but a troubled child will see this as another rejection. When you
suspend a truly troubled child, you lose far more than you gain."*[1]

L. Tobin

School got off to a bumpy start that fall. There were many changes
going on at Landmark which meant a lot of extra stimulation for the kids.
The biggest change was a move to a new and bigger building. Besides
being in a new building, the Landmark Elementary Program and the Landmark High School Program were combining to form one school. Although
the facility was newer and much nicer, the changes were unsettling for
Ryan and many of the students.

Along with the physical changes there were many staff changes. Abby
got another promotion, and a new Landmark mental health director named
Barbara took her place. Wayne and Leslie were still there, but some other
aides were new.

During the first few weeks of school Ryan's daily point sheets noted
periodic goofiness. His personal goal at school was "I will not give up and
will turn it around." At home we were working on his getting up and ready
for school on time, having good personal hygiene, not being verbally or
physically abusive, and following directions with only one prompt.

By the end of September we were seeing a downward spiral in his behavior both at school and home. At school he was argumentative and acted goofy and immature. There was an increase in foul language and he had a few episodes of "screaming out." (He said he felt like he *had* to.) He vacillated between good days and bad. Some days he stayed focused on earning his points and working toward his goal. Other days he could not care less.

We were still not having particularly good success with Chuck, our mental health liaison. During one of our home visits, Chuck asked if we had ever considered putting Ryan on Haldol. This was particularly disturbing to me because Ryan was already taking 8 mg. of Haldol a day.

Chuck then asked what other medications Ryan was taking. He acted shocked when I told him Ryan was taking 100 mg. of Ritalin. He said he had never heard of a child taking that much Ritalin. It really upset me that the person County Mental Health was sending to help us did not even bother to know what medications Ryan was taking.

Chuck also confessed to having little knowledge about Tourette's, even though we had supplied him with much written material. For several months I had requested that the Landmark staff have an "in-service training" on Tourette syndrome. I knew of five other students at Landmark with Tourette's and it was evident that some of the staff did not have a clear understanding about how to handle a child with TS.

I had been serving as our local school district's representative to the Community Advisory Committee (CAC) and I was actively involved in special education issues in our county. It was during the fall CAC retreat that I first heard about the "Hughes Bill."

The Hughes Bill is California Assembly Bill, Number 2586, authored by Assemblywoman Theresa Hughes. The legislation was developed to provide a way to assess, analyze and provide positive behavioral interventions and monitoring for students exhibiting serious behavioral problems that significantly interfered with the goals and objectives of their IEP.

The Hughes Bill definitions of serious behaviors are:

- behaviors which are self-injurious, assaultive or causing property damage which could lead to suspension or expulsion

- other severe behavior problems that are so pervasive and maladaptive that they require a systemic and frequent application of behavioral interventions.

I also learned at the retreat that our County SELPA (Special Education Local Plan Area) had formed a task force regarding the Hughes Bill. The purpose of the task force was to review the legislation, establish county guidelines and develop a training program for county educators who would be implementing the new "behavioral intervention plans" in the classroom.

I asked the SELPA coordinator if there were any parents on the task force. She said there were mainly school psychologists from the various districts on the committee, but she thought it would be a good idea to include a parent. I immediately volunteered.

While working on the committee I learned the purpose of the Hughes Bill was to teach educators to look differently at the behavior of students who were in special education. The old way of trying to change a child's behavior usually did not work that well. Teachers needed to hear that they cannot wait for a child to "get his behavior under control" before they start teaching. It only made sense to try to change the environment before trying to change the child. The Hughes Bill also mandated "mutual responsibility" for the teacher, along with the child, to change behavior.

Some of the benefits of "positive" behavioral supports were:

- a longer lasting change in the child's behavior
- it would focus on positive aspects of the student instead of the negative
- it would maintain the dignity of the staff and the students
- it would teach an alternative, appropriate behavior the student could use to get their needs met.

The Hughes Bill certainly made sense to me. So many times Ryan would do something impulsive, totally out of his control, and the staff would suspend him or issue a harsh consequence. The suspensions and consequences never, and I do mean never, prevented Ryan from committing the same impulsive infraction again.

Traditional behavioral programs work well for "normal" kids. For children with TS, their misbehavior is most often neurological, not psychological in origin. Although at times it may look purposeful, it usually is not.

If a TS child has a "temper tantrum" or loses control, he is more than likely not doing it to get attention or because of any emotional problems. He is not full of "repressed" anger that he has to get out. He is also most likely not instigating a power struggle, or doing it to inappropriately seek attention.

The child with TS loses control when his brain cannot process information and stimuli properly. Unfortunately, most behavioral programs are a "one size fits all" approach that often is useless for children with Tourette syndrome.

I was excited to be part of the Hughes Bill Task Force for our county and started attending the meetings right away. I was anxious to see how the new interventions would work.

At home we were beginning to experience neighbor conflicts again. Ryan's obsession with tigers had also spawned an interest in endangered species and animal "rights." Ryan knew that one of the neighbors, who lived a few houses away, was a hunter. He had been in the neighbor's home and knew they had various stuffed heads of deer, bear, squirrels, and other animals the man hunted and killed.

One day something triggered in Ryan's mind and he went to the neighbor's home uninvited. He rang the bell and when the man's wife answered, he told her she was a "mother fucking bitch" because her husband killed animals. Then he came home and proudly told me what he had done.

Several weeks later something much worse happened. Another neighbor had a beautiful, young, black Labrador retriever. They were not always careful about keeping their back gate closed and many times the dog would escape. Several times, Ryan saw the dog running loose and he happily caught and returned it home. I used to always say, "That dog is going to be killed someday if they aren't more careful." I said it in part to make Ryan realize that he, too, needed to be careful about letting Biskit loose.

One evening, as we were coming home from the store, we saw the owner running toward the corner calling frantically for her dog. A short time later we learned the dog was killed by a car. The dog's death deeply affected Ryan. He was sad the next day at school and told Luke and the rest of the staff about it.

That afternoon Ryan was riding his bike in front of the house and Jim and I were working in the garage. The next thing I knew, the owner of the black Labrador was shouting at Ryan and chasing him down the street. Ryan rode into the garage with the neighbor in hot pursuit.

When the man saw Jim he screamed, "I'm going to kill that little bastard!"

"What did he do?" I asked. Jim and I had no idea what had happened. "He called my wife a whore and a dog killer!" the man shouted.

Ryan, who was standing behind us, yelled, "You *are* a dog killer! You didn't take care of your dog and you made it get killed!"

By this time the man was livid. He lunged toward Ryan and Jim stepped in front of him to block his way. He attempted to calm the man while I tried in vain to grab Ryan and force him into the house. It was an ugly scene.

I had been trying for months to set up a meeting with the principal at Landmark to discuss some suggestions that I wanted to offer. Although the Hughes Bill was already law, our county task force was still working on the guidelines. None of the teachers had received training yet in "positive behavioral interventions." Even so, I knew that some of the Landmark School's policies needed to change *before* the guidelines were developed.

Finally, in early October, I was able to arrange a meeting with Principal George Flint, Abby from County Mental Health, and Barbara Fairbanks, the new Landmark Mental Health Coordinator. I also invited Janice Baker from the Special Parents group to join me in meeting with the staff.

One suggestion I felt was important involved the school's policy on suspensions. Usually, whenever a student behaved inappropriately, the school would call the parent and then send the child home. I felt the staff should develop strategies that would permit students to stay in school instead of sending them home. I felt students should not be suspended for infractions that were many times due to their handicapping condition.

It also concerned me that the students at Landmark had only "play time" instead of regular PE. I suggested that Landmark students be given instruction in physical fitness and run laps, do push-ups, rope climbing, volleyball, etc., instead of just playing basketball every day.

Since Ryan had been attending Landmark classes for the past three years, he had missed the opportunity to have a school picture taken. I suggested that the school make arrangements for school pictures the same as they do at other "regular" schools.

I also recommended that Landmark students have an opportunity for recognition and that an "honors" program be established. Other schools offered recognition for "student of the week" and I felt it would be good reinforcement if Landmark students could have the same opportunity as their brothers and sisters who attended other schools.

I also requested that the school work with local universities to get art or music students to volunteer to work with the Landmark kids. In addition, most of our public elementary schools offer a D.A.R.E. (Drug Abuse Resistance Education program), yet the students at Landmark received no information on alcohol or substance abuse. I suggested the principal look into initiating such a program with the local police department as it would also add the dimension of establishing a positive relationship between the students and law enforcement.

I stressed my concerns to the principal about the haphazard way the staff had administered medications in the past. I urged him to put a system in place that would safeguard against mistakes in dosages. I suggested that they have a log that would state the time and name of the person dispensing the medication.

I suggested a midweek award and a long-term goal such as a class trip to Disneyland. I suggested a Career Day and classes on coping skills. I urged the principal to establish a system that would educate the bus drivers about our kids and their special needs.

I had a list of over twenty suggestions. He listened favorably to all of my requests and promised he would discuss them with the rest of the Landmark staff.

On October 7, I received a call around 2:00 P.M. to pick Ryan up from school. When Jim and I arrived shortly after 3:00 P.M., Ryan was running around outside the building. There were no staff members in sight.

Jim immediately went toward Ryan in an attempt to capture him while I went inside to find out what was happening. Wayne, the "time-in" counselor, was standing inside the building. When I tried to enter, I was shocked to see he was holding the automatic door shut. I motioned for him to open the door to let me in but he refused.

I could see Wayne was very angry. He shouted at me through the door, "Susan, you need to control Ryan!"

Since I was not able to get inside, I walked back to our truck where Jim and Ryan were standing. I asked Ryan what had happened while Jim tried to go inside. Wayne was still holding the door shut. When he saw Jim, he opened it slightly and threw Ryan's point sheet at him. He quickly shut the door again without saying anything.

As Jim was walking back to our truck, Chuck came running toward us with Ryan's point sheet in his hand. Jim and I told him how appalled we were at the way Wayne was behaving. We did not understand what was happening, or what Ryan had done to cause Wayne to behave so unprofessionally. Chuck asked me to come inside with him while Jim and Ryan waited in the truck.

He explained that Ryan had a wonderful day at school, earning practically all A's. Because of his points, he earned the privilege of going to the school store to buy something. Ryan had been saving up his points for a long time to buy a model car. He had placed the car on layaway several weeks earlier, just waiting until he had earned enough points to make it his.

Evidently, just a short time after buying the shiny red car from the store, Ryan accidentally dropped it and a piece of the metal broke. He became obsessed with getting the car fixed "right now." Even with the staff's suggestion of gluing it together, Ryan was not able to calm down. When he could no longer contain his disappointment over the broken toy he flew into a rage, slamming the car onto the floor and causing it to break into little pieces.

Chuck did not tell me what interventions they used, but I learned that someone allowed Ryan to go outside while still in a highly agitated state. Evidently, he was outside, running around unsupervised for a considerable time. When his bus arrived, Ryan began to run off and on the bus and persisted in opening and shutting the bus windows. That's when we were called to come get him.

When we got back home and finally got Ryan settled, I read the comments Wayne had written on the point sheet. He suggested that we use "home interventions" in the future to control Ryan's manipulating bus situations. It always amazed me. When mental health professionals failed in their attempts to manage the kids, they always resorted to blaming the parents.

That evening, after having a chance to review the situation, I expressed to Chuck my outrage at Wayne's unprofessional behavior. Knowing how he had handled situations many times before, I suspected that Wayne's inappropriate reactions to the car incident had probably escalated Ryan's behavior.

The next day, I called George and Abby to let them know how I felt. I explained my concern that Wayne had mishandled the situation and had caused or allowed it to spiral out of control. I felt that if Wayne had been successful in helping Ryan handle his disappointment over the car that none of the other behaviors would have occurred.

I also pointed out that the bus incident would not have occurred if the staff had not permitted Ryan to run around outside unsupervised.

I conveyed my worry that if Wayne could behave so childishly toward parents, how could we have confidence that he was acting appropriately toward the students? Abby and George assured me they would look into the incident.

When Ryan returned to school after the weekend, he was ready for a fresh start. However, when he got to school that Monday morning, Ryan was told he could not have any breaks or recess that day because of the bus incident four days prior.

Of course, Ryan became upset. He felt he had already ruined his new week. He started crying and began acting out. He was acting goofy and giddy. He then refused to take a "time-in" and called another student a fat pig. While they were escorting Ryan to the time-in room, he spit on a staff member, began screaming obscenities, and started kicking over furniture. Then, of course, they called me to come get him.

When I arrived at school I found out that all four of the mental health professionals who normally worked with Ryan, (Chuck, Abby, Wayne and Barbara), were absent that day. None of his support staff were there. During a time of crisis, Ryan was passed off to a new mental health worker who had no knowledge of Ryan or his disabilities.

The next day I talked with the principal and suggested it was not appropriate to invoke a consequence for a behavior that occurred four days prior. Children with TS, I told him, usually do not perform for rewards or punishments anyway. It's like punishing an epileptic child for having a seizure, I explained. You should teach him the proper way to handle his disappointment and anger. Don't punish him because he lacks the neurological control to inhibit the outburst.

After putting up with Wayne for the past few years I decided it was time to finally address my concerns to Abby, who was now his immediate supervisor. This was not the first time we had witnessed unprofessional behavior from Wayne. I had seen him lose his temper many times before. I remembered that Wayne had slammed the door in my mother's face one day when she went to pick up Ryan. Another time he physically held the door shut, keeping her from entering the school, much the same as he did to Jim and me.

I also told Abby how Wayne frequently seemed to become overwhelmed by many of Ryan's behaviors. Landmark was a school for children with severe behavioral problems. "Why then," I questioned, "did Wayne act so outraged when Ryan exhibited the very behaviors that caused him to be at the school?"

I also reminded Abby about another day that I had arrived to pick up Ryan and found him messing up the office and throwing small objects around. Wayne was just standing by watching, doing nothing to intervene. I was very suspicious and apprehensive about how Wayne was handling situations when I was not around.

Unfortunately, Wayne was not the only staff member causing me some apprehension. One day, when Wayne was not available, the staff sent Ryan to see Leslie, another mental health worker. When Ryan entered her room Leslie said, in the presence of other students and staff, "Oh no, not him again."

Ryan responded by calling her a "big fat bitch."

Leslie then retorted with sarcasm, "What did you do, Ryan, look in the mirror?" Then, there was another incident when Leslie reportedly shoved Ryan into the time-in room.

There were also other things occurring at Landmark that troubled me. One day Ryan arrived home complaining that two other students had been smoking at school. When I asked if the staff knew about it Ryan told me that Wayne knew and he just watched them take turns passing the cigarette around. Ryan also told me that another student carried a lighter in his pocket every day and that no one ever took it away from him. Knowing that the staff was allowing kids with severe behavioral problems to carry lighters to school was a big worry to me.

Of even more significance was the behavior of the other students. Ryan was not the only student to "go off" on a regular basis. In one incident, a larger boy, who was six feet, four inches tall and weighed about two hundred and forty pounds, picked Ryan up and threw him against the wall.

Ryan was much smaller, barely five feet, two inches and more than one hundred pounds lighter. This boy was also involved in other incidents of "beating up" smaller students. Because of confidentiality laws, the school never informed us about specifics concerning the other Landmark students. It was evident that many were adolescents with a history of drug abuse. One student boasted of being a devil worshiper and a few were gang "wanna-bes."

It really bothered me that children with TS had to be in a school with students who had much different problems. Ryan exhibited very difficult and challenging behavior, but it was not due to willful defiance, rebellion, conduct disorder, drug use or a propensity to be a gang member. His problems were neurological, not simply delinquency. I worried about the influence that the other student's attitudes and behaviors might have on Ryan. I wished he could be around students that modeled good behavior.

Another incident happened which reinforced my fear that some of the staff were not always responding appropriately and sometimes doing more to hurt than help Ryan. He lost major points one day because he turned the hose on and soaked himself all over with water. I later found out he did it because he had accidentally wet his pants. By soaking himself all over with water he was "covering it up" so that the kids would not find out and make fun of him.

Why couldn't the staff have discovered that? I wondered. Why did they have to punish him? Couldn't they have used the incident to 'teach' Ryan a better way he could have handled the embarrassing accident?

Too many things were beginning to occur which I felt were becoming obstacles to Ryan's success in the program. While Luke, his teacher, was wonderful, many reactions from other staff members were certainly not helpful and often were very detrimental.

By responding with sarcasm, the staff was provoking Ryan and causing him to misbehave even more. By responding with shock they were empowering him. By not responding at all they were allowing him to escalate beyond the point where he could regain self-control without restraint or outside intervention.

I was sure that if the staff employed pro-active techniques instead of negative consequences, they could have successfully de-escalated many of the incidents.

By this time I had already given up any attempt to work. After years of trying to juggle a career and Ryan's urgent needs, I finally succumbed to the emotional and physical strain and quit my job selling real estate.

The past year had been especially difficult. It was nearly impossible for me to conduct business at home when Ryan was around. It had also become impossible to conduct business at the office. Soon after getting to work each morning, someone from the school would call. Could I please talk with Ryan? Could I please come and have lunch with Ryan? More frequently it was, Could I please come pick up Ryan and take him home?

As hard as I tried, I just could not handle selling real estate and taking care of Ryan. Both were fulltime jobs and he was the more important of the two.

On November 3, Ryan had a great day at school. At the very end of the day, while waiting for the bus to come, he became hyper and started to provoke and rough house with another student. He ran onto one of the other buses and playfully and lightly "punched" another student on the arm "three" times.

I was attending a special education meeting next door and when I saw that school was out, I walked over to get him so he would not have to ride the bus home. When I arrived, Luke told me what had just happened. He described it as rough-housing and I had the distinct impression that it was not a big deal.

When we got home, there was a message on the answering machine saying that Ryan was being suspended the following day for "physical aggression" and "willful defiance."

I was flabbergasted. When I talked with Luke just thirty minutes earlier he had made no mention of suspension. I called the school to speak with the principal, but he was not in that day. Wayne, it seemed, had made the decision to suspend Ryan.

That evening Chuck came for a home visit and I told him that I did not agree with the suspension. After all, I argued, Ryan had a great day at school. Somehow, roughhousing on the bus had turned into physical aggression and willful defiance. Chuck sat on the sofa as he always did and sighed. He had a pained look on his face. Finally, he confessed he was "frustrated" at not being able to help Ryan and not knowing what to do.

He was frustrated? How did he think Jim and I felt to have a "professional" tell us how frustrated he was? I asked why he didn't call Dr. McCracken, or avail himself of the services of the school psychiatrist if he was feeling frustrated. He just looked at us and sighed again.

The next morning Ryan stayed home. I was still upset and called the principal to express my outrage at the suspension. I was really miffed. I conceded that Ryan needed a consequence for his behavior, but I maintained that it should not be an out-of-school suspension. "Suspending Ryan is like giving him a reward," I told the principal. "He likes staying home with me. Also," I argued, "if he is not in school, how can he benefit from the behavior program and the mental health counseling?"

George, the principal, agreed with me that Wayne should not have suspended Ryan. When I talked with Abby that day she also agreed that the suspension was inappropriate. We all agreed that we needed to research additional ways to handle those types of behaviors.

I was planning a trip to Houston, Texas a few days later to attend the national Tourette Syndrome Association conference. I was really looking forward to going and getting away for a few days.

On Monday evening, November 8, I returned home rather late from a Special Parents Support Group meeting. I could tell when I walked in the door that something was terribly wrong.

Jim was standing in the kitchen with a strange look on his face. I put my purse on the counter and waited to hear what had happened. Instead of speaking, Jim took me in his arms and held me tightly. He had tears in his eyes.

"It's your dad," Jim said softly. "He's gone."

It took a few seconds for the words to register. I slumped to the floor. My dad had died. How could that be possible? I wondered. He had just had a birthday a few days ago.

When I finally recovered from the shock of Jim's words, I called my stepmother in Cincinnati to find out what had happened. "It was very sudden," she said, "a massive heart attack. He died on the way to the hospital."

I spent that night trying to reschedule my flight plans so I could be in Cincinnati to attend my father's funeral. The next morning, I broke the news to Julie and Ryan.

Ryan was very young when we moved from Cincinnati and he had never had an opportunity to spend much time with his Grandpa Jenkins. When he learned I would be traveling to the funeral by plane he worried more about me dying than his grandfather.

The next day I called Chuck at school to tell him my father had died and that I would be leaving town to attend his funeral. I emphasized to Chuck my concern that Ryan might have difficulty in dealing with me being away from home. I explained to him that Ryan had a very confused idea about death. I told him it worried me because Ryan had been acting depressed again lately. He had brought up the general subject of suicide with his grandmother on several occasions and I felt the staff should know about it. Ryan was extremely nervous about me being away from home for five days. He had already started to "obsess" that I was going to die in an airplane crash.

I specifically cautioned Chuck, "If Ryan has any problems tomorrow at school or exhibits any acting-out behaviors, I wanted you to know what is going on in our family. In case any behavior problems occur, there may be an underlying reason for them."

I left before dawn the next morning to catch my flight. When Ryan got to school, he immediately started to worry that his mom was going to die. He began "obsessing" that my plane was going to crash. There were several acting out episodes that morning but nothing major. Later that afternoon, Ryan's friend Brad flew into a rage. While the staff was trying to restrain Brad, Ryan decided that he needed to help his friend and joined in the fracas.

At that point, the situation quickly deteriorated and Wayne became involved. When Wayne challenged him, Ryan began to rage. Wayne then physically forced Ryan into the time-in room where there was a small wooden table. Wayne then stood outside the door and held it closed.

While in the time-in room, Ryan picked up the small table. He threw it, breaking off the leg and putting a hole in the wall. He stayed in the room and finally, his rage subsided. Even after Ryan was completely calm, Wayne stood outside the door, firmly holding it closed. He kept Ryan locked in the room for over an hour until my mom arrived to get him.

During that time, Ryan made repeated requests to Wayne, pleading that he needed to use the restroom. Wayne ignored his requests and continued to hold the door shut. Finally, Ryan yelled that he could not hold it any longer, that he was going to use the floor if Wayne didn't let him go to the restroom.

Ryan had a history of needing to urinate frequently. He usually consumed a lot of liquids due to excessive thirst from taking Lithium. He often had episodes of wetting his pants at school from drinking so much water and then being afraid to go into the restroom alone. Wayne knew that about Ryan, but he did not seem to care.

Ryan tried to get his shorts unzipped, but he didn't make it in time. He was too late. When my mother got there, Chuck led her to the room where Wayne was holding Ryan. Wayne told her that Ryan could not leave school until he cleaned up his mess on the floor.

My mom helped Ryan look around for some paper towels, but they did not see any. She spotted a bucket of dirty water and a mop, but it was large and Ryan had difficulty picking it up. Mom tried to pick up the bucket, but she too, had trouble. As she was struggling with the bucket, she glanced up and saw Wayne sitting at a desk, laughing at them. Chuck was watching too. My mother was crying by the time she and Ryan left. As she was leaving Wayne told her he was suspending Ryan and that he could not return to school the following day.

I was emotionally drained after attending my father's funeral. Months of taking care of Ryan had also left me physically exhausted. My grief at losing my dad and the sadness of the entire day had taken its toll. Before going to bed that evening I called home to see how Julie and Ryan were doing. When Jim told me about the incident at school I was heartsick. I felt awful thinking about how Wayne had treated my mother—and about how he treated Ryan. I knew I would have to deal with it when I got back home.

When I received a copy of the suspension report, it indicated that Ryan had "possessed a weapon." Wayne insisted that because Ryan picked up the leg of the table that had broken off that he was "in possession of a weapon." It also stated he had destroyed school property. Wayne also noted on the report that Ryan had urinated on the floor. He did not mention that it was because he had kept him in a locked room and would not allow him to use the restroom.

I immediately made a request to the principal that the suspension report be corrected. I also requested that my statement be added to Ryan's file. I wanted it to reflect that I believed Wayne acted inappropriately by putting a child who was in a full-blown rage into a room with a table and then holding the door shut. If Wayne had handled the situation in a professional and competent manner, the table would not have been damaged.

I also suspected that Wayne's incompetence had escalated and perpetrated Ryan's sustained loss of control. I knew that this time I needed to consider filing a formal complaint. I had learned enough from working on the Hughes Bill task force to know that Wayne had used several interventions that the Education Code strictly prohibited. I scrambled to find the materials that would refresh my memory.

Under California Education Code Section 56365 I found several interventions Wayne had used that were prohibited:

- Any intervention which denies adequate sleep, food, water, shelter, bedding, physical comfort, or access to bathroom facilities

- Any intervention which is designed to subject, used to subject, or likely to subject the individual to verbal abuse, ridicule or humiliation, or which can be expected to cause excessive emotional trauma

- Locked seclusion

- Any intervention that precludes adequate supervision of the individual

I thought about the things Wayne had done:

- Denied Ryan access to the bathroom facilities

- Had subjected him to ridicule and humiliation in front of the other staff, students and his grandmother

- Had laughed at him while he was mopping the floor

- Had held him in locked seclusion (holding the door shut)

- Had not provided adequate supervision by jailing him
  in a room where he could damage property or cause
  harm to himself.

Besides the possible Education Code violations, I suspected that Wayne had committed a civil rights violation too. I called the U.S. Department of Education, Office of Civil Rights and spoke with a hearing officer. Before I could even finish telling him about the episode he said that he would be sending me the paperwork to file a complaint. "Holding the door shut to keep a person inside," he explained, "was the same as locking a door. Not allowing a student access to the bathroom," he said, "was also a civil rights violation."

I debated over what to do. I talked with Janice Baker from Special Parents and Paul Rhodes at County Mental Health. I seriously considered filing formal complaints with County Mental Health, the County Superintendent of Schools Office and the Office of Civil Rights.

I immediately called for another IEP. During the meeting the staff agreed to distribute written material regarding Tourette syndrome to all staff members. They also agreed to invite a speaker to do a presentation about TS.

Jim and I agreed that we would discuss a possible change in Ryan's medication with Dr. McCracken. We all agreed that we would work together to develop an interim behavior plan that would target physical aggression, property destruction, spitting, etc. We all agreed that some of the antecedents to Ryan's escalating behavior were:

- roughhousing
- joining in with peers' negative behavior
- verbally denigrating peers
- badgering staff for immediate desires
- verbalizing the urge to hit something
- fixating on immediate desires

The staff agreed that when they observed the antecedent behaviors, they would give Ryan up to two verbal prompts for redirection. If those were unsuccessful, they would give Ryan up to two verbal prompts to take a time-in.

If he refused time-in, two staff members would physically escort Ryan to time-in using NCPI (National Crisis Prevention Intervention) approved methods. If Ryan was unable to use the time-in process because he was out of control, we agreed that the staff could use NCPI techniques to contain him until he could regain control and complete the time-in.

The principal requested that Jim and I agree to pay for restitution for property damage. We maintained that we would *not* be responsible for any property damage Ryan caused due to the staff's inappropriate responses (like the table incident) but that we would agree to pay at other times. We all agreed to make this decision on a case-by-case basis.

We also agreed that the staff would initiate a "functional assessment" pursuant to the Hughes Bill as soon as possible. We also agreed to hold another IEP within fifty working days.

After the IEP meeting, I felt satisfied that the principal and most of the staff were genuine in their desire to help Ryan. Jim and I decided not to file a formal complaint against Wayne with County Mental Health or with the Office of Civil Rights. I was comfortable that the Landmark staff now had a very clear understanding that we expected them to follow the letter and the spirit of *all* the laws written to protect students with disabilities. We also made it very clear we would no longer tolerate Wayne's unprofessional conduct.

Although Barbara was the mental health coordinator for the Landmark School, Abby asked her to act as our family liaison. We all shared concern that Ryan had suffered from all the many changes and staff turnover at Landmark.

Over the next few weeks I could sense a sincere and determined effort from the entire Landmark staff. Everyone seemed to be very conscientious and did their best to help Ryan. Except for Wayne—he stayed away from Ryan.

Unfortunately, despite all of our creative interventions and valiant efforts, Ryan's behavior continued to be unmanageable.

It had become a family "tradition" to go to Knott's Berry Farm the day after Thanksgiving for their "Christmas Craft Faire." We always looked forward to ushering in the Christmas season listening to the carols, shopping for crafts and enjoying fried chicken and biscuits. Grandma Polly was planning to go with us and Ryan was excited because he had some money to spend.

Not long after we arrived Ryan spotted a game of chance where you could win a stuffed animal by tossing a ball into an inverted basket.

"I wanna try, I wanna try," he squealed with delight.

When he got Dad's permission to use one of his dollars he proudly walked up and plunked his money down on the counter. He threw both balls and they quickly bounced out of the basket. Then, he whipped out another dollar.

Seeing what had happened, I called to him, "Come on, Ryan. Let's go."

Before I could get the words out of my mouth he whipped out three more dollar bills and threw them on the counter. His dad and I both took off toward him at the same time.

"Leave me alone!" Ryan shouted, as he picked up two balls and quickly threw them over the top of the baskets.

Jim tried to talk to Ryan, but he would not listen. He was compelled to get a ball into the basket. When all of his balls were gone, he demanded that his dad give him some more money. Jim and I both tried to calm him down, but when he realized that we were not going to give him any more money for the balls, he exploded.

For the next few minutes he had one of the most horrific rage attacks we had ever experienced. He began hitting and kicking his dad and me. He shouted obscenities and called us horrible names.

Grandma Polly tried to intervene to no avail. People were gawking and staring. I warned Ryan that I would call the park security if he did not sit on the curb and give himself some time to calm down. He spit in my face and called me a "motherfucker."

I was at a loss what to do. I spotted a park groundskeeper and asked if she could please call security for me. Before anyone arrived we were able to get Ryan inside a large barn where there were tables for eating. I sat at a table with him and he continued to shout obscenities. The barn was full of people and they were walking by the table staring at us.

I warned Ryan if he did not be quiet I was going to get up and leave. He continued the tirade. When I stood to leave, he shoved me hard. I decided that I could not win either way. Going or staying, he was driven to vent his anger. He continued to shove and hit me.

When we got outside the barn, Jim was able to persuade Ryan to go to the car. He was leery of trying to physically force him in case someone would misinterpret and think he was committing child abuse. Then, almost like someone turning off a light switch, Ryan's demeanor changed and he walked quietly and calmly to the car with his dad. My mother and I were both visibly shaken and upset. After the "storm" was over we had a pleasant time. But it was a day I will never forget.

It was about three weeks before Christmas and Ryan was in the throes of his "high holiday anxiety." We had been seeing Dr. McCracken fairly often, but nothing seemed to be working. One day, as had happened so many times before, I received a call to pick up Ryan from school. When I got there, I saw three police cars parked in front of the building.

At the time I did not even know why Ryan was being sent home. Seeing the police cars frightened me. I hoped against all hope that Ryan was not involved. When I went inside, the secretary asked me to have a seat. She assured me that Ryan was fine. A few minutes later Luke came around the corner and started walking toward me. When I asked what was going on he explained that the police were going to arrest Ryan and two other boys. Suddenly I felt weak and sick to my stomach. Luke explained what happened as I followed him to the room where the police officers were questioning him.

Evidently, two of the other boys had gotten into an altercation. There was a scuffle of some sort and Ryan decided to join. He evidently jumped on the teacher's back and "nooggied" his head. The staff eventually called the police and all three of the boys were going to be arrested.

When I got to the back room where they were holding Ryan, a police officer came out to meet me. I heard him comment to the principal that Ryan Hughes seemed to be the only one that had any remorse for what happened.

When Ryan saw me, he looked pale. He was scared to death. The police officer asked me to join him in a different room. The father of one of the other boys had also arrived and he followed us inside. The officer asked the principal if he was sure that he wanted all three boys arrested.

"Yes," the principal replied. "I think it's important that we set an example for the rest of the students. These boys need to learn a lesson."

The officer began to write and then asked me if I understood what was happening. I confessed I didn't, that it was all new to me. He explained that the boys would most likely be cited and then placed on probation. He asked how I felt about it.

I told the officer that I did not believe that the arrest would "teach Ryan a lesson." I explained that Ryan had Tourette syndrome and that he took twenty-one pills a day to control his behavior. I told him that being arrested would not stop his impulsivity and, that instead of being arrested, perhaps we should consider another brief hospitalization to help stabilize him.

When the officer heard that Ryan was taking twenty-one pills a day, he informed the principal that he would not arrest Ryan. "It would be a waste of everyone's time," he said, ripping up the paper he had started.

While he continued with the paperwork to arrest the other two boys, I excused myself from the room to call Dr. McCracken. I was able to have him paged and he responded immediately. Ryan went back to University Hospital for two weeks during which time Dr. McCracken started him on the anti-seizure medication Depakote.

Depakote, which works much like Tegretol (which Ryan had taken previously), often controls aggressive behavior. We noticed some initial improvement with the new medication, although Ryan was still extremely difficult to manage.

Although not as aggressive, he was really "squirrely" and he never stopped talking. He was goofy and giddy most of the time. He was constantly provoking, annoying and badgering. He was in our faces every waking moment, and Jim and I were going crazy. He was not sleeping well—and neither were we. His bug fears were worse than ever. He was afraid to take a shower because he "imagined" things were coming out of the drain.

For the first time I was facing a new year without my usual sense of hope. Residential treatment centers had again become a topic of conversation. In fact, Jim and I had even visited a few of them. They were terrible. Only one was even a remote possibility for us to consider.

I was beginning to wish that *I* could go to a "facility" of some type. I often joked that jail sounded pretty good. At least in jail I could get three square meals a day, some quiet time, and all the books I could read.

I desperately struggled with my fear of getting to the point of not being able to take care of Ryan. In my hours of deepest despair I even thought of running away. I knew I could never leave Jim and my children, but I dreamed of what a different life would be like, what a normal life would be like.

I prayed that 1994 would be a better year. I was certain it could not be worse. I was wrong.

Chapter 26

A Time For Tears

*"It opens the lungs, washes the countenance,
exercises the eye, and softens down the temper; so cry away."*[1]
Charles Dickens

The TSA conference I attended in Houston was a wonderful experience, but again I returned wishing there had been less talk about tics and more emphasis on the associated "behaviors." My feelings were reinforced when one of the physicians presented a diagram he entitled, "TS Myopia."

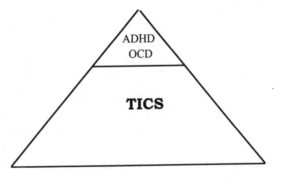

I recognized one of the adults with Tourette syndrome as a man who was featured on a television news program about the disorder. I had seen him at an earlier conference and I found him to be quite interesting. Despite all I knew about TS, this man's manifestation of symptoms mystified me.

During many of the sessions, he would spontaneously blurt out words.

It seemed as if he was "set off" by something the speaker was saying. Many times, his remarks were offensive, but at other times they were quite comical and elicited laughter from the audience.

One afternoon I attended a session on self-advocacy and civil rights and Jerry was sitting directly across from me. I watched with fascination how he seemed to feed off the audience's attention to his outbursts. After each eruption, he would gleefully glance around to see who was watching. With interest, I jotted down his outbursts during the hour-long session. During the presentation Jerry repeatedly shouted out:

> hurry up, tic me off, Mommy, what's a sheep?, fuck, Last Tango in Paris, What About Bob?, shut up, uh-oh, suck tic, what's a puppy?, hello, I got a gun, I tic for you, purple nigger, country western, book 'em Dano, and Jew you.

Each of the speakers just continued on, ignoring Jerry's outbursts. I remembered from the television program that Jerry preferred not to take medication for his symptoms.

I could not help marveling at the strange phenomenon of TS. Jerry and Ryan were one hundred and eighty degrees apart in their symptoms; however, each of them was equally challenged. I wondered how Jerry behaved as a child. I wondered about his mother. I wondered about his future, and, as always, I wondered about Ryan's future.

On the night of January 16, I was up late waiting for Julie to come home from a date. It had been a difficult day with Ryan and I was feeling exhausted. Julie had left me a note saying she wouldn't be late. By midnight I was starting to become worried. Julie was always punctual about being home on time and I could not imagine why she had not called.

By the time she and Joe pulled in the driveway after one o'clock I was a total wreck. My imagination had been working overtime and I was sick with worry. Before she even had a chance to come inside, I walked out to the car and gave them each a good tongue-lashing. I didn't care if they did have a good excuse, I was in no mood to listen. When I finally dropped into bed around 1:45 A.M., I could not go to sleep. The last time I remember seeing the clock it was nearly 3:00 A.M.

It seemed like only minutes later that a loud rumbling sound awakened me. When I felt the steady shaking and rolling motions, I realized we were having an earthquake. Without hesitation, I bolted from bed and ran toward Ryan's room. I met Julie halfway and guided her with me down the dark hallway. The whole house was shaking. I could hear things falling all around us. Ryan was screaming for me. Julie and I jumped on his bed and the three of us held each other close.

It seemed like forever before the shaking stopped. Usually, our California earthquakes are brief—before you realize what is happening, they are over. But this one was different. It just kept going. When the shaking stopped, there was total darkness, both inside and outside. Jim began searching for the flashlight he keeps under our bed. We finally remembered that Ryan had used it the day before and had not put it back.

We were fortunate to have no serious damage. Just a few miles away, my grandmother's nursing home had been destroyed. Although none of the residents were seriously injured, their building was demolished. That afternoon my mother, Julie and I went to be with Grandma during the evacuation process. The staff and ambulance attendants were moving all the residents to local hospitals until they could locate another building for them.

I was stunned by what I saw when we arrived. A large crack ran from the street, through the parking lot and across the floor of my grandma's room. Her window was shattered. Fortunately, Grandma and most of the other residents slept through the worst of the quake. Most were unaware of what happened until someone wheeled their beds into the dark parking lot that morning.

Ryan's fears intensified during the weeks after the earthquake. To make matters worse, Barbara, his mental health liaison and several other workers at Landmark left to help earthquake victims in another nearby town.

In the weeks following the earthquake Ryan's behavior at home deteriorated dramatically. We scrambled for solutions. We increased his appointments with Dr. McCracken. We adjusted the medications. We set new goals and award incentives. We reminded him that if he was not able to control his behavior he would need to go back to the hospital or to a residential treatment facility. Hearing that only increased his anxiety more. Nothing we tried worked.

During those weeks he was extremely hyper and goofy. He was irritable much of the time and flew off the handle frequently. There was an increase in hitting, kicking and spitting. He was also digging his nails into our head or arms when he became angry or he would pinch. He was demanding and oppositional, while at other times he was "clinging" and whiny. He vacillated from high anxiety to moods of sadness and depression. Mocking and provoking were constant along with verbal abuse and swearing. His fears were at an all-time-high and he was constantly "in our faces," afraid to be alone in his room or another part of the house. His speech was much too rapid and his voice was always very loud. He wouldn't (couldn't?) be quiet.

It was impossible to have a phone call and, if anyone came into our home, it was a disaster for everyone. There was the constant burping, farting and "rapping" noises. At the dinner table he would spit in our food or put his hands in his plate and squish the food around.

He would knock over laundry I had just washed and folded or jump or sit on pieces I had ironed. In the evenings he would hit us with his towel and throw his underwear in our faces. In the car he would yell out the window and poke us in the back of the head while we were trying to drive. At the market he would ram me from behind with the shopping cart or step on the back of my heels.

I was becoming physically sick from trying to care for Ryan. I was barely making it from one of his doctor visits to another. Even during the visits with Dr. McCracken, Ryan was non-compliant, demanding, obsessive and goofy-acting. I was drained after every visit. It did not help matters that we were having problems in scheduling our appointments with Dr. McCracken. There were a couple of mix-ups when we drove all the way to University Hospital and found the doctor was unavailable.

After one particularly disastrous week we arrived at the hospital and took our seat in the waiting room. Ryan was all over the place. He helped himself to some hot tea and then promptly spilled it all over the table full of magazines. After waiting nearly an hour, we finally asked one of the secretarys if she could page the doctor.

When Dr. McCracken answered the page we learned he had needed to leave early and had gone home. Evidently, his secretary had tried to call, but failed to reach us before we left home. Because the hospital was forty-three miles from home we needed to leave an hour-and-a-half before the appointment. The secretary suggested we call the next day to make another appointment.

I was devastated and didn't know what to do. We were desperate for help. I was also nervous from the hectic drive on the freeway during rush hour traffic and from the hour in the waiting room I had spent wrestling with Ryan.

On the elevator ride to the ground floor I became overwrought from the emotional strain. I started to cry uncontrollably. I felt as if I was going to faint and hurried to get outside where I could get some fresh air, but the fresh air didn't help. I could not stop crying. I sat down outside the building and the tears continued to pour. It was as if every feeling and emotion I had was fighting to get out.

Jim tried to comfort me, but I was barely aware he was even there. I began to feel nauseous and soon started to vomit. Even then, I could not stop crying. Jim went back into the hospital and requested that the secretary call Dr. McCracken again. When the doctor learned what had happened he seemed very concerned and offered to call us when we returned home.

True to his word, Dr. McCracken called and we had a visit by phone. He made several suggestions, including an increase in medication. I felt more encouraged after talking with him. Even so, I was aware that something had to change and quickly. I knew Jim and I could not take much more.

One day in early February, I took Ryan along with me to visit my grandma. She and several of the other seniors were moved to a private hospital until the nursing facility could make arrangements for a more permanent home.

During my frequent visits with Grandma, I always liked to take her outdoors in her wheelchair. Although she was blind, she loved to feel the warmth of the sun. As I pushed her, I would describe things like the colors of the flowers we passed, the kinds of cars parked in the lot, and the shapes of the clouds in the sky.

Ryan was cooperative about going with me to visit Grandma, but he quickly became bored. I suggested we both take Grandma outdoors for her walk and Ryan offered to push her chair. When we were outside the door, I moved aside so that Ryan could push his great-grandmother.

As soon as he gripped the handles, Ryan started to run with the wheelchair. I quickly caught him and scolded him for being reckless with Grandma. I reached to take the handles and he forcefully shoved me away and started to run with the chair again.

I had to fight with him to regain control of the wheelchair. Despite my screams for him to let go he continued to overpower me and push the chair. At one point, I looked down and became aware of how dangerously close the back wheel of the chair was to the edge of the curb. I shoved him out of the way and screamed at him to stop.

It was at that exact moment that I made the most painful decision of my life. I realized Ryan needed more help than I could give him—more than any of us at home could give him. All of my hard work, all of my advocacy, all of my devotion, all of my love—none of it was enough anymore. It was time for residential placement. From that moment of decision, there was no turning back for me.

My body fought an internal war over the next few weeks. My heart was crying out, "No, you can't do this!" My head, however, was saying, "You *have* to, for Ryan's good." Although it was I who first reached the decision, Jim was in full agreement. We knew that our marriage, our daughter, and even our very lives were at risk if we did not make a drastic change.

The staff at County Mental Health and Landmark were highly supportive of our decision. They knew how desperately we had struggled over the years to keep Ryan at home. I knew too, despite our occasional disagreements, that each of them had made tremendous efforts to help Ryan.

Gordon, the school psychologist from our local district, initiated the paperwork that would authorize Ryan's out-of-home placement. The first order of business was to change his special education eligibility from OHI (Other Health Impaired) to SED (Severely Emotionally Disturbed).

By changing the classification, Ryan would qualify for full funding while at the residential treatment center. Our local district would pick up the cost of his schooling, while County Mental Health would pay for all of his residential expenses. In addition, he would qualify for Social Security Supplemental Income. That check would go directly to the facility to help pay for his food, clothing and other living expenses. Medi-Cal would cover all of his doctor's visits and medications while he was away from home.

Over the next few weeks Jim and I visited several residential facilities and revisited others we had seen before. After careful scrutiny and much deliberation, we finally chose a facility in West Los Angeles. Many factors went into the decision. The fact it was one of the closest to home made it even more appealing. So many of the others were very long distances away.

Jim and I could not believe it when we learned the school we picked had decided not to accept Ryan. It had never even crossed our minds that any of the schools would reject him. Disappointed, we scrambled to find another.

By this time Ryan knew we had made the decision for him to go to residential. Knowing we had finally made the decision seemed to relieve his anxiety, at least for a while. He had lived under the threat for several months. He knew if he "blew out" of Landmark that he would have to go to residential. We had also tried to impress upon him the very real possibility that he would need to be in residential if he continued to be abusive at home. In the end, he accepted the decision valiantly and vowed that he was "going to get some help and get better."

Jim and I next chose a small residential facility located in a beautiful mountain town. The only concern we had was the distance from home—one hundred and fifty-five miles. Compared to the others we had seen, we felt that Pine Ridge would best meet Ryan's needs.

It wasn't a huge place—only twenty-nine boys in the program. The staff assured us they were familiar with Tourette syndrome. (How often had we heard that before?) The school's director told us they already had one Tourette boy who was doing quite well. He offered to show us a poem the boy had written about having TS.

None of the facilities we had visited were a mother's dream. Although most were clean, there were holes in the walls, dents in the furniture, stains on the carpets and tears in the curtains. They all looked as if many boys with ADHD lived there. I knew I had to get beyond the aesthetics. I had to keep reminding myself why Ryan was leaving home. I relied heavily on motherly instinct in making our decision. Of all the places we visited, I could mentally picture Ryan at Pine Ridge and had a "feeling" it was the best place for him, considering all the others we saw.

Despite my feelings about Pine Ridge's suitability, we still did some checking. I was able to obtain the names of two parents whose children were in the program, both of whom were also from our county. I spoke with each mother by phone and got as much information from them as possible.

I also called the county's Community Care Licensing Bureau to ask if there had been any complaints or any serious violations filed. The officer I spoke with informed me of two very minor incidents. I felt satisfied after speaking with him that Pine Ridge was a safe place and that they would take good care of Ryan.

While we were waiting to learn if Pine Ridge was going to accept Ryan, Daisy (a.k.a. Harvey) the hamster died. I found her already entered into eternal glory when I went in one morning to wake Ryan for school. He took the hamster's death fairly well and seemed to find comfort in handcrafting a "tombstone" out of plywood.

A short time later we received word that Pine Ridge was going to accept Ryan into their program. We began making arrangements to prepare him for the transition.

At school, they quickly planned a good-bye party. The staff and all the boys in his class went to a local pizza restaurant to eat and play video games. His teacher Luke brought a delicious chocolate cake that he had made and decorated himself. Ryan's friend Michael won a stuffed animal in one of the games and gave it to Ryan as a going away present. Everyone was upbeat and Ryan seemed to avoid becoming too emotional about leaving his friends and the staff that had been so much a part of his life for the past four years.

At home, Ryan's upcoming departure was met with sad resolve. As the day approached, I found it increasingly difficult to contain my sadness. I knew I could not let Ryan know how much I was hurting, yet I felt he needed to know how desperately we wanted him to be able to stay at home. My biggest fear was that he would feel that we were "giving up" on him or that we did not want him. As much as we reassured him, I knew that he must have his doubts.

A couple of days before he was to leave, we had a family party at Grandma Polly's house. It was Jim's and my birthday also, but the celebration was in honor of Ryan. He always loved it when the whole family gathered for a party or special dinner together. This night, it was clear that his mind was on leaving. Despite the brave facade, I could see the sadness underneath.

The night before he left home, Jim, Ryan and I went to the park behind our house to fly his paper airplanes. As I sat on the hill watching father and son, it was almost as if I were having a dream. It was all so perfect. We were together, playing in the park and having a good time.

Why can't it be this way all the time? I wondered. Why does Ryan have to leave us tomorrow? Too soon it was time to go home and start packing his things.

Julie's boyfriend (and Ryan's best friend) Joe came over to say good-bye. He helped Ryan pack his trunk with all the things he wanted to take—his stuffed tigers, CD player, Walkman, tapes, Nintendo player and games, magic tricks and several decks of cards. I tucked in a photo album of family pictures, his Bible, and some stationery with pre-addressed stamped envelopes to mom.

That night, before he went to sleep, Ryan came in my room as I was getting ready for bed. He handed me a small plastic figure of a baseball player that he had saved from one of his birthday cakes years earlier.

"Here Mom," he said in a low voice. "Keep this on your dresser so you will remember me while I'm gone." I could no longer hold in my tears.

I reached down to hug him, to hold him, hoping to somehow make him realize that we could never, ever forget him—that he would be with us in our hearts and thoughts every day.

I couldn't sleep that night. My heart was breaking. Even though I knew we needed to give the residential treatment center a try, the thought of sending Ryan away to be cared for by strangers was more than I could bear.

Doubts flooded my mind. What if they got his medications mixed? What if they mistreated him? What if another student hurt him? What if he were sexually abused? What if there were an earthquake and we couldn't reach him? What if he were bitten by a rattlesnake while in the mountains? What if he were homesick? What if he felt depressed? What if he tried to run away? What if he broke an arm? What if?, etc.

All night long I came up with "what if" questions and then tried to reason them out in my mind. It seemed as if I never even got to sleep before the alarm was ringing.

Jim, Julie, Grandma Polly, and Ryan and I piled his things into the back of our truck. It was time for us to leave for the long ride to Pine Ridge. We decided we would stop for breakfast midway to help break up the long drive. We all ordered big breakfasts, but none of us could eat much.

Ryan sat in the back seat between his grandma and me. He hardly spoke but held my arm tightly and rested his head on my shoulder. We all tried our best to be upbeat. We talked of all the fun things he would get to do at Pine Ridge, and we made plans to see him in two weeks. Knowing that he would see us in just a couple of weeks seemed to please him, but he hardly did more than manage a half-smile.

The one hundred and fifty-five miles to Pine Ridge seemed like one million that morning. When we finally arrived and turned into the long driveway leading to the main building, Ryan spotted a small dilapidated-looking shack. He bolted upright in the seat and asked with a frightened look, "Is that where they put you when you're bad?"

My heart sank. Somehow, we had not fully convinced him that no one would mistreat him. I had talked with him about the importance of telling someone if anyone ever did anything to hurt him. Somehow, he must have envisioned that residential was a place they would lock you up if you mis-behaved. How many other unspoken fears did he harbor? My stomach was churning with anxiety and raw nerves.

When we arrived at the administration office, the school's director Marty ushered us into his office. Assistant Director Lorraine, Residential Supervisor Donna, and Karen, the school nurse, soon joined us. I had only been seated a minute when I felt the sting of tears in my eyes.

I can't cry, I thought to myself. I can't let Ryan see me cry. I had promised myself I would not cry. I hated my body for betraying me.

I suddenly felt as though the room was closing in on me. I knew I had to get out of that room before I exploded. I quietly excused myself and walked out onto the wooden porch. I was trying hard to fight back the tears and was having no success. I fumbled in my pocket to find a tissue but could find none. I heard the door open behind me and suddenly felt Ryan's arms around my waist.

"Don't cry, Mommy," he said. "I'm going to be okay here."

"I am so sorry, honey," I blubbered. "I know you are going to be just fine here." I quickly wiped my tears on my sleeve and followed Ryan back inside the office.

We filled out the paperwork and signed release forms. Jim and I made it very clear we did not want the school's psychiatrist changing any medications without conferring with Dr. McCracken first. They all assured us that would not be a problem.

The school's psychiatrist was not on site. His office was in a small town, twelve miles away at the foot of the mountain. The boys would visit the doctor only once each month. If there was a medical emergency, they would go to a local clinic just four miles away.

One of the hardest things for me that morning was turning over Ryan's medications. At the time he entered Pine Ridge he was taking six of them: Haldol, Lithium, Depakote, Ritalin, Anafranil and Synthroid.

Keeping track of his medications and making sure Ryan got them all at the correct times was a tremendous job for me. I worried immensely that the school staff would make a mistake. It took all the strength I could muster to hand the bottles of pills to the nurse. I questioned her at length about the procedures the staff would follow. She assured me there were only certain staff members authorized to administer medications and that they were all very careful.

After we finished the paperwork it was time to take Ryan's things to his room. Normally, all new students had to start in Dorm Three, the dorm that was nearest the cafeteria and the staff room. I was nervous about Ryan being in Dorm Three. That dorm, besides being for new kids, was also the dorm for the "worst" kids. It was also the worst-looking dorm. The walls were dirty and had holes in them.

I could not bear the thought of Ryan being in a dorm with a bunch of violent kids. Evidently, expressing my concerns made a difference. When they led us to Ryan's room, it was in Dorm Two, which was a much nicer dorm.

The kids in Dorm Two typically needed less supervision. The bedrooms all opened into a large "family room" with a sofa, game table and a television set. Two boys were assigned to each bedroom. Ryan's roommate was Anthony, a boy from our county. Ryan had met Anthony at Landmark several years before and seemed happy that he already knew someone at Pine Ridge.

While unpacking Ryan's things, we heard a commotion outside. One of the boys in the TV room saw us looking out the window and said, "Don't pay any attention to that. It's only Isaiah. They'll catch him."

I cringed when I saw a small boy running across the lawn being chased by two older-looking men. He had only gone a short distance when one of the men grabbed the boy's arm and pushed him to the ground. In a second, both men were kneeling, holding the boy face down on the ground.

The boy on the sofa continued, looking up at Ryan. "You wanna stay away from Isaiah," he cautioned. "He's crazy." Ryan looked up at me with a scared look in his eyes. I put my arm around him and assured him that we would talk to Marty and Donna about Isaiah.

When I mentioned it to them, they told us Isaiah was just having a little difficulty because he was new. They assured us that he was usually no problem and that the staff always kept him under supervision. They promised Ryan he had nothing to fear.

Ryan wanted to take his sister, Julie, on a tour of his new school. Donna led the way and we all went for another look at the classrooms, the laundry room, the gymnasium and the cafeteria. Much too soon, it was time to say good-bye.

I was determined not to cry again, if it killed me. Donna stood with us beside the truck as Ryan hugged his dad, Julie and Grandma Polly. By the time he came to me he was crying.

"I don't want you to go, Mommy," he said, brushing tears from his cheek.

Seeing Ryan cry caught me completely off guard. I hugged him tightly and we each cried softly. Then, I gently pushed him away. Donna reached for his arm and he obediently let go of me. I turned to get into the truck, afraid to look at Ryan. As Jim slowly turned the truck onto the driveway, I glanced up and saw him holding Donna's hand with one hand and waving with the other. Tears were rolling down his face.

As the truck slowly moved away I flashed him our "I love you" hand sign and he did the same. I watched out the window as Donna coaxed him to walk up the hill to one of the buildings. As the truck moved farther and farther away, I strained for a last glimpse. Then, it was over. He was gone.

I could hear my mother weeping in the back seat. Julie was pale and Jim's face looked pained. I wept silently for the next hundred miles. I was glad no one felt like talking. I wanted to be alone with my thoughts—alone with my pain.

After we had driven a couple of hours, we decided to stop for coffee and something to eat. Once inside the restaurant we could barely talk. With no warning at all, tears would start to fall.

My mom commented on how much taking Ryan to Pine Ridge felt like going to a funeral. I thought it felt worse. I felt as if my heart were being ripped from my chest when I saw my son walking away with a stranger.

When we arrived home that night I could not bring myself to look in the direction of Ryan's room. I wondered how I could bear seeing his things again. It would hurt too much. I was eager to drop into bed. I was exhausted. If I'm asleep, I reasoned, then I can't feel the pain.

Chapter 27

Just What
the Doctor Ordered

*"Keep away from people who belittle
your ambitions. Small people do that, but the really
great make you feel that you, too, can become great."*[1]
Mark Twain

The next morning, I barely remember hearing Jim get up for work. I vaguely remember him hugging and kissing me good-bye, but I fell right back to sleep again. Around eight o'clock, I was awakened by a familiar rumbling sound. I was still half asleep and it seemed like part of a dream until a loud horn jolted me into awareness. It was Ryan's school bus!

I raised up enough to see the bright yellow bus sitting in front of our house. Why is it here? I wondered. The school had said they would let the bus company know about the change.

The horn sounded two more times. Finally, it slowly pulled away from the curb.

Having Ryan's bus come was more than I could bear. I started to cry again. After what seemed like a long time, I got out of bed and slowly made my way into Ryan's room. I fell onto his bed and sobbed, hugging his stuffed animals tightly. I cried until I thought I could cry no more. Then, more tears would erupt again. I was overwhelmed with grief. The phone rang but I could not answer. I didn't know who would be at the other end.

I needed to talk to my friend Cheryl. She had been through this situation when her son was only nine and somehow she survived. I called her at work and started blubbering incoherently.

"When will it quit hurting, Cheryl?" I pleaded. "It just hurts so much.

When will the pain go away?"

That morning, Cheryl gave me the best advice possible. We had been friends for several years and had shared many similar difficult situations with our sons. She and her husband had been with Jim and me throughout the past few painful months. I knew that she, more than anyone else, could help me put things in perspective. I will never forget what she told me that morning.

"Please don't get mad at me," Cheryl said. "But I really think you should call the doctor and get on Prozac. It has really helped me. I think you should quit trying to be so damn strong and take something to help you through this rough time."

I fussed, like I always do with Cheryl, but this time she was dead serious. She would not hang up until I promised to call the doctor, immediately. Worse yet, she threatened to call back in ten minutes to check and see if I had called him yet.

I knew Cheryl was right. For years, at my annual check up, the doctor would ask if I wanted something to "help" me in dealing with Ryan. "No, thank you," I was quick to say. "I can handle it myself."

I hated taking medication. I was determined I didn't need to take anything—that I could handle everything on my own. I had even perfected ways to cope with the waves of depression that taunted me. I would pour myself into my volunteer work with TSA. I would write, diet or exercise, pray, and listen to music—anything to divert my thoughts from my sadness over Ryan's difficulties. This time, however, was different. I was ready for Prozac.

I wasn't feeling strong enough to deal with Cheryl's wrath so I called the doctor and made an appointment. He was happy to write the prescription and said it might take a couple of weeks to work. I found that it only took a couple of days. Jim and Julie were the first to notice.

My grandmother died only two days after Ryan went to Pine Ridge. My grief for the next few weeks seemed unbearable. I was grateful to have the Prozac and feel that it was extremely beneficial in helping me through a time of overwhelming emotional pain and despair.

After our painful separation, Ryan seemed to adjust fairly well to being at Pine Ridge. We spoke to him every day. I could always tell by the tone of his voice how things were going.

Just a couple of weeks after being there, he seemed particularly sad one evening. I coaxed him into telling us what was wrong and he finally said that some of the staff were being mean to the kids.

Ryan related an incident that occurred in the dining room. Two of the staff members were physically restraining one of the other boys while Ryan was present. According to him, one of the female staff members taunted the boy by saying, "Come on, do it again. *Give* me a reason to slap you." It upset Ryan that the two staff members were laughing and joking while restraining the student. He talked about this incident the next three evenings.

Another incident happened around that time involving the same female staff member. Her comments disturbed Ryan so much that he went back to his dorm and copied the words down so he wouldn't forget. They were: "You are a very unpleasant little boy. I don't know what universe you came from. You are spoiled."

When Ryan told us about the woman's comments we encouraged him to speak with Marty or Lorraine. We did not want him to think he could "tattle" on the staff to us, and we emphasized the importance of him handling these types of situations himself in an appropriate way. Several nights later Ryan told me he had "tried" to talk to the staff but that no one would listen to him. Another incident had also happened with a different staff member who grabbed Ryan and screamed at him that he was "spoiled." Ryan admitted he had been acting like a jerk. Even so, the way some of the staff was responding to his behavior concerned me.

I wrote a letter to Marty, the director of the school, outlining my concerns. In the letter I noted that Jim and I have worked extremely hard over the years to learn how to deal appropriately with Ryan's behavior. One of the first things we learned was that the language you use in dealing with these types of children is very important. You attack the child's behavior, not the child himself.

I assured Marty that we realized how extremely taxing and frustrating Ryan's oppositionality can be. We stressed our hope that the staff would react with words and interventions that did not involve sarcasm, or demean Ryan and ultimately escalate his behavior.

Ryan's weekly level scores were erratic the first two months at Pine Ridge. I had requested that the staff mail or fax me a copy of his level sheets each week so I could see the times of day he was having difficulty. I also wanted to know so that Jim and I could commend him for the times he had positive scores and encourage him to keep trying in the areas where he was having difficulty. Although Lorraine promised to send copies to me and to Gordon Miller, we found it difficult to get them.

Gordon and I had tried to impress on the school the importance of incorporating a Behavioral Intervention Plan. We had already completed a "functional analysis" before Ryan left Landmark and we thought that Pine Ridge could use that in helping to develop their plan. Unfortunately, Gordon and I learned that the Pine Ridge staff had done nothing to implement the Hughes Bill regulations, even though they became law in May of 1993.

In my letter to Marty, I asked when the Pine Ridge staff would be receiving training in positive interventions (Hughes Bill), and I asked who they would designate as the Behavioral Intervention case manager. Marty later told me they were "working" on finding out more about it.

One of the first things I noticed when I received the score sheets was that Ryan was losing an inordinate amount of points for a single instance of noncompliance. If, for example, Ryan refused to take directions, a staff member might threaten to take away more points. Then, instead of complying, Ryan would respond with an inappropriate comment that would cause him to lose more points. If the staff member then commented that he had lost the additional points, Ryan would usually escalate more and could lose hundreds of points in just a couple of minutes.

Gordon Miller and I had to constantly remind the staff to work within the frameworks of the Behavioral Intervention Plan we developed. As part of that plan the Pine Ridge staff agreed that a "chain" of behaviors would count only as one incident.

Also, we encouraged the staff to increase the number of points Ryan could earn for "positive" behaviors. The ones that we added included bonus points for following directions, staying on task, ignoring provoking, asking for a time-out and consulting a staff member when he had a problem.

The administrative staff was generally cooperative in working with us on the use of the Behavioral Intervention Plan. We found, however, that the information seldom made it down to the staff who worked with Ryan— especially the ones on the evening and weekend shifts.

I knew I was a nuisance to the staff at Pine Ridge. Many, maybe even most, of their students did not have parents who were involved. There were some boys there whose parents never visited or allowed their sons to go home for a pass. Many of the boys' stories were very sad. Some had histories of being sexually abused. One boy was autistic, and several had Tourette syndrome. Another boy, Mark, had been there for nearly five years.

None of the parents had ever requested to see copies of the weekly level sheets and none had ever mentioned a "Behavioral Intervention Plan." We were also one of the few parents who talked with our son every day and visited often. Many of the parents, it seemed, were happy to have someone else caring for their child.

To me, having Ryan in a residential treatment facility required a fulltime "hands-on" approach. There was always something going wrong or someone doing something wrong. One day in early May, Ryan told his dad and me about a teacher named Roland.

Roland, he explained, had embarrassed him in front of the class. He had ridiculed him about his fear of bugs and spiders and his other phobias.

When we questioned Ryan we learned that Roland had told him, in front of the class, that he really didn't have Tourette syndrome at all. When Ryan tried to convince them that he did have TS, Roland said, "I don't see you having any tics. If you had Tourette syndrome, you would have tics."

Ryan persisted, telling Roland that his doctor had *told* him he had Tourette's. Roland then said, "That's how your doctor makes money—if he didn't tell people they had Tourette syndrome, he wouldn't make any money." Ryan gave up trying to convince the teacher. The other boys were all laughing and taunting him that he really did not have Tourette's. He felt embarrassed and humiliated.

Of course, when Jim and I heard what happened, we were livid. I immediately called Betty, one of the supervisors, and asked that she investigate. She called me back a short time later and assured me she had resolved the situation. She said that Roland would be calling me the next day.

When he called (three days later), I told him he was not seeing many tics because Ryan was taking a lot of medication to control them. He told me he was not aware of that and had no idea that Ryan took twenty-one pills a day. Roland apologized and told me that he would be more sensitive in the future and would try to learn more about Tourette syndrome. I suggested it would be appropriate for him to apologize to Ryan in front of the class and he said that he would.

It really made me angry that the staff members did not know anything about the students' disabilities. They did not know which ones were taking medication, which medications they were taking, or for what reason.

It seemed that we were always putting out little fires that erupted with various staff members. It was a classic case of the right hand not know what the left was doing, or in this case, the administrative staff not knowing what the "working" staff were doing and vice versa.

I was also disappointed that no one was making Ryan keep his room tidy. No one was checking to see if he did his laundry and he often ran out of clean clothes. One time when we were there for a visit we found he had washed his clothes, but had piled them, still wet, into a large plastic bag, where they stayed until we arrived. No one seemed to be checking up or following through with making the boys do their chores.

There was also a problem with allowance money. Each Friday the boys earned an allowance based on their level scores. If they were on the highest level of five, they earned five dollars—level four would earn four dollars and so forth.

If they had a campus job, they could earn even more money. The boys who earned at least level four or five could go off campus on Friday nights. Most weeks they went down the mountain to the "Fun Zone" where they could get sodas and play arcade games.

Ryan had a job of clearing the dining room tables after meals. He would often earn nine dollars a week extra for his job, and when combined with his allowance for being on level five, he would have fourteen dollars accumulated. Practically every week the staff would take Ryan to the Fun Zone where he would blow all his money on video games in the first fifteen minutes. Then, he would have to do without money the rest of the week. He wouldn't even have enough left to buy a soda.

Every week, Jim and I talked with Ryan and urged him to put part of his money into his savings account. We encouraged him to not take it all to the Fun Zone. He would agree, but the next week it was the same thing again. We talked with the staff about helping Ryan to make good decisions about his money, but week after week, month after month, they allowed him to spend all his money at the Fun Zone.

Because Pine Ridge was in the mountains, there were not many places for the kids to go on outings. When they did go places, like to a shopping mall, they had to ride nearly fifty or sixty miles in vans. Recreational activities were somewhat lacking too. Ryan had an opportunity to go fishing once and he got to go horseback riding once. Other than that, the kids mainly watched TV, played Nintendo, cards or basketball in the gym.

Another problem arose during those first few months Ryan was at Pine Ridge. I received a call one day from the principal at the Landmark School. He was calling to tell me that our county district attorney might subpoena Ryan to testify against one of his former classmates.

The boy, Vince Davis, had shot and killed a friend shortly after leaving Landmark. He and his attorney insisted the shooting was accidental. The district attorney, however, was not so sure. The boy had a history of physical aggression while at Landmark and had attacked three smaller boys while he was there. Ryan was one of the three.

I barely remembered the incident. Ryan had flipped a rubber band and Vince, who was much taller and weighed one hundred pounds more, had picked Ryan up and thrown him against the wall. I remembered that Ryan was frightened at the time because Vince was so big.

Now, the district attorney was subpoenaing the school's records so they could interview Ryan and the other boys. They wanted testimony they could use against Vince in his trial.

Jim and I did not want Ryan to have to testify. He was having too many problems of his own. We sought advice from people at County Mental Health and from our local school district's attorney. Everyone told us we should hire an attorney to protect Ryan's rights and to keep him from having to appear in court. It really upset us that Ryan might become involved in the situation. He was so immature and had no idea of what court was.

When the school principal called saying they had disclosed Ryan's name pursuant to subpoena, Jim and I decided we had better try to prepare him—just in case they called him to testify. During a home visit, we turned on the O.J. Simpson trial and tried to explain what was happening in the courtroom. He did not seem too interested—until we told him what had happened with Vince.

Before we had a chance to find an attorney, a deputy district attorney called me. I explained what little I knew about the situation and expressed my grave concern about Ryan having to testify. He said he could not promise anything, but that his office would do everything possible to keep Ryan and the other boys from having to personally go to court.

A couple of weeks later we learned the prosecutors were satisfied with testimony from the Landmark School staff and that Ryan would not have to testify. It was another obstacle overcome, but more were yet to come.

In early May I received a summons for jury duty and served on a civil trial for a full month. That Mother's Day, Jim, Julie and I drove to Pine Ridge and picked up Ryan for the afternoon. We had dinner at a small cafe and Ryan gave me a card he had bought with the two dollars allowance he had earned that week. Inside he had scribbled:

> *Roses are red, Violets are blue,*
> *Thanks for your love, the whole year through.*
> *The times we've been through, the good and the bad,*
> *Are love stays the same, no matter what's said.*

*I love you Mom. I'll always be your boy who loves you
very much. Your cool. Your the best Mom in the world.*

We spent a wonderful afternoon together. Again, it was hard to leave him and face the long drive home.

That month Jim received a special honor. He was selected as one of fifteen teachers in his district to receive a "Golden Wings Award." Several hundred people attended the beautiful banquet and ceremony at the Doubletree Hotel. Each of the fifteen teachers was lauded for their unique programs and hard work. At the end of the evening, two of the teachers would be selected for the coveted "Teacher of the Year" award.

Julie was with us to see her Dad honored. Several times throughout the evening I wished that Ryan was with us too. I knew, even if he was not at Pine Ridge, he probably would not have been able to come. We could not have trusted his behavior on such an important occasion.

After dinner, when all the teachers had been honored and all the speeches made, the superintendent stepped up to the microphone to announce the first 1994 Teacher of the Year. We all sat in suspense, waiting for Dr. Hansen to call out the name.

When he announced Jim's name, everyone at our table jumped up screaming. Suddenly, everyone was standing and cheering. Jim walked to the platform to accept his award and I glanced over at Julie, who was beaming with pride at her dad's accomplishment. Even then, in the middle of one of our family's happiest moments, I thought of Ryan. I felt sad that he could not be there to enjoy the moment with us.

Late in May, I received a frantic call from Ryan telling me about Edward, one of the boys in his dorm. Ryan was sitting on the sofa in the television room when he noticed Edward crawling out of his bedroom. Just as Edward reached the doorsill he collapsed. What Ryan saw next scared him to death. Edward had a cord tied tightly around his neck. According to Ryan, the boy's face was a blackish-blue color and his eyes were "bugging" out. Ryan was terrified. One of the staff members was able to cut the cord from Edward's neck and they rushed him to the hospital. When Ryan called us, he still did not know if the boy was going to be all right or not.

I worried about how witnessing Edward's attempted suicide would affect Ryan. It worried me that his anxiety might trigger or exacerbate obsessions he had experienced in the past about death and seeing images of scary faces. I asked the staff if there was a "crisis unit" available from the

County Mental Health Department that could help the boys deal with their feelings and anxieties about the incident. Marty told us the school staff would be talking with the boys about what happened but that there was no special counseling available.

Edward was not the first boy to attempt suicide while Ryan was at Pine Ridge. There were quite a few suicide attempts. Bryce, the boy with Tourette syndrome whom we met the very first day, also attempted to kill himself. Fortunately, none of the attempts were successful, at least to our knowledge.

At the end of May we brought Ryan home for the Memorial Day weekend. I arranged to pick him up early so that we could keep an appointment with Dr. McCracken. Although the facility's psychiatrist wrote the prescriptions each month, he had agreed that we would consult Dr. McCracken every couple of months for medication monitoring.

Dr. McCracken had told us earlier in the year about a new medication that would soon receive FDA approval—one that he thought might hold good promise for Ryan. The medication, called Risperdal (Risperidone), was an anti-psychotic originally developed for treating patients with schizophrenia. Dr. McCracken told us he was encouraged about reports from Europe where some early trials had found Risperdal to be extremely promising in treating Tourette syndrome.

At our visit in May, Dr. McCracken wrote Ryan's first prescription for Risperdal and with it, a suggestion to the Pine Ridge psychiatrist to gradually discontinue Haldol. He suggested that Ryan continue with Lithium, Anafranil, Ritalin, Depakote, and Synthroid.

Jim and I were optimistic but a bit nervous about starting the new medication. I worried he might have side effects from the new drug that might go unnoticed by the staff. Dr. McCracken told us it might be several weeks before we noticed any improvement, but it seemed like only a few days until we noticed a change. Almost immediately, Ryan seemed to be calmer, more "aware" and "in tune" with what was going on around him. His daily scores improved and his mood was much brighter. Within a week he was completely off Haldol and experiencing no visible side affects with the Risperdal.

The dramatic change amazed Jim and me each evening when we talked to Ryan on the phone. He was so thoughtful, so caring. "How are you tonight, Mom? How was your day today?" he would ask. Before, he never seemed to realize that I even had a day, let alone care about how it was!

Over the next few weeks and months his level scores soared. By mid-

August, Dr. McCracken suggested that the Pine Ridge psychiatrist discontinue Lithium. He first eliminated the afternoon dose for four weeks and then stopped the noon dose for the next three weeks. Then he discontinued the medication entirely.

We were eager to see what would happen and were ecstatic when Ryan was able to tolerate the elimination of Lithium with no noticeable change. Ryan was doing so well that we were finally able to concentrate on some of the "problem areas."

His therapist, Sandie Holland, and I did not always agree on the treatment plan. We both agreed that he needed to learn to take more responsibility for his needs and his actions. But I also felt Ryan needed help in learning to live with his lifelong disabilities of TS and OCD. Sandie, on the other hand, felt it was important that we not give Ryan the impression that he was a "sick" kid.

We went round and round over the issue several times and finally, I prevailed.

"Listen, Sandie," I said. "Ryan takes over twenty pills a day. He's not stupid. He knows there's something wrong. Let's help him accept it and learn to live with it."

Risperdal made a tremendous difference in Ryan's ability to function. Finally, after many years, he was able to retrieve and use all the things that so many people had tried to teach him for so long. He was finally able to respond to "behavior modification."

Risperdal also made Ryan very cognizant of where he was. Although he had been with behaviorally disordered kids for the past five years, he suddenly became aware that he was different, that he did not belong there anymore.

We noticed he was having bouts of depression and was desperately homesick at times. When we would leave after visiting for the day, Ryan would sit outside alone on the porch, very despondent and melancholy. Although he was doing well in school and his levels remained high, Jim and I were becoming very worried about his emotional well-being. Many times he would lament, "I don't belong here with these kinds of kids, Mom. You don't know what goes on in this place."

Over the next couple of months I became more aware of what was "going on." I learned there were several boys who were "gang" members and that they were trying to form a group on campus. Although a couple of the troublesome students were eventually removed from the school, there were still a few tough ones left. A couple of them had been threatening

Ryan and one of the boys had stolen his CD player. There were other suicide attempts among the students, including one by Ryan's good friend Michael, who had also left Landmark to come to Pine Ridge.

During the Thanksgiving holiday, I also learned there was frequent sexual acting-out among several of the students which terrified me. I immediately called Marty, who assured me he was taking steps to ensure all the boys would be safe. After all we had experienced, Marty's word was no longer good enough for me. I also called the County Licensing Bureau and asked them to investigate.

Jim and I decided it was time to bring Ryan home. Donna convinced us he needed to go through a period of "closure" and have an opportunity to say good-bye to his friends and the staff.

I kept Ryan at home for two weeks until I felt confident he would be totally safe. We then agreed that he would return to Pine Ridge only until the Christmas break at which time we would bring him home for good.

Ryan was right. He did not belong there.

Chapter 28

There's No Place Like Home

"If you bungle raising your children,
I don't think whatever else you do well matters very much."[1]
Jacqueline Kennedy Onassis

Making the decision to bring Ryan home was easy. Deciding where he would go to school was not. We consulted with Gordon from our local school district and Sherry O'Brien, our case manager from County Mental Health.

Although all of us were ecstatic about Ryan's tremendous improvement, everyone agreed that Ryan might benefit from a short stay in a residential program closer to home. Although he was doing exceptionally well, we were still concerned about his ability to maintain over time. We did not want to place too many expectations on him too soon.

Jim and I explored three other facilities that seemed promising. After several weeks of interviews and visits, it seemed to us that none of them would specifically meet Ryan's needs. The facility we thought had the best school had a horrible psychiatrist on staff. Our initial impressions of the doctor were less than positive. We subsequently learned that she had caused many problems for one of the other families in our local TSA support group.

After Dr. Mills and Dr. Lehrer, Jim and I were determined we would never again allow Ryan to see a doctor who did not have a proven track record in treating children with Tourette syndrome.

We asked Gordon about the feasibility of Ryan staying at home and attending our local high school on a part-time basis. Gordon, who has always been remarkably supportive, agreed to look into the possibility. We also asked Sherry to find out what, if any, counseling services would be available for Ryan and our family.

One reason we thought attending our local high school might be a possibility was the Special Day Class teacher. Ryan's favorite teacher, Marlene Rigby, had taken a job at our local high school when she left Landmark. When Gordon spoke with her about Ryan being in her class, Marlene was extremely encouraging and supportive. Although she did not have any behavior-disordered students in her class, she felt certain Ryan could and would be successful and she enthusiastically urged us to give it a try.

Sherry, too, was helpful by obtaining outpatient mental health services for Ryan. A new social worker, Kathleen Adams, was assigned to work in our area and she would be starting the same time Ryan would be returning from Pine Ridge. County Mental Health offered to have Kathleen meet with him weekly at school and weekly or bi-weekly with our family. It seemed as if everything was finally working out for Ryan to come home.

Ryan was elated about leaving Pine Ridge. He was eager to come home and attend Marlene's class at the high school. It had been over five years since he was in a "regular" school and he was extremely motivated to show everyone he could do well. He was determined to try his hardest so that he would never have to go back to Landmark or to another residential treatment center.

It was mid-January when Ryan started classes at our local high school. We live only a half-block away so he was able to walk to school with Julie each morning. Although she was a senior and Ryan was a freshman, Julie was wonderful about helping him learn his way around the campus. She also included him during lunch with her friends. For the first time in a very long time, Ryan really felt like he was a "normal" kid.

Marlene was remarkable. She welcomed Ryan with open arms, boosted his morale and made him feel confident that he could succeed. Even when she taught him at Landmark, Marlene had "the magic touch" when it came to making learning exciting for Ryan. It always amazed me how she could extract levels of work from him that I thought were impossible.

At the high school, she was no less effective. Ryan soared and was even able to "mainstream" to a keyboarding class where he earned a solid B each quarter.

In the spring he helped with the varsity baseball team, working to prepare the field and getting the equipment ready. Although he was disappointed that he wasn't able to play, he enjoyed being with the older boys and feeling as if he were part of the team.

By the end of ninth grade he had made it through the year with not a single episode of violence or aggression. In fact, there were no "episodes" of any kind.

If Ryan became wound up or felt a little hyper in class, Marlene would send him out to the rose garden to work with the horticulture teacher until he felt ready to come back inside. There were no trips to the principal's office and the campus guards did not even know who he was! His behavior was exemplary.

Even though Ryan's behavior was finally under control, he still found it difficult to make friends. He relied mainly on Julie's friends at school and at the church youth group.

Julie was good about including him, at least some of the time. She would drive him to McDonald's or take him shopping when she could. She would also take him to youth group and encouraged him to go with some of the other kids to concerts, ice skating, swimming, beach parties, etc. It was the first time in many years that Ryan finally had a chance to socialize with "normal" teenagers.

One of the things that Jim and I did when Ryan came home from Pine Ridge was to start a behavioral program similar to the one they used. On the computer, we created "level sheets" like they used, only substituting goals that would be more appropriate for home.

We also increased the positive points Ryan could earn for things such as following directions, staying on task, taking his meds on time, having his book bag and lunch ready in the morning, and asking to speak with his parents when he was upset.

Some of the negative behaviors that would result in a loss of points were: swearing, being assaultive, oppositional, non-compliant and obsessing. We also tracked other problem behaviors such as whining, bothering the dog, getting into other people's things and making unnecessary noises.

We scored him on getting up, personal hygiene, and keeping his room clean. We also tracked his bathroom cleanliness, completion of assigned chores and homework, dinner behavior, shower time and bedtime. Scores would range from one to five. A score of five would mean he was being independent and needed no prompting. Four would reflect that he complied with only one reminder. Three meant that he was doing a good job but needed two prompts. Two meant that he was late in complying or had a poor attitude. A one meant he had made no effort and was making poor choices. A zero was for noncompliance or refusing direction.

We also modified some of the rules from Pine Ridge to make them more suitable for home.

HOUSE RULES

1. Ryan will be awakened by 6:30 A.M. on school days and by 8:30 A.M. on non-school days.

2. Bedroom and bathroom will be checked by 7:15 A.M. on school days and before 10:00 A.M. on non-school days.

3. Breakfast is served at 7:00 A.M. on school days and between 8:30-9:00 A.M. on non-school days.

4. Snack times are at 2:30-3:00 P.M. and 8:00-8:30 P.M.

5. Bedtime will be based on level score for that week as follows:

Level 0, 1, 2	8:30 P.M.
Level 3	9:00 P.M.
Level 4	9:30 P.M.
Level 5	10:00 P.M.

GENERAL EXPECTATIONS

1. Ryan must be properly dressed/covered when outside of his bedroom.
2. Ryan is expected to knock once and wait for an answer before opening a closed door.
3. Ryan may not enter anyone's room without permission.
4. Property damaging or destruction, physical or emotional abuse of family members or any endangering behaviors will result in at least one level drop.
5. AWOL episodes and out-of-bounds behavior (leaving without permission, going outdoors, going to another person's house or in someone's

room without permission) will not be tolerated
and will result in at least one level drop.

6. Swearing or use of foul language in the presence
of family members will result in a loss of points.
Foul language that becomes directed at family
members or becomes abusive may result in a
level drop.

NON-NEGOTIABLE CONSEQUENCES

Loss of 25 points:

- Going away from home without permission
- In Julie's room without permission
- Horseplay that endangers another person
- Physical aggression or hands on another person in anger
- Directing obscene language toward parents or other family member
- Noncompliance with medications
- Lending, borrowing, buying, selling without permission
- Asking another person for unearned money
- Stealing
- Inappropriate sexual remarks
- Obscene gestures
- Abusive to dog
- Throwing objects at property or people
- Spitting on someone
- Self-endangerment
- Threatening parents or Julie
- Stealing (borrowing batteries) from someone else's things
- Racial remarks of any kind

Loss of 15 points:

- Refusal to participate in mealtimes or family outings
- Throwing away food
- Refusing directions
- Badgering

Loss of 10 points:

- Horseplay
- Rudeness
- Poor table manners (language, unfriendly attitude, expressing anger at the table)
- Climbing in or out of windows
- Kicking car seats, inappropriate use of car windows, radio, etc.
- Operating VCR, TV, Stereo, or Walkman that belongs to someone else
- Leaving for school late (anytime after 7:20 A.M.)

Loss of 5 points:

- For every washcloth or towel found in bedroom
- Not attempting to control bodily functions
- Not putting dirty clothes in laundry hamper
- Spitting on floor
- Playing with a ball in the house
- Bringing roller blades indoors

TELEPHONE

1. Outgoing calls are to be made with permission only.
2. Ryan is expected to answer the phone appropriately and treat callers with courtesy.
3. Ryan is not to be disruptive while others are on the phone. This will result in the loss of points for being disruptive.

PERSONAL PROPERTY

1. Electronic equipment must not be disturbing to others. Violation of this rule will result in losing the use of equipment for 24 hours.
2. TV and Nintendo are not to be used before 3:00 P.M. on school days without special permission.
3. No personal items are to be taken to school without permission from school staff and parents.
4. Allowance will be paid on Friday afternoons and will be based on level score for that week:

> Level 5 — $5.00
> 4 — $4.00
> 3 — $3.00
> 2 — $2.00
> 1 — $1.00
> 0 — $ 0

5. Extra money may be earned by:

- Washing car
- Mowing grass
- Collecting cans
- Other jobs agreed upon in advance by Ryan and parents

By the end of the year we found that we no longer needed to use the behavioral chart—not that Ryan's behavior was perfect, by any means. It's just that he was finally self-motivated to do well and was able to accept direction. We were not seeing the extreme behaviors at all and the "little" annoying behaviors were much easier to manage.

At the end of school we debated on the subject of summer school. Jim and I were certain Ryan could use some extra help in math. We were just as certain, however, that he could not handle a large class without any extra assistance—especially since the instructor would not be a special education teacher.

Gordon Miller had always been very interested in Transition Planning for special education students and had even hosted a transition workshop for parents in our local district. At the workshop I learned about various programs such as the Job Training Policy Council (JTPC).

When I spoke with Gordon about it, he encouraged Ryan to apply for the Summer Youth Employment Program sponsored by JTPC. The Summer Youth Program is a federally-funded program that provides summer jobs for teenagers from low income families or for teens with disabilities. Marlene helped Ryan fill out his application and she and Gordon provided a letter from the school district documenting his disability.

On the day of his eligibility interview, Marlene went with us to lend her support. Ryan was extremely nervous and he worried he would not be selected for a job. Marlene was great in helping him overcome some of the anxiety and remain confident in himself and his abilities.

A few days after the eligibility interview, someone from the JTPC called and asked Ryan to come to their main office to take a math and reading test. The job counselors assured us the tests were for informational purposes only—that failing a test would not prevent Ryan from getting a job. As it turned out, Ryan did extremely well on the reading test but did poorly in math. The JTPC counselor sent us home with the promise that someone in our area would call in about a week regarding a summer job.

That week was one of the longest ones I can remember. Ryan obsessed and fretted that he was not going to get a job. He was sure they had lied to him. In his mind, he could not imagine why anyone would be willing to hire him. When the call finally came, he was beside himself with excitement.

Larry, the job counselor for our area, called and asked Ryan to come in that very afternoon. When we arrived, Larry told him he needed to fill out a lot of paperwork and that it might take as long as two hours. As an incentive, they would pay Ryan for the time he spent filling out the forms. Larry also asked to see his work permit.

While Larry was helping Ryan with his pre-employment paper work, I set out to track down a school administrator who would authorize the permit. When I returned with the signed paper, Ryan was finishing a self-directed test that would assist Larry in determining his areas of interest.

When he tallied up the scores, Larry discovered that Ryan enjoyed working with animals and that he was very creative. Larry wasn't sure what jobs he could find in those areas, but he said he would definitely find something. He promised Ryan he would call the animal training program at the local college and the County Animal Shelter to ask about job possibilities. He told us to give him a couple of days to work on it.

Each time the phone rang Ryan lunged for it. Finally, Larry called and said he was not able to obtain a job for Ryan working with animals. He did say, however, that the director of personnel for the city had an opening that he thought Ryan might like.

The job, he explained, was working for the Police Resource Center and the Building and Safety Department. Both offices were in the same building and Ryan would work as a clerical assistant for whichever office needed him. The Summer Youth Program paid minimum wage—$4.25 per hour. Although Ryan would be working for the city, his salary would come from federal funds through the Job Policy Training Council. Larry would be checking in on Ryan while he was on the job and would help him fill out and turn in his time sheets.

Ryan was especially excited to get the job because he wanted to earn money to buy a computer. He was happy when he learned that he could work as many as eight hours a day for the next six or seven weeks. His salary, combined with the money in his savings account, would be just enough to buy the computer he wanted and even a couple of games.

It amazed us how well Ryan handled his first job. He was extremely conscientious about being on time. I met him for lunch each day so that he would not have to eat downtown alone. He was always watching the clock while we ate, making sure he would not be late getting back.

While working for the Building and Safety Department and the Police Resource Center, Ryan filed blueprints and alphabetized files. He also did some light typing and copied addresses onto file folders. One of the surveyors took him out on a road construction job a couple of times, which Ryan really liked. One of the guys gave him four tickets to a Dodger game. Another man brought in scraps of leather to help Ryan with his leather-working hobby. Everyone was patient with him and very supportive.

None of the people he was working with knew anything about Ryan's background. He told them he had Tourette syndrome, but only to explain why he needed to take pills several times each day.

At the end of the first four weeks, Ryan had finished his work and there was nothing left for him to do. Larry then found him a job at the library where he worked full time for the next three weeks. He liked it so much he decided when his job was over he would like to "volunteer" at the library.

The staffs at the library, Building and Safety and the Police Resource Center were incredibly supportive of Ryan. They set expectations he could meet and he enthusiastically worked to meet each goal. I don't think any of them will ever realize how much their influence and the experience of having those jobs will have on Ryan's development.

Toward the end of the summer Larry called with some wonderful news. The JTPC had selected Ryan as the Summer Youth Employee of the Year in our area.

Ryan and all of our family were invited to a formal reception for the JTPC honorees. It was at the Radisson Hotel and they presented him with a beautiful certificate.

I was bursting with pride as I watched Ryan walk up to the front to accept his award. He was neatly groomed, wearing dress clothes and a tie. I could not help remembering how different he looked just a year earlier when I had tearfully driven away, leaving him behind at Pine Ridge.

What had made the difference? Was it the medication? Was it being in a residential treatment facility? Was it that he was getting older and maturing?

I am convinced Ryan's improvement was not due in any significant part to his experience at Pine Ridge, but that he improved despite the time he spent there. If there was any good that came from the residential experience, it was that Ryan gained a greater appreciation for his home, and Jim and I got a much-needed rest.

I do believe Risperdal played a major role in his drastic improvement. He has successfully maintained for over two years now. Ryan is currently taking Risperdal, Depakote, Anafranil and Ritalin. The medications have worked well and have "made him available" neurologically to put into practice all that he has learned throughout the years. I do not, however, believe that medication has been the only factor. Medications are a wonderful "tool" but they are not the total answer.

I believe that age, too, has been an important factor. Although still developmentally behind in some areas, with each passing year we have seen Ryan achieve monumental milestones in maturity. It gives us continued hope that eventually his mind and body will meet and work in harmony, allowing him to accomplish all that he dreams of doing.

Although age and medication have been major players in helping Ryan to enjoy the success he does today, many people have also played a vital role in helping him and our family.

Wonderful, caring and dedicated teachers and social workers have invested hundreds of hours and even a part of themselves to help Ryan succeed. Extraordinary doctors such as Dr. Comings and Dr. McCracken have been willing to try, fail, and try again. They have worked fervently to do whatever was required, even when it was not conventional or convenient.

Exceptional professionals such as Gordon Miller, Paul Rhodes, Abby Stevens, Sherry O'Brien, Luke Wagner, and Marlene Rigby have been willing to go the "extra mile" and then keep on going.

Despite all he has been through, Ryan is a very lucky young man. He is fortunate to have a devoted family who has given unconditional love, even when his behavior was, at times, unlovable.

Loving and caring for a child with severe Tourette syndrome and ADHD has required sacrifice. Jim, Julie and I have each paid an individual and collective price in raising and nurturing Ryan. It was a decision we made by listening to our intuition and our hearts. Only with God's grace did we have the strength to endure.

What does the future hold for Ryan and our family? Of course, we remain fiercely optimistic that he will have continued success. Today, he is a sophomore attending high school on a regular campus. His grades are good. In fact, he even made the honor roll this past semester, and his most recent report card showed a 3.5 average! Even more exciting to Ryan, after physically pushing himself to overcome the effects of taking twenty-three pills a day, he was able to compete and land a spot on the high school junior varsity baseball team.

Ryan is one of the first kids to grow up on the "forefront" of Tourette syndrome research and treatment. He has been one of the first to try many of the newest medications, and has been a product of the innovative "Collaborative Model" that joins mental health and educational services. He has been given every chance available to assist him in becoming a successful and contributing member of society.

Yet, there are no guarantees. Despite the great strides that have occurred over the past ten to twelve years, there still remains no cure for Tourette syndrome.

The other day, as we were riding in the car, Ryan remarked on a song that was playing on the radio.

"Listen Mom," he said solemnly, "this song sounds just like me."

I turned up the volume and listened closely to the ballad about a young man who saw other people getting things that he was wishing for. He felt discouraged by his bad luck, surmising that all of his wishes must be landing on someone else's star.

It saddened me to learn that Ryan was internalizing the words of the song. I suddenly realized there were things about him I didn't know—things I may never know. I will never know the depth of the pain he has suffered. He has been through more than many of us will suffer in our lifetime. I may never know the height of his hopes, but I do believe he will be stronger because of all he has endured. I now understand that I need to listen to Ryan's dreams and nurture those as well as caring for his needs.

Dr. Mort Doran, an inspiring Canadian surgeon who has Tourette syndrome, ended one of his keynote speeches with a quotation from Vince Lombardi, coach of the Green Bay Packers. The coach's powerful message is one I will gladly pass on to Ryan and hope that he will always remember.

"It's not whether you get knocked down in life that counts, it's whether you get up again."[2]

Congratulations on "getting back up again," Ryan. We always knew you would.

Chapter 29

Epilogue:
Just A Parent

"Snowflakes are one of nature's most fragile things,
but just look at what they can do if they stick together."[1]
Unknown

Parents of children with neurobiological disorders such as Tourette syndrome, ADHD and OCD are intimately familiar with the word frustration. Many times we get so exasperated that we scream, explode, give up, or threaten to run away.

It's understandable that parents feel or experience frustration in dealing with the challenges of a special needs child. With TS in particular, the ups and downs, the highs and lows, and the peaks and valleys all seem to invoke an extremely cruel frustration.

The symptoms erratically come and go, wax and wane, lessen and worsen. Even during periods of stability, parents of children with a severe case of TS often feel as if they are waiting for "the other shoe to drop." Parents learn quickly that they can take nothing for granted. Each success, however small, must be celebrated, yet tempered with cautious optimism.

Far too often we "set ourselves up" for frustration by grabbing onto the elusive "miracle" cure. We hang our hopes on the newest medication, the newest doctor or the newest alternative therapy. When the medication stops working, the doctor (who seemed enthusiastic in the beginning) is slow to return calls, and the biofeedback sessions don't seem as promising as they did at first—frustration creeps in. Unfortunately, it often saps the strength we desperately need to help our child.

I have often thought that dealing with Ryan's TS, ADHD and OCD was the easy part. Coping and dealing with "everything else" has, for me, often created the most stress and feelings of frustration. The "everything else" includes neighbors, family, friends, teachers, principals, social workers, psychologists, doctors, hospitals and insurance companies.

For years we solicited help from psychologists and psychiatrists who knew nothing about Tourette syndrome. They just happened to be on the insurance company's "approved" list. We sacrificed hard-earned money and benefits, only to hear that Ryan's problems were the result of our inadequate parenting skills. The message was clear. If we would just fix ourselves, he would not have a problem. We have truly suffered as we tried to rise above outdated, conventional psychiatric wisdom that blames parents for everything and then forces a "one size fits all" approach to treatment.

We, too, have been entangled in the HMO insurance nightmare that traps many parents and prevents them from seeking competent care for their child. Even with the most favorable of insurance companies, we are often forced to use limited, inadequate mental health benefits to pay for a disorder that is biological.

Most psychiatric benefits lag far behind those offered for other illnesses. How unfortunate that even the service providers we hire perpetuate and reinforce the prevailing stigma. They, too, embrace the notion that having something wrong with our brain is less important and worth less money than having something wrong with another less-complicated part of our anatomy.

Dealing with these added frustrations on top of dealing with your child can be overwhelming at times. It is what parents do with these feelings of frustration that make the difference in their success at helping their child and themselves.

I learned very quickly that no one could advocate for Ryan as well as

I could. Certainly no one knew him as well or loved him as much. Instead of sitting back and waiting for the "professionals" to decide what was best for him, I began to educate myself. I learned all I could, not only about TS, ADHD and OCD, but also about special education laws, the mental health system, Transition Planning, Social Security and insurance benefits.

I became an active participant in our local school district's special education parent's group. I became our district's representative to our county's special education Community Advisory Committee. I joined a local parent support group for children with emotional and behavioral disorders and I attended meetings of Ch.A.D.D. (Children and Adults with Attention Deficit Disorder) and LDA (Learning Disabilities Association).

Because our community did not have a Tourette syndrome support group, I volunteered to start one and, by doing so, formed a large network of friends who are also parents of children with TS. From an original list of thirteen names, we now have contact with over three hundred families in our county.

Becoming better informed and educated has empowered me to assume an equal role as a decision maker concerning services for Ryan. By working with various professionals in a cooperative and collaborative way, I have been able to be a more effective advocate for him and for our family. I strongly believe parents must not only assert their rights, but that they must assume their responsibility in obtaining competent and appropriate care for their child.

If you are still in denial that your child has a problem, then you *must* get out of it. You cannot begin to help your child or your family until you admit there is a problem. Learn about TS, ADHD and OCD. Knowing more about the disorders will help dispel some of the fear you may be feeling.

If a physician is not knowledgeable about your child's disorder, or blames you for your child's neurological problems, then change doctors! If you have received inadequate care from a physician, let your insurance company know by writing a letter detailing your experiences. If you have had a bad experience with a hospital, write the director of the hospital.

If your insurance company denies a claim, appeal it as many times as necessary to reach an equitable solution.

If the school district says your child with TS (or ADHD/OCD) does not qualify for special education services, you have the right to a Due Process Fair Hearing. Don't be afraid to take that step. Get an advocate to help you or hire an attorney, if necessary. There are agencies to help parents who cannot afford to hire an attorney or advocate.

If a teacher, principal or school psychologist tells you there is no room in a program the IEP team has deemed to be appropriate for your child, insist that they make room. Remember, "waiting lists" are not legal.

Do not agree to wait for testing or placement. Know your rights and do not be afraid to use them. Similarly, be fair and willing to compromise. Remember that the most "appropriate" placement does not always mean the "best" placement.

Work on honing your assertiveness skills. I have learned from years of experience that speaking out, if done in an assertive and non-confrontational manner, can make a positive difference in the help and services you can obtain for your child.

I often remind myself that it was because of one mother's frustration and determination that MADD (Mothers Against Drunk Drivers) came into existence. When Candy Lightner's daughter was killed by a drunken driver, she channeled her frustrations into action. The MADD organization has been highly successful in effecting important legislative changes. These changes have resulted in the strictest drunk driving laws and most severe penalties in our country's history.

We need some Candy Lightners involved in the Tourette syndrome community. We need parents to speak up for their children, to advocate for their children and even to fight for their children when necessary.

We need parents who will challenge ineffective doctors and insurance companies.

We need parents who will keep an eye on Washington and be aware how our Senate and Congress are voting to address the needs of people with disabilities and children with special needs. We need to know who our local senators and members of Congress are and we need to communicate with them.

We need to let them know how we feel about Social Security benefits for disabled children. We need to let them know how we feel about job training programs for our young adults with TS.

We need parents who will become advocates for children's mental health issues and parents who will keep abreast of local political decisions that affect children. We need parents of special needs children to sit on their county board of supervisors or the county mental health board.

We need parents who will serve on their local Community Advisory Committee (C.A.C.) and become involved in special education decisions in their county. We need to elect school board members who are knowledgeable about and sensitive to the needs of special education students.

We need parents who will work with schools and teachers—parents who want to be part of the solution, not just ones who scream about the problems.

We need to make sure that every principal and every teacher know what Tourette syndrome is. Then, we must be sure to provide them with whatever information they need to do the best job they can in helping our children with TS become successful at school and in their community.

I would encourage every parent of a child with Tourette syndrome to move from being a "spectator" to "participator." It's simple—just follow the A,B,Cs.

A	Attend a local TSA support group meeting
B	Belong to the Tourette Syndrome Association
C	Commit to serving

As parents of children with TS, ADHD and OCD, we must resist the urge to scream, explode, give up, or run away from our frustrations. We must work to overcome the stigma and discrimination that has held us back in seeking appropriate services for our children. We, too, can make important changes in the quality of medical care, insurance benefits, and educational services available to our children.

By refusing to become victims and wallow in our disappointments, we can channel our frustrations into action. We can, and must work tirelessly to make important and positive changes—changes that will help our children with Tourette syndrome live with, cope with, and even overstep the challenges of their neurobiological disorders.

Chapter 30

A Word from Ryan

Hi!

My name is Ryan Hughes and I have Tourette syndrome. Having TS has made my life very hard, but I have learned that with a little bit of patience and a lot of med changes that there is always hope.

Tourette syndrome has made my life tough, but it has also made me strong by showing myself that no matter how hard the times are, I can always turn it around and make things better.

I feel that having this problem has changed my life over the years by drawing people away from me instead of toward me, thus making it harder to make friends and harder to live with my family.

I didn't like having to be at Pine Ridge because the times away from home were rough and I always felt depressed. I was depressed because I couldn't be home with my mom and my family. Also, the kids there had many problems that were so different from my problems. They always got into fights and stole things from each other.

The times that I had to be in the hospital I felt terrible because I didn't understand why I had to be locked up. I felt like I was an animal in a cage. Being in the hospital, though, helped get my meds straightened out and helped me a little bit with my behavior.

I used to have a hard time controlling my anger. All that went through my mind when I was being held down was rage. I know that the physical stuff happened so fast I couldn't stop it. I never did want to hit my mom or dad but sometimes, out of rage, the impulse just happened before I knew it.

Over these past two years I have shown remarkable improvement in the way I live and how I act toward other people. I have made many improvements, yes, but not without the help of my friends and family that have always been there for me.

I don't mind taking medication, but I hated taking Lithium because it made my hands shake really bad and made me very thirsty. My feeling about Risperdal is I am very glad they have this medicine because it has helped me be able to lead a normal life.

Sometimes when you have TS you will get made fun of by other kids. When I get made fun of, it doesn't feel very good at the time. But I just always remember that they are just words and they don't matter at all.

I really like attending school now because I feel that I am starting to fit in with the other kids. The thing I like most about school is being able to be with my friends and knowing that I have a good teacher to help me succeed.

After I graduate, I'd like to go to college because I want to be a counselor. I'd like to be a counselor so that I can help kids who have behavior problems. I think I can be a big help to them because I have gone through the same thing and I would like to help them through their hard times.

I would like to tell all the other kids who have TS, ADHD and OCD that no matter how hard your time is, no matter how much you think you won't be able to have a normal life—keep on trying. And never stop believing in yourself.

Chapter 31

Bruised But Not Broken

*"You gain strength, courage and confidence
by every experience in which you must stop
and look fear in the face...You must do the
thing you think you cannot do."*[1]

Eleanor Roosevelt

During the past five years I have received dozens of letters from mothers across the country. They have written to share their experiences, frustrations, and hopes for their children with Tourette syndrome and its associated disorders.

Their experience with doctors

"Needless to say, we've been through our share of doctors. Over a period of time I've begun to let go of the resentment and bitterness toward many of them for not listening to us."

"I left the doctor's office feeling like the world's worst mother."

"I read about TS in a magazine and made the appointment with a pediatric neurologist by myself. I bypassed our pediatrician who I am sure was convinced I was an overprotective fussy mother."

"I am a neurosurgical nurse manager and I have taken him to many doctors. He has been through four child psychiatrists—three of them knew nothing about TS."

"He was hospitalized and the staff decided they would break his will. He got worse and finally they gave up. I pulled him out when I found out they had him heavily drugged twenty-four hours a day."

"We've changed doctors three times and are still experimenting with different medications in various doses."

"The hospital has done an EEG (nothing wrong), blood tests (nothing wrong), and a CAT scan (nothing wrong)."

Their experiences with psychologists

"Psychologists don't realize the depths of his trouble. He is a hard study."

"I am frustrated because psychologists, therapists and clinicians all think they can help him by using conventional methods and these methods do not work for him."

"The psychologist he sees in the hospital says our son is just spoiled and we have to learn to 'control' him."

Their fears

"We pray everyday that he doesn't fall prey to someone who wants to hurt him or blame him or that he doesn't do something that will get him into trouble."

Their frustrations

"Sometimes, by the day's end, I felt like I had no more emotional strength left because of the things I found out my son has done."

"We're at our wit's end, scared to death, frustrated and I cry a lot because I don't want our son ending up in a youth home at 16."

"I know there are other people going through this but have yet to meet one person I can talk to."

"We love our son very much and desperately want to help him, but we can't get any support from anyone."

"I had Hodgkin's Disease eleven years ago and my sister has Down's Syndrome, but of everything, this is by far the hardest."

"Day care is one of my biggest problems."

"I can't even keep up with his med changes."

"Time-outs, restricting him, no TV, sending him to bed early, didn't work at all."

"My medical expenses are outrageous."

"Every time we try to do something positive for him he turns it into a negative."

"I have had periods of severe isolation due to this and the fact that people with normal children don't understand."

On aggression, rage attacks, storms

"There's not much in our home that has not been scratched, dented, broken, etc."

"One day I sent him to his room for a sassy mouth. Not only did he refuse to go, he screamed, yelled and cursed at me for several minutes. After letting him blow off steam, I tried to escort him to his room. He pushed me away and we ended up in a physical battle. He had me by the hair, pulling me down to the bed where we wrestled for quite sometime. I ended up with a black eye, bruises on my arms and losing a great deal of hair."

"When he loses control, he later feels true remorse and truly regrets his actions."

"At times he would seem almost possessed by an unknown force."

"We learned to walk on 'eggshells' at all times around our son."

"He goes into these 'mood swings'...gets the glazed look in his eyes and has very violent temper tantrums."

"He's helpful, very loving, respects property, goes to school - but when he 'swings over' - no one wants him around."

"Wearing a beeper is a necessity I required."

On their pain

"He's been through the kids teasing him and I've held him while he's cried."

On getting a diagnosis

"At age twelve, after fighting years of tics, depression and school problems, he was finally diagnosed with TS and ADHD."

"My son is thirteen and he was diagnosed at two and a half by my pastor and his wife, a registered nurse, when I took him to be exorcised for demon possession."

"He clears his throat, pulls at his crotch/pants, bites his nails, chews his clothing, and licks his lips until they are raw. He has a "thing" that he does which is lick his lips and then pull his shirt on the right shoulder area up to meet his mouth and then wipes it off. He does this at least twenty times an hour. Our county Mental Health Department workers have dismissed all of these activities as "nervous habits."

The systems

"I've been battling 'the system,' so to speak, for nine years and can't seem to make any headway."

"Financially, I feel stuck because we have no insurance to cover medical costs, but make too much money to get government aid."

On medications

"He's on medication for aggressive and compulsive behavior. Like the medication for tics, sometimes I think it's working great, then there are times when I wonder if it's doing anything at all."

"He'll never be obedient but with Tegretol, he's within normal limits."

"The older he gets, the more tools are available to reason with a more mature mind, as long as his medication gives him that choice."

On their child with TS

"My most important task is to keep on loving and caring."

"He has a wonderful loving heart and a real desire to help others."

"He's sarcastic, witty, humorous—a brilliant mind with an immature orientation."

"The oppositional behavior was present since birth."

"He told me his heart wants to succeed but his brain won't let him."

"I saw him in the kitchen last night pressing a heated metal spoon into his arm. We spent the next few hours on an emotional roller coaster, talking quietly, loudly, sitting silently, and crying."

Their hopes

"Taking one day at a time is the key to our surviving life with our son. We pray he will learn ways to deal with his handicap when he gets older."

"My husband and I are worried about the future but we pray a lot."

"I love my son dearly. Praying helps me most."

Chapter 31. Bruised But Not Broken

"What has helped me most is taking him to church."

"I'm hoping that he outgrows it."

End Notes

Chapter 1
1. Quotation from: *A Treasury of the Art of Living*,
Published by Wilshire Book Company, North Hollywood, CA. Used by permission.

Chapter 2
1. Quotation taken by permission from Robert Andrew's *Columbia Dictionary of Quotations* © 1993, Columbia University Press, New York, New York.

Chapter 3
1. Quotation taken from *Kip Quotes* © 1987, Parker Chiropractic Resource Foundation, Fort Worth, Texas.

Chapter 4
1. Quotation taken by permission from Robert Andrew's *Columbia Dictionary of Quotations* © 1993, Columbia University Press, New York, New York.

Chapter 5
1. Quotation taken by permission from Robert Andrew's *Columbia Dictionary of Quotations* © 1993, Columbia University Press, New York, New York.

Chapter 6
1. The Serenity Prayer, Reinhold Nebhuir, 1926

Chapter 7
1. Quotation taken by permission from Robert Andrew's *Columbia Dictionary of Quotations* © 1993, Columbia University Press, New York, New York.

Chapter 8

1. Quotation taken by permission from Robert Andrew's *Columbia Dictionary of Quotations* © 1993, Columbia University Press, New York, New York.

Chapter 9

1. Quotation from: *A Treasury of the Art of Living,*
Published by Wilshire Book Company, North Hollywood, CA. Used by permission.

Chapter 10

1. Quotation from: *A Treasury of the Art of Living*, Published by Wilshire Book Company, North Hollywood, CA. Used by permission.

Chapter 11

1. Quotation from: *A Treasury of the Art of Living,* Published by Wilshire Book Company, North Hollywood, CA. Used by permission.

Chapter 12

1. Scripture taken from the Holy Bible, New International Version®. Copyright ©1973, 1978, 1984 by International Bible Society. Used by permission of the International Bible Society.

Chapter 13

1.Quotation from Heartland Samplers, *Catch the Wind*, Copyright © 1991, Edina, Minnesota.

Chapter 14.

1. Quotation from: *Taking It to Heart - Thoughts for Teens,* Copyright © 1988,Thoughtful Books, Marshalltown, Iowa. Original source unknown.

Chapter 15

1. Quotation from Heartland Samplers, *Catch the Wind*, Copyright © 1991, Edina, Minnesota.

Chapter 16

1. Quotation from: *A Treasury of the Art of Living*, Published by Wilshire Book Company, North Hollywood, CA. Used by permission.

Chapter 17

1. Original source unknown. Quotation from: *Taking It to Heart - Thoughts for Teens*, Copyright © 1988,Thoughtful Books, Marshalltown, Iowa.

Chapter 18

1. Quotation taken by permission from Robert Andrew's *Columbia Dictionary of Quotations* © 1993, Columbia University Press, New York, New York.

Chapter 19

1. Quotation taken by permission from Robert Andrew's *Columbia Dictionary of Quotations* © 1993, Columbia University Press, New York, New York.

Chapter 20

1. Quotation from Heartland Samplers, *Catch the Wind*, Copyright © 1991, Edina, Minnesota.

Chapter 21

1. Quotation taken by permission from Robert Andrew's Columbia Dictionary of Quotations © 1993, Columbia University Press, New York, New York.

Chapter 22

1.Quotation taken from: Barbara Johnson's *Splashes of Joy in the Cesspools of Life*, Copyright © 1992, Word Publishing, Dallas, Texas. Original source unknown.

Chapter 23

1. Quotation from *"The Remedy Worse than the Disease" by Matthew Prior* (1727), as quoted in The Oxford Dictionary of Humorous Quotations.

Chapter 24

1. Quotation from: *A Treasury of the Art of Living*, Published by Wilshire Book Company, North Hollywood, CA. Used by permission.

Chapter 25

1. Quotation from: *"What Do You Do With A Child Like This?* Copyright ©1991 by L. Tobin. Published by Whole Person Associates, Duluth, Minnesota. Used by Permission.

Chapter 26 1. Quotation taken by permission from Robert Andrew's *Columbia Dictionary of Quotations* © 1993, Columbia University Press, New York, New York.

Chapter 27

1. Quotation taken from *Kip Quotes* © 1987, Parker Chiropractic Resource Foundation, Fort Worth, Texas.

Chapter 28

1. Quotation taken by permission from Robert Andrew's *Columbia Dictionary of Quotations* © 1993, Columbia University Press, New York, New York.

2. This quotation is recorded in a talk by Mort Doran, M.D., at the Tourette Syndrome Association's Western Regional Conference, Pasadena, CA, October 1994.

Chapter 29

1. Original source unknown.

Chapter 30

1. Quotation from: *The Best of Women's Quotations*, Published by Exley Gift Books, Watford, Herts, Gt. Britain.

If you would like to communicate with the author, please send a self-addressed stamped envelope to:

Susan Hughes
c/o Hope Press
P.O. Box 188
Duarte, CA 91010

Appendix

Resources

Tourette Syndrome Association, Inc.
(National Headquarters)
42-40 Bell Blvd.
Bayside, NY 11361
(718) 224-2999

Ch.A.D.D. (Children and Adults with Attention Deficit Disorders)
National Office
499 Northwest 70th Ave., Suite 308
Plantation, FL 33317
(305) 587-3700

Obsessive Compulsive Foundation
P.O. Box 9573
New Haven, CT 06535
(203) 878-5669

Learning Disabilities Association (L.D.A.)
National Headquarters
4165 Library Road
Pittsburgh, PA 15234
(412) 341-1515

Orton Dyslexia Society
National Headquarters
600 La Salle Road
Baltimore, MD 21204-6020
(301) 296-0232

Office for Civil Rights
U.S. Department of Education
400 Maryland Ave., S.W.
Washington, D.C. 20202-4135
(202) 401-3020

Reading List

Anderson, W., Chitwood, S., and Hayden, D.
Negotiating the Special Education Maze: A Guide for Parents and Teachers
Woodbine House, 1989

Buehrens, Adam
Hi, I'm Adam
Hope Press, 1991

Chase, T.N., Friedhoff, A.J. and Cohen, D.J.
Tourette's Syndrome: Genetics, Neurobiology, and Treatment Advances in Neurology, Volume 58
Raven Press, 1992

Comings, David E., M.D.
Tourette Syndrome and Human Behavior
Hope Press, 1990

Comings, David E., M.D.
Search for the Tourette Syndrome and Human Behavior Genes
Hope Press, 1996

Dornbush, Marilyn P. and Pruitt, Sheryl K.
Teaching the Tiger: A Handbook for Individuals Involved in the Education of Students with Attention Deficit Disorders, Tourette Syndrome or Obsessive Compulsive Disorder
Hope Press, 1995

Fowler, Mary Cahill
Maybe You Know My Kid: A Parent's Guide to Identifying, Understanding Helping Your Child with Attention-Deficit Hyperactivity Disorder
Birch Lane Press, 1990

Hallowell, Edward M., M.D. and Ratey, John J., M.D.
Driven to Distraction
Pantheon Books, a Division of Random House, Inc., 1994

Hughes, Susan
RYAN, A Mother's Story of Her Hyperactive/Tourette Syndrome Child
Hope Press, 1990

Johnston, H.F.
Obsessive Compulsive Disorder in Children and Adolescents: A Guide
Child Psychopharmacology Information Center, University of Wisconsin
1993

Kurlan, Roger, Ed.
Handbook of Tourette's Syndrome and Related Tic and Behavioral Disorders
Marcell Dekker, Inc., 1993

Rapoport, Judith, M.D.
The Boy Who Couldn't Stop Washing: The Experience and Treatment of Obsessive Compulsive Disorder
Plume Books, 1990

Helpful Pamphlets

These pamphlets may be ordered by contacting the Tourette Syndrome Association's National Headquarters, 42-40 Bell Blvd., Bayside, NY 11361   (718) 224-2999

Problem Behaviors & Tourette Syndrome
Discipline and the TS Child
Educational Rights for Students with TS
Coping with Tourette Syndrome in the Classroom
An Educator's Guide to Tourette Syndrome
Tourette Syndrome and the School Psychologist
Coping With Tourette Syndrome
Guide to the Diagnosis and Treatment of Tourette Syndrome
Know Your Rights
Tourette Syndrome: Information for Insurance Carriers

Order Form

1. Books:

Quantity			Amount
	Tourette Syndrome and Human Behavior		
_____	1S Softback	$39.95	_____
	Search for the Tourette Syndrome and Human Behavior Genes		
_____	8H Hardback	$34.00	_____
_____	8S Softback	$29.95	_____
	The Gene Bomb Does Higher Education and Advanced Technology Accelerate the Selection of Genes for Learning Disorders, ADHD, Addictive and Disruptive Behaviors?		
_____	9H Hardback	$29.95	_____
_____	9S Softback	$25.00	_____
	RYAN — A Mother's Story of Her Hyperactive-Tourette Syndrome Child		
_____	2S Softback	$9.95	_____
	What Makes Ryan Tick? A Family's Triumph over TS and ADHD		
_____	10S Softback	$14.95	_____
	Hi, I'm Adam - A Child's Book about Tourette Syndrome		
_____	4A Softback	$4.95	_____
	Adam and the Magic Marble		
_____	4B Softback	$6.95	_____
	Hi, I'm Adam + Adam and the Magic Marble		
_____	4C Both together	$11.50	_____
	Echolalia - An Adult's Story of Tourette Syndrome		
_____	5A Softback	$11.95	_____
	Don't Think About Monkeys - Extraordinary Stories by People with Tourette Syndrome		
_____	6A Softback	$12.95	_____
	Teaching the Tiger - A Handbook for Individuals Involved in the Education of Students with Attention Deficit Disorder, Tourette Syndrome or Obsessive-Compulsive Disorder		
_____	7A Softback	$35.00	_____

Subtotal for Books ━━━━━

2. Tax: **California residents please add 8.25% sales tax** _____

3. Mailing and Handling:

- ☐ Fourth Class: $4.00 lst item $1.00 each additional item
- ☐ U.P.S. Ground: $6.00 lst item $1.00 each additional item
- ☐ U.P.S. Air: $10.00 lst item $2.00 each additional item _____

Total ━━━━━

Name: _____

Address: _____

City: _____ State:_____ Zip: _____

Country (if other than U.S.A.): _____

Check Enclosed _____   **or**   Visa ____ Mastercard____

CC#_____ Expiration Date _____

send to: ☐┬○ **Hope Press P.O.Box 188,
Duarte, CA 91009-0188**

or Fill out this form with credit card # and FAX it to 818-358-3520

or Order by phone **1-800-321-4039** — 24 hr service

[Foreign buyers outside North America please: a) send bank check in U.S. dollars, or b) order by credit card with charge in U.S. dollars, or c) FAX in the form. For surface mail add $6.00 shipping for first book and $1.00 for each additional and allow 4-6 weeks. For air mail add $25.00 shipping and $2.00 for each additonal book and allow 1 week.]

Order Form

1. Books:

Quantity   Amount

Tourette Syndrome and Human Behavior
_____ 1S Softback $39.95   _____

Search for the Tourette Syndrome and Human Behavior Genes
_____ 8H Hardback $34.00   _____
_____ 8S Softback $29.95   _____

The Gene Bomb   *Does Higher Education and Advanced Technology Accelerate the Selection of Genes for Learning Disorders, ADHD, Addictive and Disruptive Behaviors?*
_____ 9H Hardback $29.95   _____
_____ 9S Softback $25.00   _____

RYAN — A Mother's Story of Her Hyperactive-Tourette Syndrome Child
_____ 2S Softback $9.95   _____

What Makes Ryan Tick? *A Family's Triumph over TS and ADHD*
_____ 10S Softback $14.95   _____

Hi, I'm Adam - A Child's Book about Tourette Syndrome
_____ 4A Softback $4.95   _____

Adam and the Magic Marble
_____ 4B Softback $6.95   _____

Hi, I'm Adam + Adam and the Magic Marble
_____ 4C Both together $11.50   _____

Echolalia - An Adult's Story of Tourette Syndrome
_____ 5A Softback $11.95   _____

Don't Think About Monkeys - Extraordinary Stories by People with Tourette Syndrome
_____ 6A Softback $12.95   _____

Teaching the Tiger - A Handbook for Individuals Involved in the Education of Students with Attention Deficit Disorder, Tourette Syndrome or Obsessive-Compulsive Disorder
_____ 7A Softback $35.00   _____

Subtotal for Books ▬▬▬

2. Tax:

California residents please add 8.25% sales tax _____

3. Mailing and Handling:

☐ Fourth Class: $4.00 lst item $1.00 each additional item
☐ U.P.S. Ground: $6.00 lst item $1.00 each additional item
☐ U.P.S. Air: $10.00 lst item $2.00 each additional item _____

Total ▬▬▬

Name: _____

Address: _____

City: _____ State:_____ Zip: _____

Country (if other than U.S.A.): _____

Check Enclosed _____   **or**   Visa ___ Mastercard ___

CC#_____ Expiration Date _____

send to: ☐┬○ **Hope Press** P.O.Box 188, Duarte, CA 91009-0188

or Fill out this form with credit card # and FAX it to 818-358-3520

or Order by phone **1-800-321-4039** — 24 hr service

[Foreign buyers outside North America please: a) send bank check in U.S. dollars, or b) order by credit card with charge in U.S. dollars, or c) FAX in the form. For surface mail add $6.00 shipping for first book and $1.00 for each additional and allow 4-6 weeks. For air mail add $25.00 shipping and $2.00 for each additonal book and allow 1 week.]

Order Form

1. Books:

Quantity			Amount

Tourette Syndrome and Human Behavior
_____ 1S Softback $39.95 _____

Search for the Tourette Syndrome and Human Behavior Genes
_____ 8H Hardback $34.00 _____
_____ 8S Softback $29.95 _____

The Gene Bomb *Does Higher Education and Advanced Technology Accelerate the Selection of Genes for Learning Disorders, ADHD, Addictive and Disruptive Behaviors?*
_____ 9H Hardback $29.95 _____
_____ 9S Softback $25.00 _____

RYAN — *A Mother's Story of Her Hyperactive-Tourette Syndrome Child*
_____ 2S Softback $9.95 _____

What Makes Ryan Tick? *A Family's Triumph over TS and ADHD*
_____ 10S Softback $14.95 _____

Hi, I'm Adam *- A Child's Book about Tourette Syndrome*
_____ 4A Softback $4.95 _____

Adam and the Magic Marble
_____ 4B Softback $6.95 _____

Hi, I'm Adam *+ Adam and the Magic Marble*
_____ 4C Both together $11.50 _____

Echolalia *- An Adult's Story of Tourette Syndrome*
_____ 5A Softback $11.95 _____

Don't Think About Monkeys *- Extraordinary Stories by People with Tourette Syndrome*
_____ 6A Softback $12.95 _____

Teaching the Tiger *- A Handbook for Individuals Involved in the Education of Students with Attention Deficit Disorder, Tourette Syndrome or Obsessive-Compulsive Disorder*
_____ 7A Softback $35.00 _____

Subtotal for Books _____

2. Tax: **California residents please add 8.25% sales tax** _____

3. Mailing and Handling:
☐ Fourth Class: $4.00 1st item $1.00 each additional item
☐ U.P.S. Ground: $6.00 1st item $1.00 each additional item
☐ U.P.S. Air: $10.00 1st item $2.00 each additional item _____

Total ▬▬▬

Name: _____
Address: _____
City: _____ State: _____ Zip: _____
Country (if other than U.S.A.): _____

Check Enclosed _____   **or**   Visa ___ Mastercard ___
CC# _____ Expiration Date _____

send to: ☐┬○ **Hope Press** **P.O.Box 188, Duarte, CA 91009-0188**

or Fill out this form with credit card # and FAX it to 818-358-3520

or Order by phone **1-800-321-4039** — 24 hr service

[Foreign buyers outside North America please: a) send bank check in U.S. dollars, or b) order by credit card with charge in U.S. dollars, or c) FAX in the form. For surface mail add $6.00 shipping for first book and $1.00 for each additional and allow 4-6 weeks. For air mail add $25.00 shipping and $2.00 for each additonal book and allow 1 week.]

Order Form

1. Books:

Quantity		Amount
Tourette Syndrome and Human Behavior		
_____ 1S Softback	$39.95	_____
Search for the Tourette Syndrome and Human Behavior Genes		
_____ 8H Hardback	$34.00	_____
_____ 8S Softback	$29.95	_____
The Gene Bomb Does Higher Education and Advanced Technology Accelerate the Selection of Genes for Learning Disorders, ADHD, Addictive and Disruptive Behaviors?		
_____ 9H Hardback	$29.95	_____
_____ 9S Softback	$25.00	_____
RYAN — A Mother's Story of Her Hyperactive-Tourette Syndrome Child		
_____ 2S Softback	$9.95	_____
What Makes Ryan Tick? A Family's Triumph over TS and ADHD		
_____ 10S Softback	$14.95	_____
Hi, I'm Adam - A Child's Book about Tourette Syndrome		
_____ 4A Softback	$4.95	_____
Adam and the Magic Marble		
_____ 4B Softback	$6.95	_____
Hi, I'm Adam + Adam and the Magic Marble		
_____ 4C Both together	$11.50	_____
Echolalia - An Adult's Story of Tourette Syndrome		
_____ 5A Softback	$11.95	_____
Don't Think About Monkeys - Extraordinary Stories by People with Tourette Syndrome		
_____ 6A Softback	$12.95	_____
Teaching the Tiger - A Handbook for Individuals Involved in the Education of Students with Attention Deficit Disorder, Tourette Syndrome or Obsessive-Compulsive Disorder		
_____ 7A Softback	$35.00	_____

Subtotal for Books _____

2. Tax: **California residents please add 8.25% sales tax** _____

3. Mailing and Handling:

☐ Fourth Class: $4.00 1st item $1.00 each additional item
☐ U.P.S. Ground: $6.00 1st item $1.00 each additional item
☐ U.P.S. Air: $10.00 1st item $2.00 each additional item _____

Total ■■■■

Name: _____
Address: _____
City: _____ State: _____ Zip: _____
Country (if other than U.S.A.): _____
Check Enclosed _____ **or** Visa ____ Mastercard ____
CC#_____ Expiration Date _____

send to: ☐┬○ **Hope Press** P.O.Box 188,
Duarte, CA 91009-0188

or Fill out this form with credit card # and FAX it to 818-358-3520

or Order by phone **1-800-321-4039** — 24 hr service

[Foreign buyers outside North America please: a) send bank check in U.S. dollars, or b) order by credit card with charge in U.S. dollars, or c) FAX in the form. For surface mail add $6.00 shipping for first book and $1.00 for each additional and allow 4-6 weeks. For air mail add $25.00 shipping and $2.00 for each additonal book and allow 1 week.]

cut here   cut here   cut here